The Quest for Professionalism

Early pioneers in management thinking, such as Henri Fayol and Peter Drucker, conceived of management as a science-based professional activity that serves the greater good. Today, however, many organizations are managed by people demonstrating anything but professionalism, resulting in mismanagement of risks as well as a one-dimensional focus on short-term results.

The key thesis in this book is that the quest for professionalism must be revitalized because the societal costs and damage caused by managerial amateurism are huge. The book is about how to address this grand challenge, for example by exploring whether and how a shared professional purpose, and a professional body of knowledge, can be developed. While most work in this area has previously focused on management education, *The Quest for Professionalism* adopts an inside-out approach, implying management scholarship is the driving force behind any intrinsic transformation of the profession at large. Without management scholars playing an active role in advancing 'science-based professionalism,' in the mould of engineering and medicine, any attempt to professionalize management practice is doomed to fail. Moreover, Georges Romme demonstrates the professionalization quest has to move away from the idea of management being confined to a few people at the top toward management as a technology for distributing power and leadership throughout the organization.

Georges Romme is Professor of Entrepreneurship and Innovation at Eindhoven University of Technology (TU/e) in The Netherlands. He studied economics at Tilburg University and obtained a doctoral degree from Maastricht University. Until 2014, Georges served as Dean of Industrial Engineering & Innovation Sciences at TU/e. In the early 1990s, he introduced Boolean comparative analysis in the field of management studies, and also pioneered the Thesis Circle, a tool for collaboratively supervising graduation projects. Moreover, he is one of the original pioneers who (re)introduced design thinking and the design sciences to management and organization studies. For his pioneering work in this area, Georges received the 2016 Tjalling Koopmans Asset award and the 2019 Distinguished Scholar-Practitioner Award of the Academy of Management. Georges also serves as a non-executive director on a variety of boards.

The Quest for Professionalism

The Case of Management and Entrepreneurship

Georges Romme

OXFORD
UNIVERSITY PRESS

OXFORD
UNIVERSITY PRESS

Great Clarendon Street, Oxford, OX2 6DP,
United Kingdom

Oxford University Press is a department of the University of Oxford.
It furthers the University's objective of excellence in research, scholarship,
and education by publishing worldwide. Oxford is a registered trade mark of
Oxford University Press in the UK and in certain other countries

First published 2016
First published in paperback 2020

Published in the United States of America by Oxford University Press
198 Madison Avenue, New York, NY 10016, United States of America

British Library Cataloguing in Publication Data
Data available

Library of Congress Cataloging in Publication Data
Data available

ISBN 978–0–19–873773–5 (Hbk.)
ISBN 978–0–19–885706–8 (Pbk.)

Preface

The Quest for Professionalism: The Case of Management and Entrepreneurship brings together a number of ideas and themes I have been exploring, studying, and applying for more than two decades. One key idea is distributed knowledge and management, to which I was first exposed as an economics student in the early 1980s, via Friedrich Hayek's work on knowledge creation. Hayek observed that knowledge about, for example, the organization in which we work does not exist in concentrated or integrated form, but is *dispersed* across many individuals in the form of bits of incomplete and frequently contradictory knowledge. Obviously, the notion of dispersed knowledge has major implications for (distributed) management and leadership. At the time, I did not anticipate how the notion of distributed knowledge, management, and leadership would become a recurrent theme throughout my career.

Another key source of inspiration is the actual application of distributed management in circular organizing. While working on a doctoral dissertation at Maastricht University in the late 1980s, I read a newspaper article about the circular approach to management. The article described several examples of organizations where power and authority appeared to flow as easily upward as downward. The pioneer of this management method was said to be a Dutch entrepreneur, Gerard Endenburg. This was an eye-opener, because here was an example of an entrepreneur who actually applied the notion of distributed knowledge and management. It was not until the early 1990s, after completing my doctoral work at Maastricht University, that I followed up on the article and contacted Gerard Endenburg and his colleagues. Ever since, the notion of *circularity* has been another time constant in my work, be it as a scholar, educator, manager, or advisor.

I was also fortunate to run into Chris Argyris' work in the late 1990s. I recall assembling a group of colleagues at Maastricht University, to together study and discuss the book *Action Science* (by Argyris and co-authors). Even today, I'm still deeply impressed by how Chris managed to combine creative theorizing, scientific validation, and actual application of ideas and frameworks in the area of defensive routines and learning processes. Chris was also a very kind and gentle person, who never stopped offering help and support, his emails typically raising questions starting with "I have a puzzle for you." Chris died in 2013, leaving us with an enormous intellectual and professional legacy. Chris' ideas about the (mis)alignment between what we actually do and what we say we do has influenced *The Quest for Professionalism* in many ways.

At a later stage, the collaborative work with Endenburg as well as the seminal work of Argyris led me to engage more deeply with the literature on design science, arising from the work of Herbert Simon and others. In the meantime, I moved from Maastricht to Tilburg University, and increasingly ran into the mismatch between mainstream social science and the kind of design- and intervention-oriented work that Argyris and Endenburg were doing. In our conversations, Gerard Endenburg often used "design" and "design science" as key terms, a vocabulary I was unfamiliar with. When I consulted Chris Argyris about this, he referred me to an appendix in *Knowledge for Action* (1993), which outlines his conception of human beings as "designers." In fact, Chris at some point confessed that, if in the 1950s and 1960s he had been exposed to any design science literature, he would never have adopted the "action science" label for the organizational learning methodology developed later with Donald Schön and many others.

A few years after I started framing most of my work around "design science," I relocated from Tilburg University to Eindhoven University of Technology (TU/e). This move also created the intellectual space that allowed me to pursue some of the ideas that ultimately led to *The Quest for Professionalism*. The department of Industrial Engineering & Innovation Sciences of TU/e, where I've been a faculty member and also served seven years in the capacity of dean, operates in the periphery of the world of business and management schools. This peripheral position implies our school largely operates outside the pressures and rituals arising from international rankings and AACSB and EQUIS accreditations—while delivering MSc graduates (e.g. in industrial engineering) that compete with the best MBA graduates from elsewhere. Until today, this peripheral position has offered an intellectual climate that supports and enables work on management and entrepreneurship at the interface between science and design, or any other work outside the mainstream.

The hands-on managerial experience as a dean also offered the opportunity to come to grips with the practical side of the professionalization equation. In this managerial role, I increasingly became aware of the gap between the theory and praxis of management as a nascent profession—even within the same building—and the various rhetorical tricks and mental routines we draw on to suppress this awareness. In the same period, I also joined the supervisory boards of several corporations and nonprofit organizations, providing direct access to how CEOs and other executives operate in and around boardrooms, including the interaction with their non-executive directors.

Over the past fifteen years, various efforts have been made to re-introduce Herbert Simon's ideas about management as a design discipline in the literature on management studies. These efforts by Dick Boland, Roger Dunbar, Armand Hatchuel, Roger Martin, Joan van Aken, Bill Starbuck, myself, and many others have led to a substantial number of articles, several special issues, and other publications. However, the overall impact on the field has been very limited. Related perspectives, such as evidence-based management (EBM) and Mode 2 and 3, seem to suffer the same fate. At a more fundamental level, all these attempts to revitalize the management discipline appear to get stuck in what Khurana and Spender have called the "intellectual stasis" of the field of management, that is, its over-emphasis on academic values and ideas at the expense of professional ones. Notably, at the heart of Herbert Simon's initial argument about management as a design discipline was his call for "science-based professionalism," that is a profession informed by science.

As a result, I decided to conceptualize the main argument in this book not around design science, but around a more fundamental challenge: do we want management to be(come) a profession informed by management scholarship, and if so, how can the quest for science-based professionalism be revitalized? This question tends to raise a sense of anxiety and discomfort in view of, for example, the fact that the notion of professionalism is still pivotal in getting MBA and other programs accredited, although as management scholars we no longer seem to care about it. In terms of Argyris' distinction between espoused and actual behavior, there is a substantial misalignment between what we say to (e.g. AACSB) accreditation committees and what we actually do once the committee members have again left the campus. In other roles, for example as non-executive director, I've been running into similar gaps between what we say we do and what we actually do. As a result of these and several other observations and experiences, I became increasingly fascinated by what professionalism in management and entrepreneurship currently is, should be, and can be. This book pulls together the initial findings of this ongoing journey.

No journey is possible without travel companions. I'm very grateful to the following "professionals" who read and commented on early versions of chapters of *The Quest for Professionalism*: Hans Berends, Jeroen van Bree, Elco van Burg, Per Davidsson, Dimo Dimov, Ksenia Podoynitsyna, Isabelle Reymen, Annewiek Reijmer, Brian Robertson, Denise Rousseau, J. C. Spender, Bill Starbuck, Madis Talmar, Pieter van der Meche, Andy van de Ven, Sharon Villines, Bob Walrave, and Mathieu Weggeman. David Musson, Clare Kennedy, and their team at Oxford University Press were a great source of professional support, especially in the early conception and final completion stages of getting this book published.

Over the past three decades, dialogical encounters with many other colleagues and friends offered opportunities to discuss ideas and engage in research. In many ways, the dialogical encounters with the following co-authors have directly or indirectly informed the argument in this book: Henk Akkermans, Elena Antonacopoulou, Marie-José Avenier, Frank Barrett, Hans Berends, Dick Boland, Jan Broekgaarden, Myriam Cloodt, David Denyer, Roger Dunbar, Gerard Endenburg, Stephan Eltink, Victor Gilsing, Gerard Hodgkinson, Jan Holmström, Sam Jelinek, Paul Kunst, Fred Langerak, Jan Nijhuis, René Olie, Krsto Pandza, Ksenia Podoynitsyna, Amandine Pascal, Isabelle Reymen, Annewiek Reijmer, Roger Rompa, Hein Schreuder, Scott Shane, Sjo Soeters, John Spangenberg, Bill Starbuck, Ken Starkey, Susan Taylor, Catherine Thomas, Liisa Välikangas, Geert Verbong, Joan van Aken, Michel van der Borgh, Rob van der Eyden, Marjolein van Noort, Woody van Olffen, Kim van Oorschot, Arjen van Witteloostuijn, Mathieu Weggeman, Uwe Wilkesmann, Nicolay Worren, and Maurizio Zollo. I also acknowledge the collaborative work and discussions with the following (former) doctoral students: Peter Berends, Sharon Dolmans, Amr Farouk, Rob Heine, Freek Hermkens, Sjaña Holloway, Janneke Hooijer, Freek Meulman, Deborah Mulders, Madis Talmar, Elco van Burg, Stephan van Dijk, Inge van Seggelen-Damen, Bob Walrave, and Mohammad Zolfagharian.

I dedicate this book to Gabi, for her companionship and unconditional love. She knew I would write this book, long before I started considering it.

Georges Romme
Eindhoven, August 2015

Acknowledgments

The author and publisher wish to acknowledge the following permissions to reproduce or re-use materials:

Figure 2.2 is reproduced, with permission from IEEE, from: J. N. Warfield, "Micromathematics and macromathematics," *Proceedings of 1986 International Conference on Systems, Man and Cybernetics*, pp. 1127–31. New York: IEEE.

Figure 2.3 is reproduced, with permission from IEEE, from: J. N. Warfield, "Micromathematics and macromathematics," *Proceedings of 1986 International Conference on Systems, Man and Cybernetics*, pp. 1127–31. New York: IEEE.

Figure 7.2 is reproduced from: R. K. Mitchell, B. R. Agle & D. J. Wood, "Toward a stakeholder identification and salience: Defining the principle of who and what really counts," Academy of Management Review 22 (1997): 853–86. Copyright © 1997 The Academy of Management.

Table 1.1 is reproduced from: D. M. Rousseau, "Designing a better business school: Channelling Herbert Simon, addressing the critics, and developing actionable knowledge for professionalizing managers," Journal of Management Studies 49 (2012): 600–18. Copyright © 2012 John Wiley & Sons.

Several text extracts are re-used, with permission from John Wiley & Sons, from: A. G. L. Romme, M.-J. Avenier, D. Denyer, G. P. Hodgkinson, K. Pandza, K. Starkey, and N. Worren, "Towards common ground and trading zones in management research and practice," British Journal of Management 26 (3): 544–59. DOI: 10.1111/1467-8551.12110 (© 2015 British Academy of Management). Published article: http://onlinelibrary.wiley.com/doi/10.1111/1467-8551.12110/abstract

The author and publisher also wish to acknowledge the re-use (in adapted form) of materials from the following articles:

"A note on the hierarchy-team debate" (author: A. G. L. Romme), Strategic Management Journal 17 (1996): 411–17. Copyright © 1996 John Wiley & Sons.

"Domination, self-determination and circular organizing" (author: A. G. L. Romme), Organization Studies 20 (1999): 801–32. Copyright © 1999 Sage Publications.

"Making a difference: Organization as design" (author: A. G. L. Romme), Organization Science 14 (2003): 558–73. Copyright © 2003 the Institute for Operations Research and Management Sciences (INFORMS).

"Construction principles and design rules in the case of circular design" (authors: A. G. L. Romme and G. Endenburg), Organization Science 17 (2006): 287–97. Copyright © 2006 the Institute for Operations Research and Management Sciences (INFORMS).

Contents

List of Figures

List of Tables

Introduction

When you're booking an airline ticket, you trust the airline company will assign a pilot to your flight who is sufficiently knowledgeable, experienced, and competent to fly the aircraft. In fact, you expect this pilot to be a professional who has gone through many hours of flight training and theoretical study, and as such is fully licensed to fly the aircraft.

Change of scenery. Recall the last job offer that you accepted. Did you check the credentials of your future boss, to assess whether (s)he is the professional "pilot" you can entrust with leading you and your colleagues to the next destination of this organization? Or did you assume such an assessment had been done by those who appointed your boss at the time? If you are an entrepreneur, what about the last venture you started? Have the investors and other stakeholders in this venture thoroughly assessed your ability to get the venture off the ground and fly it to commercial success?

You might answer these questions with a straightforward *no*, recall some form of informal assessment, or refer to your (boss's) track record and possibly educational background (e.g. MBA). In all instances, however, there probably is a striking difference between the level of professionalism naturally expected from an aircraft pilot and the more ambiguous and undefined expectations we have regarding a manager or entrepreneur. This is one of the observations that motivates the search for ways to revitalize *The Quest for Professionalism* in management and entrepreneurship.

Background

Historically, pioneers in management thinking and practice such as Frederick Taylor, Mary Parker Follett, Henri Fayol, and Peter Drucker conceived of management as a *science-based professional activity that serves the greater good* (Taylor 1911; Follett 1927; Fayol 1949; Drucker 1974). At the beginning of the twenty-first century, however, the nature and level of professionalism of management is under close public scrutiny. For example, many of the large banks on Wall Street that failed so badly in the fall of 2008 were managed by people demonstrating anything but professionalism, resulting in mismanagement of risks and a one-dimensional focus on short-term profitability. The CEOs of these organizations "strayed from their strategies and took unwise and unsustainable risks, thus ignoring potential long-term consequences," as observed by Beer (2009: 53). Moreover, executives and other managers in these organizations intimidated and silenced employees who sought to challenge these risk-management practices, resulting in an organization-wide focus on short-term gains (Beer 2009; Williams 2010).

Not only do managers of financial institutions demonstrate amateurism in situations where professionals are needed. Enron, ICI, Worldcom, Global Crossing, Adelphia Communications, Tyco International, AOL Time Warner, Bristol-Myers Squibb, Kmart, Xerox, and many other companies have been observed to suffer from mismanagement and lack of direction (Fox 2003; Cooper 2008; Kay 2014; LawBrain 2014). Other recent cases include the mismanagement of megaprojects such as the Berlin Brandenburg airport, San Francisco Transbay Terminal, the 2014 Soccer World Cup in Brazil, and the 2014 Winter Olympics in Russia (Flyvbjerg 2013). Non-professionalism can also be observed in many supervisory boards, or boards of directors. A recent example is the supervisory board of Vestia, the largest public housing association in the Netherlands. When Vestia's CEO mismanaged the organization for many years, its supervisory board failed to effectively monitor the CEO's performance and later also failed to properly manage his exit (The Guardian 2012).

Of course, the level of professionalism shown by managers, directors, and administrators is not the only determinant of organizational performance and viability in these examples. A variety of institutional, cultural, macro-economic, and other mechanisms and conditions also affects organizational viability and performance. But if we zoom in on those factors and variables that managers and their stakeholders can to a large extent *influence* if not control (Kenworthy and McMullan 2013), then all these examples appear to have a common denominator: the low level of professionalism among managers who struggle, and often fail, to meet the growing demands and expectations of employees, investors, and many other stakeholders. The fact is that the vast majority of assessments and decisions made by executives and other general managers are highly amateurish compared to how, for example, pilots and surgeons make up their minds and take decisions. As a result, about half of the managerial decisions made in organizations fail (Nutt 1999, 2011) and most managers fail to effectively lead and motivate their staff (Haney and Sirbasku 2011). In addition, what they actually do is not consistent with what they say they do (Argyris et al. 1985; Argyris 2004).

Similarly, management and entrepreneurship scholars have increasingly abandoned the quest for professionalism in their discipline. They therefore tend to operate in "tribes that form around rigor and relevance, sequestering themselves into closed loops of scholarship" (Gulati 2007: 775) primarily talking and writing to members of their own tribe and dismissing work done outside their tribe (Bedeian 1989; Bradbury Huang 2010; Gulati 2007). Moreover, the publish-or-perish system prevailing in most business and management schools encourages scholars to emphasize productivity at the expense of innovation and prioritize the theoretical relevance of their research at the expense of its relevance for professional practice (Bouchikhi and Kimberly 2001; Starkey and Madan 2001; De Rond and Miller 2005). One perverse implication of the publish-or-perish system is that some scholars are under so much pressure to produce and publish papers that they are tempted to engage in plagiarism and to mischaracterize and manipulate data (Honig and Bedi 2012; Matlack 2013).

Key Thesis and Audience

Despite the high expectations and ambitions of the early pioneers, the level of professionalism within management today is rather low. My key thesis is that the search for professionalism in management and entrepreneurship needs to be revitalized, because the societal costs and damage caused by managerial amateurism are huge. This quest for professionalism is, in fact, a grand societal challenge that requires a collective and sustained response, for which I will map and explore several paths. These paths open up ways to develop and align the professional purpose, knowledge, conduct, and expectation of management. Whereas most previous work in this area is about management education, I adopt an *inside-out* approach, by focusing on management scholarship as the driving force behind any intrinsic transformation of the profession at large. Without an active role of management scholarship in promoting science-based professionalism, similar initiatives and changes in management education are doomed to fail.

The target audience of *The Quest for Professionalism* includes management scholars as well as practitioners interested in revitalizing this quest. In addressing management scholars, I hope *The Quest*'s arguments and findings will appeal to both senior scholars and their junior counterparts (e.g. graduate students). On the practitioner side, I am particularly addressing "reflective practitioners" (Schön 1983), that is, managers and entrepreneurs who want to explore ways to further professionalize their practice.

Whereas most ideas developed in this monograph also apply to specialized areas such as marketing, financial, and supply chain management, the main interest here is in *general* management, entrepreneurship, strategic management, change management, and related areas. These managerial efforts are at the heart of how any organization creates value by coordinating people and resources, and are therefore central to management as a (nascent) profession.

Professionalism

The quest for professionalism has four dimensions or levels: purpose, knowledge, behavior, and expectation. At the heart of any profession is a shared sense of *purpose*, a "commitment to a good broader than self-interest" (Despotidou and Prastacos 2012: 437) that facilitates conversations between highly different voices in the profession and communicates what the profession is essentially about.

Another dimension of professionalization is the *knowledge* the profession can claim and draw on (Abbott 1988). This body of knowledge involves expertise, that is the insights and tools required to perform professional work; these insights and tools are constituted by a "vocabulary" that serves to define and describe problems and challenges as well as a "language" in the form of conceptual frameworks, models, and theories (March and Smith 1995). This body of knowledge is inherently ethical in nature. Therefore, the values guiding professional conduct and performance are, or should be, explicit elements of this body of knowledge.

The *behavioral* dimension, broadly defined, refers to how professionals divide and coordinate work, organize the work flow, monitor the quality of their work and that of others, perform on key outcome measures, account for their performance, and so forth. Finally, the *expectation* dimension primarily refers to what a variety of stakeholders expects of the profession. True professions raise high expectations among internal as well as external stakeholders (e.g. employees and investors), and in turn, these expectations inspire and guide professionals to perform and deliver their best.

Professionalization is often also equated with the conditions and regulations for entry to the profession as well as sanctions and penalties regarding non-professional conduct. However, these regulations and sanctions tend to have perverse effects on professional conduct. Mechanisms to control and regulate entry to a profession as well as the behavior of its members are therefore not fundamental to "professionalism"; rather, these regulatory mechanisms are outcomes that may arise from professionalization efforts.

Moreover, any professionalization effort that aims at regulating entry and conduct, while professional purpose and knowledge are not yet well developed and widely shared, is doomed to fail. Accordingly, *professionalism* is defined as the alignment between:

(i) the shared purpose (*P*) of the (nascent) profession
(ii) the body of knowledge (*K*) these professionals have access to
(iii) their actual behavior (*B*) in terms of actions and decisions, and
(iv) the expectations (*E*) of a variety of internal and external stakeholders.

In a simple equation: *professionalism* $= P \times K \times B \times E$ with *P*, *K*, *B*, and *E* measured on a scale from 0 to 1. Accordingly, each of these four dimensions directly affects the level of professionalism. Moreover, this equation is multiplicative rather than additive in nature. Even when most dimensions are relatively high, a low score on one dimension will thus dramatically affect the overall level of professionalism.

This equation serves to assess the professionalism of the management discipline in a concise manner. First, *P* is low because there is hardly any shared sense of purpose (e.g. Khurana and Nohria 2008; Rolin 2010). Moreover, *K* is low as the academic body of knowledge is highly fragmented (e.g. Walsh et al. 2006) and only loosely connected to practical knowledge (e.g. Hughes et al. 2011). Both *B* and *E* are also rather low, because our ignorance about organizations and managing them "is so great that forms of malfunctioning and the suffering which results from it are ubiquitous and are widely accepted as normal and unavoidable" (Elias and Scotson 1994: 181). The *overall* level of professionalism of management is therefore rather low. Given that the quest for professionalism in management has been largely abandoned, any attempt to revitalize it will need to aim at raising all four dimensions.

Small Pockets of Excellence

This assessment of the overall level of professionalism in management might raise the counter-argument that it is extrapolating from a few bad apples. Indeed, there are many examples of highly professional managers and management practices, the most prominent ones being celebrated as global role models (e.g. Kelly 2009; Willis 2013). However, these examples represent small pockets of professional excellence that are exceptions to the rule, rather than reflecting the standard case. The highly skewed distribution of professionalism in management—with many very badly managed organizations and relatively few ones with professional management practices—will be discussed in more detail in Chapter 1.

The broader systemic issue here is that management scholars, consultants, and practitioners have largely abandoned the development of integral management approaches and technologies (cf. the aircraft in the pilot example earlier), to focus on partial aspects of management that propagate economic thinking at the cost of moral responsibility (Ghoshal 2005). As a result, the idea of professionalism has become closely linked, if not almost entirely defined by, the following two key constructs.

First, the idea of management as a (nascent) profession has become confined to a *few people* at the top of the organization. For most people, therefore, words like "management" and "managing" immediately evoke the image of someone in a leadership position. This image appears to be incomplete. Professional management is as much about the knowledge and evidence informing professionalism as it is about the people using this knowledge. Moreover, in a new category of management systems currently emerging, leadership is not confined to a few people at the top but distributed throughout the organization. I will discuss this type of management approach in the the quest for professionalism in this book.

Second, professionalism and related (e.g. capability) notions have become tightly coupled to *financial performance and other outcomes*. That is, the ability to accomplish something has become equated with performance and results. This of course raises a tautology problem: if the organization performs at a superior level in terms of, for example, profitability, then the leadership of the organization apparently possesses a large professional capability; if this performance is not superior, its leadership apparently scores lower on professionalism (cf. Zahra et al. 2006; Teece 2007). This tautology problem is pervasive in management scholarship and practice, which explains why many people misunderstand and underestimate the generative role of management capabilities and technologies. *The Quest for Professionalism* will serve to explore ways to decouple capability and performance—similar to how the capabilities of an aircraft are assessed and tested while on the ground, between the flights during which it actually performs.

Discovering New Paths

Whereas the $P \times K \times B \times E$ definition of professionalism serves to characterize the current state of the management discipline, in itself this definition does not provide any directions toward future solutions. The quest for professionalism therefore also needs to draw on creative discovery and design. Herbert Simon argued "design" is at the heart of the business and management discipline. That is, engineers are not the only professional designers because,

> everyone designs who devises courses of action aimed at changing existing situations into preferred ones. The intellectual activity that produces material artifacts is no different fundamentally from the one that prescribes remedies for a sick

patient or the one that devises a new sales plan for a company or a social welfare policy for a state. (Simon 1969/1996: 111)

Discovery and design thus provide metaphors that open up ways to think about the future of management and its scholarship. As such, *The Quest for Professionalism* is about discovering and designing paths out of the "intellectual stasis" (Khurana and Spender 2012) that currently characterizes the field of management.

Donald Schön (1979) provides an example of how purpose, knowledge, and discovery interact to create a fresh perspective. He observed a group of designers trying to improve the performance of a paintbrush made of synthetic bristles. This paintbrush failed to give the same smooth finish as its established counterpart, a natural-bristle paintbrush. These designers knew the paint had to attach itself to the bristles and then be spread on a surface. In contrast to the natural-bristle paintbrush, the synthetic paintbrush delivered paint rather unevenly, in a "gloppy" way. The design group experimented with different synthetic materials and diameters for the bristles; when observing that natural bristles had split ends, members of the group also split the ends of the synthetic bristles—all without significant improvements. One day, after many attempts in these various directions, someone suggested "You know, a paintbrush is a kind of pump!" (Schön 1979: 257) based on the observation that, when a paintbrush is pressed against a surface, paint is forced through the spaces *between* the bristles onto the surface. As a result, the designers started noticing that the paint flows through channels, whose size is controlled by the painter's bending of the brush. To facilitate the flow of paint, a painter would even vibrate the brush.

Talking about a brush in terms of a pump radically changed the designers' conception of the problem. Instead of focusing on the bristles, they started observing what happens in the capillary spaces in-between, and soon found out that synthetic bristles bend differently than natural ones. Inspired by the novel perspective of paintbrush-as-pump, these designers transformed their initial conception of the assignment (i.e. making synthetic bristles better) to one of controlling the system of capillary spaces that soak up the paint and enable the painter to apply it to a surface by manipulating and curving the bristles. This new metaphor brought a new vocabulary into the conversation that radically transformed the perception of the assignment, and led to several patents and better synthetic paintbrushes (Schön 1979).

Similarly, in *The Quest for Professionalism: The Case of Management and Entrepreneurship*, I intend to (re)discover the "professionalism" metaphor, by developing a vocabulary that might re-ignite and transform the discourse on the purpose, knowledge, behavior, and expectation dimensions of management as a professional activity.

Professional Engagement

The quest for professionalism in management is highly contested. Critical observers have argued that established professions, such as law and medicine, draw on a formal body of knowledge shared by all members of the profession, monitor behavior and performance of these members, regulate entry to the profession, and so forth (e.g. Barker 2010). Accordingly, in the absence of a formal body of knowledge and elaborate regulatory mechanisms, it would make no sense to pursue the professionalization of management.

However, this critique draws on a rather naïve image of established professions, as Adler et al. (2008), Barends et al. (2012), and others have demonstrated. The fact is that professional work in, for example, accounting, law, medicine, and health care continues to be highly contested (e.g. Sullivan 2000; Suddaby et al. 2009; Flood 2011). The nature and context of work in these established professions is still evolving in often unpredictable ways. Moreover, professionals in these areas are increasingly employed in corporate or other organizational settings (Evetts 2011). Consequently, many accountants, legal experts, and medical doctors increasingly find themselves torn between their professional commitment and their loyalty and commitment to the organization paying their salary (Muzio and Kirkpatrick 2011). This is no different to the role of general managers in the same organizational settings. These tensions are fundamental to all professional work in organizational settings, and we cannot make them go away by simply abandoning the journey toward professionalization. By revitalizing the quest for professionalism in managerial and entrepreneurial work, these issues and challenges again take central stage.

The experiences in other disciplines therefore suggest that the essence of professionalization is not only in its (intermediary) outcome or destiny, but also in the journey itself. This is not merely a philosophical matter. External bodies use "professional" values and standards to assess whether business and management schools accomplish "an appropriate balance and integration of academic and professional engagement" (AACSB 2015). Therefore, management scholarship and education are to a large extent justified by what we espouse about *professional engagement* to research funding agencies and accreditation bodies such as AACSB and EQUIS. If management scholars and educators truly believe that managerial work and systems cannot be effectively studied, shaped, and improved, this would raise an enormous misalignment with what is actually said to funding agencies and accreditation bodies. If it really makes no sense to invest in professionalizing management, the logical consequence would be to eliminate all business and management schools. In other words, without the quest for professionalism, the external legitimacy of management scholarship and education is likely to break down entirely.

As in any quest, the target is not well-defined. Established professions such as medicine and law do not provide a target, because any professionalization process in the twenty-first century is entirely different to one in the nineteenth or early twentieth century. Moreover, in view of the ongoing evolution of these professions (e.g. Evetts 2011), it would amount to a moving target. A traditional conception of professional work as being heavily regulated is also not very appealing (Timmons 2011). We do not want managers and entrepreneurs to follow detailed protocols, and write reports and logs on every single action and decision they take. No one would want to work for such a boss. Here, *The Quest for Professionalism* serves to explore and define alternative conceptions of, and routes for, professionalizing management and entrepreneurship.

Key Findings and Conclusions

The Quest for Professionalism serves to create *paths* for professionalizing management (cf. Garud and Karnøe 2001; Pandza and Thorpe 2010). Overall, the following paths arise.

Developing a Shared Sense of Purpose and Responsibility

At the heart of each (emerging) profession is a shared sense of purpose and responsibility toward society. For example, civil engineers share a sense of purpose regarding the reliability, robustness, and user convenience of the roads, bridges, tunnels, docks, and other artifacts they design and create (Muller and Gewirtzman 2004). The respect for human life and the commitment to heal people, expressed in the Hippocratic oath, reflects the sense of purpose and responsibility among medical professionals (Miles 2004).

The Quest for Professionalism serves to develop a prototype statement of the purpose and responsibility of management and its scholarship. In sum, this prototype says:

> Management should be(come) a profession that serves the greater good by bringing people and resources together to create value that no single individual can create alone. In this profession:
> - practicing and knowing co-constitute each other;
> - professionals share an interest in outcomes and implications, and are committed to learning to see things from different perspectives;
> - professional development is fueled by a pluralism of voices as well as dialogical encounters between different voices.

The shared interest in outcomes and implications arises from the pragmatist nature of management as a nascent profession, and invites conversations about how financial, social, or moral implications are defined and interpreted. This shared interest might serve to facilitate conversations between highly different voices in the profession.

The dialogical encounters proposed here are meant to expose professionals to fundamentally different views, to provide opportunities for reconsidering and reflecting on their central beliefs and assumptions. In these encounters, management practitioners and scholars learn to see themselves, their personal background, their organizational settings, and their own beliefs from a range of different perspectives, thus enabling them to engage reflexively with their profession and work.

While a shared sense of purpose and responsibility will enhance the identity of management as an emerging profession, only a sustained collective effort can bring it about. Given the embryonic stage of the discourse on the purpose and nature of management, any attempt toward closure is not likely to be successful at this stage. In this respect, the statement of professional purpose and responsibility outlined earlier is a prototype, intended to revitalize and re-open the debate.

Toward a Professional Body of Knowledge

In their quest for academic respectability, most management scholars have retreated from creative and action-oriented work. Management practitioners largely focus on the latter, but tend to avoid or minimize efforts to validate and reflect on their work. Central to any attempt to revitalize the transformation toward science-based professionalism is a body of knowledge informed by both creative discovery and scientific validation.

The framework for a science-based professional body of knowledge, arising from *The Quest for Professionalism*, provides a map of the research inputs and outputs (i.e. values, constructs, models, principles, and instantiations) and the research activities and methods in the area of discovery and validation required to develop and sustain professional knowledge. This body of knowledge goes beyond the academia–practice divide as well as conventional demarcations such as constructivism-positivism. While many elements of a professional body of knowledge on management and entrepreneurship are already available, many opportunities to connect them have thus far remained untapped.

A key insight arising from the case of circular organizing is that the intellectual and professional stasis in management, evident in for example shareholder value maximization, can only be resolved by raising fundamental questions about values and power. Moreover, management scholars should engage more in discovering and validating constructs and models that help practitioners respond to challenges such as empowerment and organizational resilience. Key theoretical constructs such as Hayek's dispersed knowledge and Simon's bounded rationality appear to offer promising opportunities for addressing these challenges.

Creating Trading Zones where Different Voices and Interests Meet

A key barrier for professionalizing management arises from the tribal nature of the behavior of management practitioners and scholars alike. Most management scholars hardly or never engage with practice, and only talk to and write for their own tribes. So-called trading zones offer opportunities for (professionals with) different voices and interests to meet and trade. Successful trading zones offer a durable and psychologically safe platform for participants to meet and collaborate.

Potential trading zones are new business incubators, management labs, and professional degree programs, some of which already appear to enable more meaningful dialogues between highly different communities and voices in management scholarship and practice. A key finding is that trading zones are most likely to come alive in areas where there is a minimum of regulatory and institutional constraints, such as in the case of incubators.

This is not to say that managers in highly regulated organizational settings—for example publicly traded corporations or government agencies—will benefit less from the quest for professionalism. The point is that profound management innovations are not likely to be created and pioneered in these highly constrained settings. Therefore, new business creation is not only relevant to the management profession because all organizations (in order to be managed) first have to be created, but also because these entrepreneurial settings provide the flexibility to discover and try out new values, constructs, and models for managing any organization.

Raising Expectations of Management as Professional Discipline

If investors, shareholders, employees, union representatives, and others raise their expectations, management professionals will tend to internalize these expectations, which in turn will inspire and guide them to perform and deliver their best. How do we trigger such a virtuous circle? Established professions such as medicine and law are often equated with conditions and regulations for entry to the profession as well as sanctions and penalties regarding unprofessional conduct. These regulations and sanctions tend to have counterproductive effects on professional conduct—especially by transforming the intrinsic commitment to professionalism into an extrinsic one.

There are several ways to initiate the self-reinforcing effect of increased expectations, without the force of regulatory mechanisms. First, the transformation of silenced employees into assertive ones serves to raise the expectation and accountability level, especially toward those employees whom managers work with on a daily basis.

Second, prevailing accounting and control systems can be broadened to include a variety of non-financial performance measures—which serves to redirect the attention of many managers who would otherwise focus on financial performance.

Third, management professors, supervisory board members, management consultants, and other nascent professonionals need to pay much more attention to tensions and gaps between their own actual and espoused behavior as well as those of others. The ultimate test of professionalism is whether our actual behavior is consistent with what we say we are doing.

Leveraging These Paths

These four pathways, or levers, for professionalization are complementary in nature. Notably, management scholars do not need a commitment from an amorphous population of practitioners to start using any of these four levers. The strategies outlined for each path can be leveraged with active contributions from a select group of practitioners who are already actively seeking to professionalize their work in collaboration with management scholars.

At the core of management as a future profession is the alignment between professional purpose, knowledge, behavior, and expectation. The key challenge is to create a shared vision on what professionalism entails, which in turn will enable a viable and productive discourse on professionalizing management and entrepreneurship.

Contribution

Most literature on the professionalization of management focuses on business and management education and its problematic relationship with management practice (e.g. Khurana and Nohria 2008; Spender 2007; Barker 2010; Dierdorff et al. 2013). Moreover, Spender (2007) argues that, following the publication of the 1959 Ford and Carnegie reports, business schools in North America and later Europe successfully transformed management *education* into a profession, with accreditation systems and a specialized body of knowledge, even as management itself has yet to become one. Education in the area of management and entrepreneurship has therefore become heavily regulated by accreditation bodies such as AACSB and EQUIS, without a visible impact on professionalizing management and entrepreneurship practice (Spender 2007).

While the educational side is also relevant to the quest for professionalism, my main focus in this monograph is on management and entrepreneurship *scholarship*—as the driving force behind any intrinsic transformation of the profession at large. In focusing on how scholarship can contribute to professionalizing management practice, I will not so much attempt to scope the entire landscape of relevant literatures (Khurana 2007), but instead engage in an attempt to create a set of paths for renewing the quest for professionalizing management practice and scholarship. Chapter 1 explores the key parameters of this project in more detail.

The focus on envisioning and designing pathways for revitalizing the professional connection between management research and management practice also differentiates *The Quest for Professionalism* from related work. For example, Khurana's (2007) historical analysis of the rise and potential fall of American business schools, Starbuck's (2006) monograph on reforming the production of knowledge in the social sciences, Van de Ven's (2007) research guide on participative forms of engaged scholarship, and Rousseau's (2012a) edited volume on evidence-based management are highly congruent with some of the key ideas developed in this book. *The Quest for Professionalism* goes beyond this earlier work by explicitly envisioning and creating paths for renewing the professionalization quest.

Terminology

The Glossary of Terms at the end of the book provides definitions of the key terms used. Several key notions are used throughout *The Quest for Professionalism*.

First, *management* is defined here as inclusive of *entrepreneurship*. That is, managing involves the act of creating value that no single individual can create alone, by connecting and coordinating people and resources (Drucker 1974, 1985; Khurana and Nohria 2008; Anderson and Escher 2010). Accordingly, throughout this book the term "management" will refer to the broad domain of organization, innovation management, entrepreneurship, and management (studies). The shortcut "management" is often used to prevent longer phrases and sentences and make the text more readable.

Second, *The Quest for Professionalism* in this broadly defined domain is consistent with a similar discourse about firms in the professional services sector (e.g. Maister 2000), but also goes beyond that. The argument in *The Quest* applies to all managerial work, whether it is in professional service firms or in any other company and organization. Moreover, the discourse on professionalism in accounting, consulting, and other services focuses on professionals conducting work for clients (e.g. Maister 2000), whereas my argument in *The Quest* addresses all management "professionals" who connect and coordinate people and resources to create value, regardless of whether they conduct any direct work for external clients.

Third, the professionalization idea implies that practitioners as well as scholars in management should be considered as members of their nascent profession. Scholars cannot exempt themselves from the code the broader profession needs to commit to. Interestingly, most management scholars and educators are formally appointed as assistant, associate, or full "professors." Of course, scholars and practitioners have different roles in building and sustaining a professional community, but this division of labor does not imply that scholars can place themselves outside the quest for a professional identity. The quest for professionalism pertains to all work in the area of management and entrepreneurship that aspires to be "professional" in nature, and therefore also about scholarship.

Overview of Chapters

The first four chapters define the quest for professionalization and explore several ways to revitalize it. Chapter 1 seeks to understand professionalism in terms of purpose, knowledge, behavior, and expectation. Chapters 2 to 4 then assess each of these dimensions in more detail, and also provide a map of the territory that might give directions for those travelling and exploring this territory. This part of *The Quest* thus invites readers, as Kessler and Bartunek (2014: 241) advocate, to "think like cartographers" in order to understand the management landscape more comprehensively.

Chapter 1 develops the professionalization framework that structures the argument in the first four chapters of *The Quest for Professionalism*. First, the historical context of this quest is explored, and then several examples serve to point out that management currently is anything but a profession. The unresolved dispute on shareholder value maximization and multi-stakeholder management illustrates the lack of shared sense of purpose and understanding. Subsequently, a set of definitions and a multi-level framework of science-based professionalization is developed that identifies and connects four generative mechanisms of professionalization: purpose, knowledge, behavior, and expectations. This framework implies professionalization involves the development and alignment of purpose, knowledge, behavior, and expectations. If one or more of these four dimensions remain underdeveloped, so will the nature and level of professionalism of management and its scholarship.

Chapter 2 addresses the most fundamental challenge in professionalizing management: its purpose. In this chapter, I first discuss the pluralistic and fragmented nature of the management research landscape, and how this affects the discourse about the purpose and responsibility of management (scholarship) in society. Subsequently, a thought experiment designed by political philosophers provides a set of heuristics for evaluating any proposals regarding the purpose and responsibility of management as a profession. Moreover, several notions of purpose and responsibility developed by scholars and practitioners are outlined. Subsequently, the contours of a shared sense of purpose are inferred from the literature on pragmatism. Moreover, a collaborative attempt by seven scholars/practitioners results in a prototype of a shared sense of purpose and responsibility. Finally, I speculatively assess the level of support among management practitioners and scholars for this proposed statement of professional purpose.

Chapter 3 turns to the challenge of developing a body of knowledge the management profession can claim. First, the notion of "knowledge" is explored, by drawing on Aristotle's categorization of knowledge as well as the distinction between explicit and tacit knowledge. I then turn to defining and framing a professional body of knowledge in the area of management. A core idea here is that this body of knowledge arises from creative discovery as well as scientific validation. Both discovery and validation activity inform the discourse on management, organizational, and entrepreneurial practices—in terms of their constituent values, constructs, models, and principles. A key observation here is that most elements of such a body of knowledge are already present in the broader literature, albeit in a scattered and fragmented manner. The framework for a professional body of knowledge presented in this chapter might help to integrate the landscape and as such facilitate dialogue between professionals with widely different backgrounds and perspectives.

Chapter 4 focuses on the actual behavior and external expectations of management as a nascent profession. In this respect, the global population of management scholars is highly fragmented and the level of interaction between management scholars and management practitioners is generally poor. These behavioral patterns in management scholarship and practice appear to arise from the evolution of the human brain over many thousands of years, which has made it hard-wired toward tribalism. The notion of trading zones is therefore adopted to explore how common ground between different tribes in the management discipline can be developed and sustained. Management labs, new business incubators, and professional degree programs offer promising (albeit currently imperfect) trading zones that enable meaningful dialogues between tribes with highly different voices and interests. Moreover, I argue that scholar-consultants are more productive contributors to this type of trading zone than management consulting firms.

Chapters 5 to 7 draw on the case of circular organizing to extend the professionalization quest to issues of power and leadership. Thus, the maps of the territory developed in the previous chapters are used to understand the territory itself in a more in-depth manner.

Chapter 5 and *6* are both about circular organizing, a management technology that fundamentally redistributes power and authority throughout the organization. The case of circular organizing is of interest because the abuse and rationalization of power in organizational and administrative settings may be one of the most pressing problems of our time. A deeper understanding of how power can be shaped and controlled in organizational settings serves to redefine the (ab)use of power in managerial settings and firmly connect it to the professionalization agenda. *Chapter 5* explores the emergence of circular organizing, pioneered by the Dutch engineer and entrepreneur Gerard Endenburg as well as the American software engineer and entrepreneur Brian Robertson. The principles informing the circular approach as well as the various instantiations created with these principles are discussed. As circular organizing initially developed outside mainstream management theory and practice, *Chapter 6* seeks to connect it to key constructs and models in the management literature. In this respect, circular organizing systematically adresses fundamental issues of authority, ownership, and power, which tend to be marginalized and rationalized in mainstream management theorizing and practices.

Chapter 7 assesses the learnings that arise from the circular approach to management. At a more fundamental level, this approach implies a shift from established notions of leadership toward systems of distributed leadership. Subsequently, the discourse on shareholder value maximization and multi-stakeholder management is compared with circular organizing as an emerging management approach. This comparison serves to demonstrate in more detail how both the shareholder value and the multi-stakeholder literatures have been marginalizing fundamental issues and challenges in the area of ownership, authority, and power. Moreover, it suggests key issues in the area of power and authority need to be explicated and addressed, to advance the professionalization quest. The overview of three management approaches resulting from this chapter, may also constitute a first step toward a professional body of knowledge on management.

Finally, *Chapter 8* outlines the key implications and conclusions arising from *The Quest for Professionalism*. Four complementary paths for professionalizing management practice and scholarship are defined and outlined. The first path allows the development of a shared sense of professional purpose and responsibility. The second path explores the idea of a professional body of knowledge informed by both discovery and validation. A third path involves growing the number of trading zones in which professionals with different voices and interests can effectively meet and collaborate. The fourth path suggests how the expectations of professionalism in management can be raised. Finally, I discuss several implications for management education. For example, both undergraduate and graduate programs in management should provide opportunities for developing professional skills that align actual and espoused behavior.

1

The Professionalization Challenge

Introduction

The history of the quest for professionalism in management goes back to the early days of the management discipline. This chapter serves to explore this history, but also illustrates that management currently is anything but a profession. In particular, the dispute on shareholder value maximization and multi-stakeholder management exemplifies the lack of shared purpose and understanding. More broadly speaking, the quest for professionalism has been largely abandoned by business schools, and this quest is therefore highly contested.

The contested nature of the professionalization challenge appears to arise partly from differences between vocabularies and definitions. In this chapter, I will therefore explore and define what a "profession" is. The latter definition also informs the subsequent argument about science-based professionalism. In this respect, a multi-level definition of science-based professionalization is presented, involving four generative mechanisms (or levels): purpose, knowledge, behavior, and expectation. As a result, professionalization involves the development and alignment of shared purpose, a specialized body of knowledge, congruent behaviors, and public expectations. If one or more of these four levels remains underdeveloped, so will the professionalism of management and its scholarship. Finally, I will draw on this multi-level approach to argue that the professionalization of management is a grand societal challenge, on par with other challenges such as climate change.

Background and History

In many occupations and disciplines, the quest for professionalism initially involved a struggle for power, prestige, status, income, and privileges (Johnson 1972). In the Middle Ages, many guilds in Europe engaged in professionalization by acquiring exclusive rights to practice their trade, including the right to train and engage unpaid apprentices (Benton 1985). As of the nineteenth century, the idea and ideology of professionalism became increasingly popular in Europe and North-America, which spurred the development of several emerging professions—initially also including management (e.g. Metcalf 1926). Charles Babbage, Andrew Ure, Charles Dupin, Frederick Taylor, Henri Fayol, Mary Parker Follett, Chester Barnard, and many others therefore set out to develop and establish management as a profession in the late nineteenth and early twentieth century (Metcalf 1927; Wren and Bedeian 2008). In this vein, the first business schools were established to train a professional class of managers in the mold of lawyers and medical doctors (Sass 1982; Augier et al. 2005; Khurana 2007).

A historical turning point in the evolution of business and management schools was 1959, when both the Carnegie Corporation and the Ford Foundation published highly critical reports on the state of American business education. As Khurana (2007: 270) observes, the "goal of both the Ford and Carnegie reports was not simply to present a set of findings but, rather, to shake business schools out of their complacency and instigate change." Both reports renewed the idea of professionalism for management scholarship and education, emphasizing that the management profession would need to rest on a systematic body of knowledge, standards of professional conduct, and other components of a curriculum informed by rigorous science. Because early drafts of the Carnegie and Ford reports had been circulating as early as 1955, several leading schools had already started implementing most of the recommendations by 1959 (Khurana 2007). Many other business schools have, since the 1960s, been repositioning and reshaping their educational and research programs, with the initial intention to transform management education and scholarship in the direction of "science-based professionalism" (Simon 1991a).

However, American business schools as well as their European counterparts ended up misappropriating the initial idea of an intellectually robust and relevant research and educational agenda, which in turn contributed to the intellectual stasis of management scholarship and its capacity to inform management practice (Khurana and Spender 2012). In this respect, the Carnegie and Ford reports redirected business schools toward pursuing "management" as a rigorous science, but also legitimated their growing detachment from business practice (Khurana 2007). As a result, most business schools today treat their students as consumers of course content rather than apprentices in a profession, and most management scholars have abandoned the quest for professionalism and hardly or never engage with practice and practitioners.[1]

Academic and experiential knowledge are therefore, at best, loosely connected (Starkey and Madan 2001; Hughes et al. 2011). As a result, management scholarship today is not an organic part of a professional community, in contrast to, for instance, the medical and legal professions that rest on a shared body of research methods and findings on which practitioners seek to base their decisions and actions. At the core of professional work in engineering, medicine, and law is the dependence on and awareness of advances in knowledge, and therefore, "all that is required is for business schools to model themselves more closely on their other professional school counterparts and less on arts and sciences departments" (Pfeffer and Fong 2002: 93). Indeed, a key factor in developing professions such as law and medicine has been, and still is, the university as "the institution of the intellectual" (Jackson 1970: 4). With its emphasis on teaching and research, the modern university provides training in the intellectual tradition of the discipline as well as offers a legitimate structure of authority and competence (Jackson 1970).

This suggests business and management schools should reclaim their initial identity as "professional" schools, to revitalize the quest for professionalism in management (Van de Ven 2007; Pfeffer 2012). In this vein, James March believes the current malaise of management research is not so much a lack of relevance, but a "lack of essence" (quote in: Fendt 2013: 7). Similarly, Khurana and Nohria (2008) argue that management needs to become a profession similar to medicine and law, but observe that such professions have codes—like the Hippocratic Oath in medicine—that the management discipline is currently lacking.

The main challenge in writing such a code for management, according to Khurana and Nohria, is reaching a broad consensus on the purpose and aims of management. This is a huge challenge, because the management discipline is divided into two schools of thought: one school of thought arguing that management's aim is to maximize shareholder wealth, whereas the other school advocates balancing the claims of all the firm's stakeholders. Any code will therefore have to accommodate the notion of shareholder value as well as the accountability required for a broad set of stakeholders (Khurana and Nohria 2008).

Sobering Facts

The observation that management currently is *not* a profession can be backed up by many sobering facts. Many managers, even those with degrees obtained at business schools, struggle to lead and motivate their staff to realize objectives (Haney and Sirbasku 2011). Also disturbing, if not alarming, are the major gaps and inconsistencies between what most managers say they do and what they actually do (Argyris et al. 1985; Argyris 2004). As a result, about half of all managerial decisions made in organizations fail (Nutt 1999, 2011). At the same time, this amateurism in managerial practices is widely accepted as normal and inevitable, because employees, investors, journalists, and others tend to be ignorant of it (Elias and Scotson 1994).

The quest for professionalism is also a major challenge in public management and governance (Bowman and West 2011). Many democratically chosen governments have long been unable to tackle, for example, high public debt levels, widespread poverty, and increasing unemployment. Moreover, public administrators suffer from high levels of distrust in public institutions and a growing sense of powerlessness among many citizens (Dalton 2004; Ansell 2011). For example, survey data demonstrate that in most European countries between 60 and 80 percent of all citizens say they distrust political institutions; while in only a small number of European countries between 40 and 60 percent of all people express some level of trust in political institutions (Hendriks 2009). However, common sense suggests these "exceptional" levels of support and trust are still far too low for any institution to function in a professional manner (cf. Bauer et al. 2013).

In the corporate world, the ongoing stream of investment debacles, accounting scandals, options-backdating schemes, and other breaches of ethical standards (Martin 2011) illustrates how widespread non-professionalism is. In the next section, I will explore the unresolved debate between shareholder value and stakeholder management advocates, and its dramatic consequences for society-at-large.

Uneven Distribution of Professionalism

In absolute terms, there are many examples of professional excellence in management (e.g. Semler 1993; Cheney 2000; Pfeffer and Sutton 2000; Quarter 2000; Nayar 2010). Fact is, however, that the distribution of professional management practices is highly uneven, or what statisticians call "skewed." Figure 1.1 pictures this skewed distribution of professionalism in management—with many very badly managed organizations and relatively few organizations demonstrating professional excellence in their management practices. This distribution can be inferred from data collected by Bloom et al. (2015), consisting of cross-sectional and panel data on core management practices in over 10,000 firms from thirty countries in the Americas, Europe, and Asia. A key conclusion arising from this study is that globally there "appear to be so many very badly managed firms" compared to a small population of well-managed firms (Bloom et al. 2015: 23).[2]

Figure 1.1 also serves to depict the preferred "target" distribution in any quest for professionalism. The dotted curve represents this ideal future. Notably, even in a very mature stage of professionalization, there will be some

Figure 1.1. Distribution of professionalism in management among firms and other organizations

"bad apples" characterized by low level of professionalism—for example in settings where there is hardly any competitive pressure or people have no access to any formal (management) training. The key challenge in professionalization is not to erase all forms of amateurism, but to make high levels of professionalism the norm rather than the exception.

Raising the overall level of professionalism in management is not only the "right" thing to do on moral grounds. Throughout the world, young people are increasingly better educated and demanding more professional management practices from their employers. For example, a large study among 40,000 employees and managers at PricewaterhouseCoopers (PwC) observed that employees under the age of 30 perceive present management practices in PwC as highly dysfunctional, causing most of them to resign within two years (PwC 2013). Moreover, Bloom and co-authors (2012, 2015) demonstrate that the level and quality of management practice, or what they call *management technology*, has a strong effect on firm performance. The preferred distribution of professionalism in management practices, represented in Figure 1.1, is therefore not only in the interest of many employees and managers but is also of great importance for investors and customers.

Shareholders and Stakeholders

Maximizing Shareholder Value

Shareholder value proponents argue that corporations and their managers should focus on maximizing shareholder value (e.g. Aretz and Bartram 2010; Rappaport 1998). The commitment of many executives, directors, and investors to shareholder value maximization has been giving rise to a string of accounting scandals, options-backdating schemes, investment debacles, and other breaches of ethical standards (Martin 2011). The ideology of shareholder value has caused large corporations like Enron and ICI, once widely believed to be too big to fail, to completely break down (Fox 2003; Kay 2014). These and many other cases of corporate failure illustrate that managers whose sole objective is to maximize shareholder value are very likely to end up achieving the opposite, that is, destroying shareholder value. Managers of many other corporations like Nike, General Motors, and Philips have—in key episodes of their history—also rather exclusively focused on shareholder value, and done so at the expense of their customers, investors, suppliers, and employees (e.g. Boggan 2001).

The failure of the shareholder value (SV) idea appears to arise from short-termism, debt financing, false accounting, and stock options for managers. First, *short-termism* makes managers focus on increasing short-term value, rather than attending to the long-term performance and viability of the company (Walrave et al. 2011). For example, the demise of Kodak can be largely attributed to the SV short-termism that motivated its top managers to decide to abandon development of digital camera technology—that it had been pioneering for many years—to avoid any reduction in the sales volumes arising from its established analog technology (Helfat et al. 2007; Tripsas and Gavetti 2000).

Another reason for the failure of SV maximization is *debt financing*. When executives and directors embrace the target of maximizing SV, they often take on much more risk and more debt than they otherwise would do. Large volumes of debt tend to increase SV in the short run, because it almost immediately leverages a (relatively speaking) low baseline of equity in more value (Lazonick and O'Sullivan 2000). However, too much debt is detrimental to the long-term viability of the company, which is evident from, for example, Enron's demise (Fox 2003) and the near-bankruptcy of Royal Bank of Scotland that in 2008 had to be rescued by the UK government (Deakin 2014).

A focus on maximizing the current value of the corporation's equity also appears to invite *false accounting* and *reporting*. As such, current profits can be artificially increased by, for example, inflating revenues with bogus accounting entries, making less reservations for future risks on the balance sheet, manipulating the value of certain assets (e.g. brand names or intellectual property), or transferring costs and debts to subsidiary companies (Srivastava et al. 1998; Martin 2011; Deakin 2014). Systematic attempts to create false impressions of earnings have been uncovered in dramatic cases such as Worldcom and Enron, and appear to be rather widespread in shareholder value-driven corporations (Owen 1983; Backover 2002; Fox 2003; Cooper 2008; The Guardian 2012).

The short-termism, debt financing, and false accounting practices arising from a (too) strong focus on SV are likely to hit fertile ground if executives participate in a corporate *stock options* program. Stock options are options to buy equity in the corporation (at a fixed price) at a certain date in the future (Yermack 1995). Boards of directors establish stock option schemes for managers to align their interests with those of the shareholders, and indeed, the obvious effect is that managers with stock options start acting like shareholders. That is, these managers have a strong interest in the value of the company's stock going up in the period until the day when the options have to be exercised (Adamo 2013). As a result, stock options promote managerial decisions and actions that are beneficial to the short-term development of the stock price, but also increase the company's total risk (Armstrong and Vashishtha 2012) and as such are detrimental to the sustained success of the corporation in the long run (Walrave et al. 2011).

Multi-stakeholder Perspective

The most prominent alternative for shareholder value maximization is the so-called *multi-stakeholder* approach. Advocates of this approach believe managers should balance the interests of all stakeholders (Freeman 1984; Martin 2011; Kay 2014), that is, "all those interest groups, parties, actors, claimants and institutions—both internal and external to the corporation—that exert a hold on it" (Mitroff 1983: 4). The multi-stakeholder perspective has also informed the search for measures and interventions that would reduce some of the risks and negative effects arising from shareholder value maximization. These measures and interventions largely focus on the composition of the board of directors, legal duties of directors, executive pay, accounting treatment of stock options, activating the power of institutional investors, and the like (e.g. Charkham and Simpson 1999; Patterson 2009; Hayes et al. 2012; Williamson et al. 2014).

One key problem here is that the multi-stakeholder approach, as the antithesis of the shareholder value approach, is less developed in terms of legal entities, organizational designs, and other guidelines (e.g. Freeman et al. 2007; Kay 2014). Moreover, most practical solutions arising from the stakeholder approach focus on a single stakeholder, such as employees (Nayar 2010; O'Grady 2014), whereas leading advocates of this approach consider the corporation as a social institution that promotes the development of its business in the interests of all stakeholders (e.g. Freeman 1984).

Unresolved Nature of this Debate

The debate between shareholder value maximization and multi-stakeholder management advocates is essentially about the purpose of governance and management. The unresolved nature of this debate makes the claim that management is a professional discipline extra hard to defend (cf. Ghoshal 2005; Khurana and Nohria 2008; Tihanyi et al. 2014). Most management scholars have therefore abandoned the professionalization quest and, as such, have lost their way and become the "hired hands" of shareholders (Khurana 2007). The professionalization challenge for the management discipline therefore also implies the more specific challenge arising from the shareholder–stakeholder dilemma.

The unresolved nature of the shareholder–stakeholder debate has major consequences for corporations owned by shareholders that have no other stake in the corporation than a financial one. But privately traded companies, firms led by owner-entrepreneurs and non-profit organizations are facing similar challenges when they define the purpose and objectives of their organization and develop management systems and processes to realize these objectives. These organizations will also benefit from the professional capability to define and accomplish organizational purposes and objectives, and effectively be held accountable by investors, employees, and other constituencies.

What Is a Profession?

As observed earlier, since the 1960s many business schools have been repositioning and reshaping their curricula and research programs in the direction of science-based professionalism, but have ended up focusing on academic scholarship and education at the expense of professional relevance. All leading business schools in the US as well as their European counterparts nowadays overemphasize the "science" dimension.

Consequently, the idea that management is a profession is highly contested. For example, Barker (2010) argues that, unlike lawyers and medical doctors, managers do not adhere to a universal and enforceable code of conduct defined by professional bodies; moreover, "the abilities and learning required to be a good manager don't lend themselves to such oversight—and business education is more about acquiring the skill of integration than about mastering a set body of knowledge" (Barker 2010: 52). These observations underscore that management is not like any of the established professions, and never will be like them. Barker is also right in pointing out that the state of the art of management is far from being a profession.

But Barker does not provide an alternative identity of management as an occupational activity. If we do not expect managers to aim at professional behavior and performance, why would business and management schools educate (future) managers and engage in management research to build the knowledge base for these educational efforts? Indeed, medicine, architecture, and other professional disciplines have been facing similar challenges in their evolution toward established professional communities (e.g. Abbott 1988; Frankford et al. 2000). For example, Adler et al. (2008) demonstrate how the medical discipline has mutated from a craft guild to a liberal profession, and is currently evolving toward a more collaborative and civic professional community. This ongoing development is contested, with many barriers and a highly uncertain outcome (e.g. Adler et al. 2008; Timmons 2011).

The contested nature of professionalization in management appears to partly arise from the (implicit) differences between vocabularies and definitions. The remainder of this section therefore serves to explore and define the key notion of "profession," which in turn will inform the argument about science-based professionalism later in this chapter.

Profession

Historians, sociologists, and economists have extensively studied what professions are, how they arise, and so forth. An extensive review of this literature is beyond the scope of this chapter.[3] Abbott (1988: 318) defines professions as "somewhat exclusive groups of individuals applying somewhat abstract knowledge to particular cases." He deliberately adopts this rather loose definition because a profession is not objectively definable in view of its (perceived) power and status in our society.

Such an approach is problematic in the context of the quest for professionalism in management, because it implies we would aim at an undefined target. Moreover, Abbott's definition is highly retrospective in nature, by defining a profession as the outcome of a historical evolution toward an exclusive occupational group with high societal status and power. Such a retrospective definition cannot inform an attempt to discover and craft ways to enhance professionalism in management or any other nascent profession. Instead, *profession* is defined here as a vocation founded upon specialized knowledge and training. There are three key elements in this definition: vocation, specialized knowledge, and specialized training.

VOCATION
The term "vocation" refers to an occupational activity to which a person is specially drawn and dedicated. While the notion of vocation originated in religious (e.g. Christian) contexts, it is today more often used in a broad variety of professional settings such as law, accounting, nursing, psychiatry, medicine, and architecture. Vocation is a key dimension of these and other professions, because if one is not intrinsically motivated and drawn to the work of the incumbent profession, what remains is a transactional notion of professional activity in which expertise is being exchanged for money.

An underdeveloped sense of vocation among managers may lead them to adopt a one-dimensional focus on shareholder value, as argued earlier. The consequences of a lack of vocation can also be widely observed among management scholars, in the form of a "moral void" in which incentives and pressures to publish undermine the practical relevance of research, which in turn motivates many scholars to engage in plagiarism, mischaracterizing data, and other immoral behaviors (Reed 1996; Starkey and Madan 2001; Ghoshal 2005; Starbuck 2006; Honig and Bedi 2012; Matlack 2013).

SPECIALIZED KNOWLEDGE AND TRAINING

The second and third elements in the definition of profession, "specialized knowledge" and "specialized training" are evidently related. Some level of specialized training in the intellectual tradition of the discipline serves to guide professional behavior and performance, and also provides a sense of authority and competence to the profession (Jackson 1970). However, the knowledge and skills one gets from completing an educational program only partly determine the "specialized knowledge" required. In any professional domain, specialized knowledge is partly also tacit and experiential in nature, involving knowledge and insights arising from on-the-job training and experiences (Wilensky 1964) or what has also been called interactional and contributory expertise (Collins and Evans 2007).

EXAMPLES

Whereas vocation is largely normative and motivational in nature, specialized training and knowledge constitute the instrumental dimension of professional work (Wilensky 1964). Together, the normative and instrumental elements of a profession explain why law, medicine, teaching, nursing, and architecture are widely considered to be professions, whereas taxi drivers, carpenters, and call center agents are not.

Newcomers and apprentices in occupations such as taxi driving are not required to have a strong intrinsic motivation for the job. Moreover, there typically is no extensive specialized training that must have been completed before entering the occupation. Carpenters and taxi drivers acquire most knowledge and skills while on-the-job, possibly complemented with apprenticeship training. Call center agents, especially those in call centers operating internationally, draw on proficiency in multiple languages that can only be acquired via extensive education and training, but this expertise is not sufficiently specialized to justify the label "professional" (e.g. several other occupations in international sales and tourism draw on a highly similar multi-language proficiency).

Obviously, occupational groups such as taxi drivers and carpenters often seek to regulate and professionalize their occupation. But that does necessarily imply they also are, or can become widely viewed and respected as a profession (cf. Wilensky 1964). As Abbott's (1988) work demonstrates, many occupations seek to become professions, but only few meet the standards that make people speak about them as a professional occupation.

SOCIO-POLITICAL DIMENSION
The definition of profession adopted earlier serves to demarcate the territory, but also illustrates what is excluded. A key dimension excluded is the socio-political dimension. This is not to say that (management as) a profession is without socio-political processes. The socio-political dimension is pivotal in any attempt to understand behavior and performance in organizational and societal settings. Moreover, established professions such as medicine and law have developed regulatory mechanisms for accrediting and controlling its members and their professional activities.

These regulatory mechanisms serve to protect the profession and control the entry of newcomers to the profession, and thereby sustain their high societal prestige. Especially when the discipline becomes increasingly professionalized, as defined earlier, its internal and external stakeholders tend to pay more and more attention to these regulatory mechanisms. Later in this chapter, I will return to the role of regulatory mechanisms.

Simon's Call for Science-based Professionalism

The definition of a profession adopted earlier also includes vocations such as priests and ministers, which suggests that non-scientific systems of thought can also provide the "specialized knowledge" base for a profession (Wilensky 1964). Simon (1967) therefore recommended that business schools pursue "science-based professionalism" rather than merely professionalism. At the time, Simon worried about business schools splitting into faculty inhabiting the discipline-oriented world and those living in the profession-oriented world; the discipline-oriented scholars would be part of the social system of scientists in the relevant disciplines (e.g. economics and psychology) and the profession-oriented faculty would be completely immersed in the social system of practitioners. As such, the biggest danger to the future of business schools would be that the barrier between these two social systems is transferred from the outside world to the business school itself (Simon 1967).

Instead, Simon advocated a dual orientation toward both professional practice and fundamental research. He argued the business school can and must be a very productive and challenging environment for scholars seeking to understand and "exploit the advantages of having access to the 'real world' as a generator of basic research problems and a source of data" (Simon 1976: 341), also to prevent profession-oriented faculty becoming entirely "dependent on the world of business as its sole source of knowledge inputs" (pp. 349–50). Business and other professional schools must therefore go to great lengths to avoid a separation between discipline-oriented and profession-oriented faculty members by developing "an explicit, abstract, intellectual *theory* of the processes of synthesis and design, a theory that can be analyzed and taught in the same way that the laws of chemistry, physiology, and economics can be analyzed and taught" (Simon 1976: 354).

Critiques and Extensions

In his call for science-based professionalism, Simon appears to draw on several problematic assumptions. Schön (1987) and Krippendorff (2006) observe that Simon draws on an implicit notion of technical rationality, in which fundamental (scientific) knowledge is applied to practical problems (see also: Crowther-Heyck 2005; Dasgupta 2003). Simon's version of science-based professionalism is therefore not concerned "with uncertainty, uniqueness, or conflict, presumably because he regards his proposed science of design as applicable, at least in principle, to the entire topography of professional practice" (Schön 1987: 308).

Both Schön (1987) and Krippendorff (2006) therefore extend the design challenge for professional schools as initially defined by Simon. In addition to the barriers between discipline-oriented and practice-oriented faculty, they point at more fundamental challenges at the level of different kinds of rationality (assumptions) pursued and the type of discourse that would effectively connect both types of scholarship and thereby support a self-reflective reproduction of management as a profession (Schön 1987; Krippendorff 2006).[4]

Rousseau (2012b) revisited Simon's original advocacy for professionalism, to identify several interventions that might redirect business schools back to their professional mission. In this respect, Rousseau points at the key role that evidence-based management and design science can play in helping business schools realize their (original) founding purpose. She also provides a hypothetical example of a so-called "organizational learning contract" that defines the expectations and commitments, to be shared by the school's leaders, staff, and students in their collaborative effort to accomplish the professional mission. Table 1.1 reproduces this organizational learning contract. Explicating these (new) expectations and commitments in business schools is important because "some existing beliefs need to be unlearned" (Rousseau 2012b: 616). Moreover, the organizational learning contract proposed by Rousseau may guide policy decisions and provide novel ways of recruiting new faculty as well as help to re-orient existing faculty.

Table 1.1. Example of an "Organizational Learning Contract" for business schools

Parties	Students, Faculty (research/practice), Dean and Senior Leadership, Administrators, Practitioners Affiliated with Business School.
Our school's core practices (all parties engaged in to various degrees)	*Professionalism:* Commit to practice based on best available knowledge. Code of conduct that is lived by all (everyone knows the Code and can explain it to others). *Collaborations across disciplines and with practice.* Scholars are engaged with practice, practice problems, and practitioners. Practitioners are engaged with science, scientific problems, and scientists. Students and administrators are engaged with both. *Critical thinking.* We're the people in room asking What's the evidence? Why do we think this? *Insistence on use of science and facts:* In teaching, designing practices, solving problems, implementation, and administration. Ongoing data gathering to evaluate mission success. *Advancement of science, active intellectual contributions to profession and education, and advancement of practice.* Research that is of significant scientific and practical value. Supports systematic reviews of what is known and what we still need to learn to guide teaching, research, and practice. Students and alumni participate in and collaborate on research.
Learning environments (Multiple settings to aid student learning and ease its transfer)	*Classroom:* The learning process and its content are models of professional practice. *Science/Practice Commons:* Opportunities, venues, and tasks create joint interactions. *Projects:* Practical problem solving using scientific and practical knowledge. *Internships:* Use of student skills, advance their learning goals. *Simulations:* Use of student skills, support their learning. *External Contacts:* Intellectual contributions to profession, businesses, alumni, associations. *Administrative Practices:* Business school leaders and managers model use of evidence from science and organizational facts in decisions, policies, practices, and interactions.
Outcome examples (Monitored for purposes of feedback and redesign)	*Student skill development*—pre-/post-tests for courses and curricular activities. *Student skill use*—internships, alumni. *New applications*—faculty/student development of patents, interventions, products, decision aids. *Teaching based on best available evidence* from science and practice. *Introduction of new science/practice-based teaching content.* *Significant scientific research*—citations, awards, impact on business education and practice.

Source: Rousseau (2012b: 615).

These critiques and extensions of Simon's initial call for science-based professionalism demonstrate that the professionalization quest in management cannot be tackled with a one-dimensional strategy.

Can Management Scholarship Transform Itself (Again)?

As observed earlier, management scholars and their institutions appear to have over-accomplished the transformation to science-based professionalism. They have been overshooting this target and thereby narrowed it to the "science" dimension (Khurana and Spender 2012). Therefore, the transformational capabilities of management scholarship, business schools, and other stakeholders involved should not be underestimated. Anyone arguing such transformational capabilities are underdeveloped or do not exist (e.g. due to institutional inertia) is proven wrong by the history of management education and scholarship over the past five decades. Indeed, a fundamental transformation from "vocationalism" to "science" was effectively made in this period (Augier et al. 2005; Khurana and Spender 2012).

The key challenge in *The Quest for Professionalism*, therefore, is to revitalize the idea of professionalism *and* effectively connect it to the relatively young tradition of management scholarship as it currently prevails. The remainder of this chapter outlines a multi-level perspective that might help address the complexity of this unfinished quest.

Professionalization: A Multi-level Perspective

This section serves to develop a multi-level definition of (science-based) professionalism that can inform the professionalization quest in management practice and scholarship. The key argument will be that professionalization occurs through four generative mechanisms (cf. Hedström and Swedberg 1996; Pawson 2006): purpose, knowledge, behavior, and expectation. Figure 1.2 provides a visual representation of these four generative mechanisms of professionalization.

Purpose

At the heart of any professionalization process is the vocational dimension, as defined earlier. This vocational dimension arises from a shared sense of *purpose*,

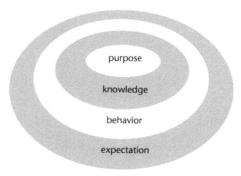

Figure 1.2. Key generative mechanisms of professionalization: purpose, knowledge, behavior, and expectation

that is, a "commitment to a good broader than self-interest" (Despotidou and Prastacos 2012: 437), or what Khurana and Nohria (2008) call a professional code. Shared purpose provides the profession with a collective identity, also by forging an implicit social contract with society: society entrusts members of the profession to perform a particular set of tasks, and in return the profession ensures societal stakeholders that its professionals are worthy of being trusted. The codes of the legal and medical professions are good examples. Frankel (1989) identifies three types of professional purpose that act as a foundation and guide for professional conduct in the face of morally ambiguous situations: aspirational, educational, and regulatory. Because the professionalization of management is still in a very early stage, *The Quest for Professionalism* focuses on the aspirational dimensions of professional purpose.[5]

Knowledge

Another professionalization mechanism is the search for, and contestation of, the *knowledge* base that the profession can claim (Abbott 1988). This body of knowledge has two key interdependent elements: expertise and values. Professionals draw on expertise in the form of insights and tools, which in turn are based on a "vocabulary" that serves to define and describe problems and challenges as well as a "language" in the form of conceptual frameworks, models, and theories (March and Smith 1995).

All professional expertise, including the scholarship involved, is inherently ethical in nature (Myers and Thompson 2006; Wicks and Freeman 1998). Therefore, the values that guide professional conduct and work are explicit elements of a professional body of knowledge. These values constitute the normative dimension of any professional activity and are a key mechanism for ensuring its capacity to guide professional work (Adler et al. 2008). Consequently, when managers and their stakeholders misrepresent and lose sight of their professional values in highly turbulent and complex settings, their professional conduct and performance is also compromised (Flyvbjerg 2006). Together, professional values and expertise constitute the body of knowledge claimed by a profession.

Behavior

The *behavioral* dimension, broadly defined, refers to how professionals divide and coordinate work, organize the work flow, monitor the quality of their work and that of others, perform (e.g. on key outcome measures), account for their performance, and so forth. The actual behavior of practitioners and scholars in the profession may raise gaps and tensions between the purpose and values they espouse and those actually being used (Argyris et al. 1985; Van

Maanen and Barley 1984), particularly when these diverge. For example, the level of engagement of management scholars with practice and practitioners is generally poor (Starkey and Madan 2001; Starbuck 2006; Gulati 2007; Hughes et al. 2011), even though the objectives and values expressed by leading academic assocations suggest otherwise (e.g. Academy of Management 2015).

Expectation

The level of *expectation* involves the expectations of a variety of stakeholders of the profession. True professions raise high expectations among external stakeholders, and in turn, these expectations inspire and guide professionals to perform and deliver their best. Whereas professionalization is often equated with conditions and regulations for entry to the profession as well as sanctions and penalties regarding unprofessional conduct, these regulations and sanctions tend to have perverse effects on professional conduct. In fact, management education has become overly regulated by accreditation bodies such as AACSB and EQUIS, without any impact on the professionalization of management practice and scholarship (Spender 2007).

Mechanisms to control entry to the profession as well as regulate behavior by its members are not fundamental to professionalization—in line with how "profession" was defined earlier. Rather, these regulatory and institutional mechanisms may arise as outcomes of "successful" professionalization trajectories (Abbott 1988), in which a group of (nascent) professionals wins the battle for claims on a body of knowledge and professional work conducted on the basis of that knowledge (Khurana 2007). The history of professions such as law and medicine demonstrates that certain groups within these occupations first had to contest and claim a unique body of knowledge in competition with other groups, typically with a major role of university education and research, before regulatory mechanisms could be developed and implemented (Abbott 1988).

More importantly, I will argue and demonstrate in Chapters 5 to 8 that the quest for professionalism in the area of management must address issues of power and authority *directly* at the level of knowledge, behavior, and expectation—rather than merely adding a regulatory layer to Figure 1.2.

Interdependence

These four generative mechanisms are obviously interdependent and complementary in any effort toward professionalization. For example, the better the members of the profession have together defined and communicated their shared purpose, the easier it will be to meet public expectations of the profession. Moreover, a body of knowledge serves to inform professional conduct and performance, and in turn, researching the latter helps to extend the body of knowledge (Rousseau 2012b). But it is also evident that the actual conduct of individual members of the profession needs to be consistent with the shared purpose as well as the specialized knowledge they draw on and espouse (cf. Despotidou and Prastacos 2012).

Defining Science-based Professionalism

This multi-level framework of professionalization now serves to define *science-based professionalism* as the alignment of:

- the shared purpose (P) among members of the profession;
- the body of knowledge (K) these professionals have access to;
- the actual behavior (B) of these professionals in terms of actions and decisions; and
- the expectation (E) of a variety of internal and external stakeholders.

This definition can be summarized in a simple equation:

$$professionalism = P \times K \times B \times E$$

Assuming that each of the four dimensions can be scored on a scale from 0 to 1, this equation implies that each of the four factors directly affects the level of professionalism. It also means that even when most of these dimensions are relatively high, a low score on one dimension will dramatically affect the level of professionalism. The latter case may be an entirely theoretical one, because in practice the four dimensions are likely to co-evolve (cf. Abbott 1988). For example, if the purpose and knowledge dimensions are underdeveloped, then it is unlikely that external stakeholders will have high expectations that professionals can actually live up to, and vice versa.

In view of the interdependence between the four levels of professionalization, *alignment* is thus a key element in the definition of professionalism (cf. the multiplicative nature of the $P \times K \times B \times E$ equation). This alignment can be shaped in various ways, such as through aspiration and commitment, economic incentive, legal restriction, and regulation (Abbott 1988; Spender 2007). At the core of any twenty-first-century quest for professionalism, however, is the aspirational and vocational alignment between purpose, knowledge, conduct, and expectation, because an intrinsic commitment to these dimensions of professionalism is what most effectively inspires and guides professional work.

Assessing Professionalism in Management

Drawing on the definition of professionalism previously developed, the level of professionalism of the management discipline can now be assessed as follows. First, there is hardly any shared sense of professional purpose (Khurana and Nohria 2008; Barker 2010; Rolin 2010; Heracleous 2011); *P is therefore low*. Second, the academic body of knowledge is highly fragmented (Starkey and Madan 2001; Walsh et al. 2006) and only loosely connected to practical knowledge and application (Hughes et al. 2011); *K is therefore low*. Moreover, our ignorance about organizations and managing them "is so great that forms of malfunctioning and the suffering which results from it are ubiquitous and are widely accepted as normal and unavoidable" (Elias and Scotson 1994: 181); that is, *both B and E are therefore also rather low*.

Therefore, the professionalization challenge in management is to create a vision of management as a collaborative profession that thrives on a viable and productive discourse on managerial work and performance (cf. Krippendorff 2006). *The Quest for Professionalism* serves to develop and propose such a vision, and also explore ways to bring this vision to life.

The multi-level perspective on professionalization in Figure 1.2 reflects the image of an inner core surrounded and protected with multiple layers. The outer generative mechanisms of professionalization are more variable and dynamic, whereas the inner mechanisms such as purpose tend to be more inert and difficult to change. Moreover, in any quest for professionalism the inner and outer mechanisms play different roles over time (Abbott 1988; Khurana 2007). Here, the development of a shared purpose and an initial knowledge base grounded in professional values serves as a prerequisite for the other dimensions of professionalization. In this respect, Khurana (2007: 82) draws on Abbott's (1988) work on professional contestation, to observe that "a key prerequisite of any professionalization project is that a cognitive basis for such claims of unique knowledge be at least approximately defined before a rising profession can stake its claim to specific tools and techniques, thereby establishing its absolute superiority over competitors." Therefore, the behavior and expectation dimensions of professionalization can only come about once an initial identity at the level of purpose and knowledge has been established.

Generally speaking, any attempt to renew the quest for professionalism in our discipline has to take the interdependence of expectation, behavior, knowledge, and purpose into account. Figure 1.3 illustrates how the dynamics at different levels may reinforce and complement each other, but can also go against and undermine each other (cf. Van Olffen 2014). Changes can sometimes be assumed to primarily occur at the "surface" levels of behavior and expectation, with limited or no changes required at other levels (Bartunek et al. 2011; Van Olffen 2014). The quest for science-based professionalism in management evidently requires substantial transformation and growth at each layer of professionalization. Moreover, the four dimensions of the professionalization quest will have to positively reinforce each other, to have any chance of success.

Figure 1.3. Visual images of how professionalization may evolve over time
Source: Adapted from Van Olffen (2014).

Professionalizing Management as Grand Challenge

The multi-level perspective previously developed suggests the quest for professionalism in management is one of the grand societal challenges of our time. Following Ferraro et al. (2015), a grand societal challenge is characterized by many interactions and nonlinear dynamics, has highly uncertain dimensions and consequences, and cuts across jurisdictional boundaries implying multiple evaluation criteria. Accordingly, grand challenges such as poverty, climate change, and professionalizing management require a collective response that allows diverse and heterogeneous actors to interact constructively over prolonged timespans, and moreover, sustains different interpretations among various audiences with different interests and backgrounds. A grand societal challenge potentially has many solutions, and therefore "there is no way of knowing in advance how best to proceed," which calls for multiple distributed experiments, to find out what works and what does not work (Ferraro et al. 2015: 376).

In addressing the widespread non-professionalism in management, *The Quest for Professionalism* therefore needs to go beyond a focus on one or two of the dimensions of professionalization identified earlier. Notably, the quest for professionalism in management is itself also highly contested—as is also the case for climate change as a grand challenge—implying that many of its (potential) stakeholders have abandoned it or are not (yet) prepared to join it. *The Quest for Professionalism* will therefore also explore the conditions under which management scholars and practitioners are inclined to engage in the professionalization of their work.

Overview of Subsequent Argument

The Introduction to this book contains a detailed overview of subsequent chapters. Figure 1.4 visualizes the key structure of the argument in the remainder of this book, using the professionalization framework developed earlier. Chapter 2 explores ways to develop a sense of professional purpose among

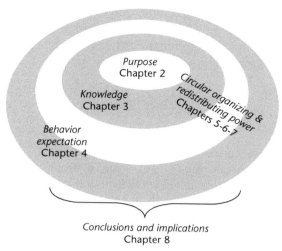

Figure 1.4. Overview of book, mapped on the four professionalization mechanisms

management scholars and practitioners. Chapter 3 serves to create a broad framework for a professional body of knowledge. Subsequently, the behavioral and expectational mechanisms of the professionalization quest are explored in Chapter 4.

Chapters 5 to 7 turn to the interdependence between these different professionalization dimensions, and consider new ways to reconnect them. This part of *The Quest for Professionalism* especially draws on circular organizing, a management approach that redistributes power and leadership throughout the organization. Finally, Chapter 8 synthesizes the conclusions and implications of *The Quest for Professionalism* in terms of several promising paths for the professionalization of management, and also outlines the implications for management education.

Concluding Remarks

Although the idea of professionalism has motivated the work of early pioneers in the management discipline, management is currently anything but a profession. The unresolved dispute on shareholder value maximization and multi-stakeholder management illustrates the lack of shared professional purpose and understanding. Attempts to professionalize the management discipline are therefore highly contested.

The key notion of profession was explored and defined in this chapter, and subsequently, a multi-level framework of professionalization was developed. This framework also informs the definition of science-based professionalism adopted here. Moreover, it suggests the professionalization quest in management is a grand societal challenge involving multiple interdependent levels. In subsequent chapters I will explore the different levels of professionalization in more detail, and also reconnect them in new ways.

Notes

1. As observed and documented by for example Khurana (2007), Heracleous (2011), Hughes et al. (2011), and Kaplan (2014). Notably, many business schools in Europe initially resisted the academicization of the field, and indeed appear to have developed a somewhat distinct (e.g. interdisciplinary) profile. However, over time they have also largely abandoned the professionalization agenda (Kaplan 2014).
2. See also Bloom et al. (2012) and Bloom et al. (2014).
3. Excellent overviews of the literature are provided elsewhere (e.g. Abbott 1988; Adler et al. 2008; Despotidou and Prastacos 2012; Khurana 2007).
4. In his autobiographical *Models of My Life*, Simon (1991a: 44) did not directly engage with these critiques, but he did admit that a time constant throughout his career was the "logical positivism" that he embraced as a graduate student and "never relinquished." A core thesis pursued in *The Quest For Professionalism* is that any foundational approach to the philosophy of knowledge and science (be it positivistic, constructivistic, or otherwise) is antagonistic to the overall pragmatist thrust of any professional discipline.
5. Management education appears to have successfully professionalized itself, but has done so without a significant impact on professionalizing management practice (Spender 2007). This book therefore focuses on management practice and scholarship. The implications for management education will be explored in Chapter 8.

2

Purpose and Professionalization

Introduction

Aristotle argued that every skill and every inquiry, and thus every action and choice of action, has some good as its object: "This is why the good has rightly been defined as the object of all endeavours...as everything is done with a goal, and that goal is *good*" (Aristotle, Nicomachean Ethics 1.1, as quoted by Strichow 2013: 184). Similarly, one of the most fundamental questions raised in the previous chapter involves the purpose of management practice and scholarship. In this chapter, I will first discuss the pluralistic and fragmented nature of the management research landscape, and explore how this affects the discourse about the purpose and responsibility of management (scholarship) in society. Subsequently, a thought experiment designed by political philosophers provides a set of heuristics for evaluating proposals regarding the purpose and responsibility of management as a profession. Moreover, several notions of purpose and responsibility developed by scholars and practitioners are outlined.

Subsequently, the contours of a shared sense of purpose are inferred from the literature on pragmatism. To specify such a shared sense of purpose in a written statement, I draw on a collaborative effort to produce such a statement by a highly diverse group of seven scholars/practitioners. The thrust of this prototype of a shared purpose is that management practice and scholarship would thrive on dialogical encounters between highly different voices, and as such exploit and enhance the pluralistic nature of the management landscape, while avoiding extreme fragmentation. Finally, I speculatively assess the level of support among management scholars and practitioners for this normative statement of professional purpose and responsibility.

Pluralism and Fragmentation

The landscape of management studies is highly fragmented and not systematically organized. Moreover, academic and experiential knowledge are, at best, loosely connected (Starkey and Madan 2001; Walsh et al. 2006; Hughes et al. 2011). As such, the quest for science-based professionalism in management is highly contested, as observed in the previous chapter. The pluralistic and fragmented nature of the management discipline is often depicted as unchangeable (e.g. Pfeffer 1993; Lampel 2011; Venkataraman et al. 2012), consistent with the idea that several existing paradigms and epistemologies are incommensurable (Deetz 1996; Jarzabkowski et al. 2010). In this respect, graduate students and other newcomers to management research are typically inducted into scholarship by means of personal mentoring, to adopt either a positivist or constructivist stance to which they then stick throughout their career (e.g. Czarniawska 2003; Donaldson 2003; Stablein and Frost 2004; Bradbury Huang 2010). As a result, the philosophical basis of management research and practice remains highly disputed.

Cultivating Dialogue, Diversity, and Dissent

Some scholars advocate a constructive dialogue and interaction between proponents of different paradigms (Hassard and Wolfram Cox 2013), or pursue multi-paradigm literature reviews and research strategies to juxtapose different perspectives and thereby foster mutual understanding (Schultz and Hatch 1996; Lewis and Kelemen 2002; Aguinis et al. 2014). For example, Schultz and Hatch (1996) developed a theory of paradigm interplay that accentuates differences and interconnections among paradigm representations; as such, paradigm interplay would foster an appreciation of how the insights and limitations from one paradigm are most apparent from an opposing one.

This multi-paradigm discourse can be used to argue that the pluralistic nature of management research cultivates diversity and dissent (e.g. Seidl 2007). However, based on a detailed philosophical assessment of the "organization studies" (OS) landscape, Rolin (2010) suggests the OS community would only be able to cultivate a research culture of diversity and dissent if it subscribed to, and acted upon, some *shared norm of responsibility*—that currently appears to be missing (see also: Palmer et al. 2009; Tadajewski 2009). In this respect, Rolin talks about a norm of "epistemic responsibility," among philosophers also known as "intellectual responsibility." She argues epistemic responsibility in OS would need to involve the strong desire to have "true" beliefs, and thus the desire to have one's beliefs produced by processes which lead to true beliefs; "true" in the sense of valid and reliable (Rolin 2010). This appears to be a circular argument, because there is no agreement whatsoever among management scholars on, for example, the notion of validity (e.g. Worren et al. 2002; Sandberg and Tsoukas 2011; Shapira 2011). Later in this chapter, I will therefore attempt to avoid this circular argumentation.

This minor definitional issue aside, Rolin's assessment provides a fundamental insight that is critical for professionalizing the management (incl. OS) discipline. This assessment suggests most management scholars are unlikely to welcome the recommendation to cultivate pluralism and dissent, unless there is a shared norm of professional purpose and responsibility. The concerns of many management scholars about the fragmentation of their discipline (e.g. Whetten 1989; Donaldson 2003; Shapira 2011) appear to arise from the idea that, first, too much diversity in values, theories, and methods will lead to fragmentation; and second, a consensus on theory and method is needed to maintain the unity of the discipline. By contrast, other scholars assume a highly pluralistic landscape of values, theories, and methods is essential to the discourse on management, and inevitably brings along a high level of fragmentation (e.g. Lewis and Kelemen 2002; Czarniawska 2003; Seidl 2007).

Addressing Fragmentation at the Level of Purpose Rather Than Knowledge

Both sets of assumptions regarding the fragmentation of the field, previously outlined, are trying to address this significant problem at the same level of thinking as where the problem has been arising—that is, at the knowledge and behavior levels in Figure 1.2. Here, Albert Einstein's recommendation that significant problems are better addressed at another level of thinking than where they were created (Hurd 1998) may serve to redirect the discourse about pluralism and fragmentation in the management discipline. As such, the multi-level perspective on professionalization introduced in Chapter 1 suggests we can only cultivate diversity, pluralism, and dissent at the level of behavior and knowledge (incl. theorizing and methodology issues), if there is a strong shared sense of professional purpose and responsibility. The need for a minimum amount of common ground is similar to a shared understanding of the purpose and rules of the game in competitive sports such as baseball, soccer, or basketball. Without such a shared understanding, spectators and (competing) players cannot engage in the game and enjoy it.

A good example of shared professional purpose as a generative mechanism is the case of Paul Farmer in health care, described by Ansell (2011) based on Kidder's biography (2003). Farmer is an American antropologist and physician that pressed the World Health Organization (WHO) for major changes. In the early 1990s, the WHO was conducting a major program to control tuberculosis using a powerful chemotherapy treatment known as DOTS. This treatment was institutionalized on a global scale and achieving impressive results. However, from local clinics in Haiti and Peru, Paul Farmer learned that DOTS for some patients was also producing substantial negative side-effects in the form of resistance to multiple tuberculosis drugs. The WHO and other stakeholders initially regarded these side-effects as unfortunate but inevitable, given the success of the program as a whole. Farmer and colleagues therefore initiated small experiments in Peru, to demonstrate that tuberculosis patients with multiple drug resistance were effectively treatable. By repeatedly present-ing their research findings on medical conferences and lobbying for change, Farmer and colleagues capitalized on the overall purpose of the health care profession—quality health care as a basic human right, also for the poor—and succeeded in getting the WHO to modify its tuberculosis treatment recom-mendations and programs (Kidder 2003; Ansell 2011).

The generative role of shared purpose has been documented in studies of, for example, collective mindfulness (Weick et al. 1999), inner knowledge creation (Corner and Pavlovich 2014), and the role of positive emotions in organizational development (Frederickson 2003). Moreover, widely used tools in the area of strategic and organizational change—such as appreciative inquiry summits (Cooperrider and Whitney 1999) and the World Café approach (Brown 2005)—emphasize and exploit the generative impact of shared purpose. The fragmented nature of management scholarship is there-fore best addressed at the level of professional purpose. With a minimum amount of professional purpose as common ground under our feet, conversa-tions amongst a plurality of voices are more likely to come alive and be sustained.

Before exploring what this common ground might look like, it is helpful to consult political philosophers regarding how a community would, ideally, agree on any shared principles.

A Thought Experiment

In political philosophy, there is long history of thought on how "social contracts" among people should come about. In his famous *A Theory of Justice*, John Rawls (1971) builds on this discourse by conducting a thought experi-ment, based on the idea that any attempt to understand and develop society would greatly benefit by specifying the correct position an individual should take in thinking about "justice." Whereas Rawls created this thought experi-ment to design the moral structure of a "well-ordered" society, resulting in a set of principles around liberty, equality, and distributive justice (Rawls 1971: 397), here it serves as a thought experiment regarding the purpose of man-agement as a profession.

THE "VEIL OF IGNORANCE" THOUGHT EXPERIMENT

Adapted to the challenge of developing a shared sense of purpose for management as a professional discipline, Rawls' hypothetical scenario runs as follows. A group of managers and management professors is set the task of reaching an agreement about the political and economic structure of their profession, which they will occupy once an agreement has been reached. Each individual in the group, however, deliberates behind a "veil of ignorance" (Rawls 1971: 136); that is, each participant lacks knowledge of, for example, his or her age, gender, religion, skills, wealth, educational background, and area of specialization. The only thing all participants know is that they can and will be members of the management profession, and that each of them possesses the basic capabilities required to fully and willfully contribute to the profession being created. Following Rawls, there are two such basic capabilities:

(i) the individual capability to form, pursue, and revise a conception of the collective "purpose" of the profession that is being created; at the start of the experiment, however, participants do not exactly know what sort of conception of this purpose they will form (e.g. whether it is vocational or transactional in nature);

(ii) the individual capability to develop a sense of responsibility for the shared purpose of their profession and a generally effective desire to act and perform according to it.

In this hypothetical scenario, all participants know only these two individual features of themselves. Under these conditions, each participant is asked to design a structure for the profession that will secure him/herself a maximal advantage. The interesting result of this thought experiment is that proposals one would ordinarily think of as unjust or unfair—such as exclusively connecting the profession's purpose to a particular educational background or area of specialization within the profession—will not be proposed anyway. It would be entirely irrational for any participant to do so, not knowing their own educational background, specialization, and so forth.

This thought experiment, for example, serves to assess the idea of shareholder value maximization, discussed in Chapter 1. Would any participant in the experiment propose "maximization of shareholder value" as the purpose of professional management? This is very unlikely, I would say. And even if someone does propose shareholder value maximization as a shared purpose, most other participants will not accept it. In general, Rawls' thought experiment suggests a shared conception of purpose is one that every member of the profession, starting from a fair position, would accept and agree to.

Other political philosophers have extended the argument proposed by Rawls. For example, Gauthier (1986: 168) in *Morals by Agreement* draws on game theory to demonstrate it is highly rational to give up the straightforward

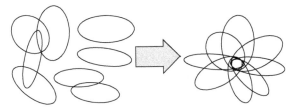

Figure 2.1. The challenge of developing a minimum amount of common ground between otherwise highly different perspectives

pursuit of self-interest and instead adopt a disposition of "constrained maximization." Accordingly, people are likely to cooperate with all those disposed toward conforming to a shared set of principles and defect on the rest, since repeated cooperation appears to provide greater yields than repeated mutual defection from agreed principles. In other words, such an agreed set of principles is justified because they make everyone better off. Gauthier (1986: 104) suggests these "moral" principles are entirely a matter of elevated utilitarian thinking, in which "morality is identified with *collective* maximization."

FUNDAMENTAL CHALLENGE
The fundamental challenge of identifying and agreeing on any shared purpose in the field of management practice and scholarship is visualized in Figure 2.1. The argument by Rawls and Gauthier suggests that all stakeholders in the management profession would ideally need to detach themselves from their particular background and interest, to be able to collaboratively define their shared purpose—as some overlap to be created between all, otherwise highly different, worldviews and perspectives at the right side of this figure. Obviously, this type of thought experiment can never be conducted as a real experiment. But the thought exercise itself suggests all stakeholders in management as a nascent profession can only create a shared sense of purpose, if they avoid carrying the full weight of their own perspective and history into the discourse.

These reflections serve as a source of inspiration for the search for a shared sense of purpose and responsibility in the management discipline. In particular, the "veil of ignorance" experiment provides a framework that, later in this chapter, will be used to assess a preliminary statement of professional purpose and responsibility.

Notions of Professional Purpose and Responsibility

Developing a shared sense of professional purpose and responsibility is a key challenge in the area of management. This section reviews several notions of professional purpose and responsibility raised in the (broader) management literature.

Before turning to this review, the notions of purpose and responsibility need to be clarified. The previous section already started to connect these two notions. Purpose was defined in Chapter 1 as a commitment to some good broader than self-interest. *Responsibility* is defined here as a sense of obligation to oneself, others, and/or a particular situation; as such it is "an expression of self-restraint guided by these obligations" (Ansell 2011: 134). In others words, responsibility tends to follow purpose, rather than the other way around (cf. Rawls 1971).[1]

Scholarly Notions of Purpose and Responsibility

Action researchers start from a professional orientation to knowledge creation in practical contexts. This professional orientation requires working with practitioners in order to understand organizational arrangements and processes, but also to affect desired change, empower managers and other stakeholders, and generate new knowledge (Argyris et al. 1985; Bradbury Huang 2010).

More specific is the professional mission and responsibility conceived by management scholars engaging in *appreciative inquiry*. Appreciative inquirers want to transform the one-way mode of communication prevailing in most organizations into an open, system-wide dialogue intended to engage stakeholders in co-inquiry and co-creation (Barrett and Fry 2005; Cooperrider and Whitney 1999). This notion of professional purpose arises from a social constructionist approach, implying that organizations are created, sustained, and changed by conversations (Cooperrider et al. 1995).

Another discourse on professional purpose has been arising from Boyer's (1990) ideas on the scholarship of *engagement*. A prominent advocate of this notion in management studies is Van de Ven (2007), who believes a more engaged type of scholarship is needed to meet the dual hurdles of relevance and rigor in management research. In particular, he argues engaged scholarship involves

> negotiation and collaboration between researchers and practitioners in a learning community; such a community jointly produces knowledge that can both advance the scientific enterprise and enlighten a community of practitioners. Instead of viewing organizations and clients as data collection sites and funding sources, an engaged scholar views them as a learning workplace (idea factory) where practitioners and scholars co-produce knowledge on important questions and issues by testing alternative ideas and different views of a common problem. (Van de Ven 2007: 7)

More broadly, Flyvbjerg (2001) argues for a more responsible approach to social science, one that draws on each of Aristotle's three intellectual virtues: episteme, techne, and phronesis.[2] *Episteme* draws on universal, invariable, and context-independent knowledge and seeks to uncover universal truths about empirical matters; it thus thrives on the idea that knowledge represents reality, and as such, on denotative statements regarding the world as-it-is. *Techne* involves practical, variable, and context-dependent knowledge that is instrumental, for example, in making or managing organizations better. Finally, the virtue of *phronesis* refers to questioning and deliberating about values, by providing concrete examples and detailed narratives of the ways in which power and values work in organizations (including their consequences) and suggesting how power and values could be changed (Flyvbjerg 2001). Based on the observation that the virtue of episteme is overemphasized in social science, at the expense of techne and particularly phronesis, Flyvbjerg argues social sience must be redirected toward scholarly work "that matters" in three ways:

> First, we must drop the fruitless efforts to emulate natural science's success in producing cumulative and predictive theory; this approach simply does not work in social science. Second, we must take up problems that matter to the local, national, and global communities in which we live, and we must do it in ways that matter; we must focus on issues of values and power like great social scientists have advocated from Aristotle and Machiavelli to Max Weber and Pierre Bourdieu. Finally, we must effectively communicate the results of our research to fellow citizens. If we do this, we may successfully transform social science from what is fast becoming a sterile academic activity, which is undertaken mostly for its own sake and in increasing isolation from a society on which it has little effect and from which it gets little appreciation. We may transform social science to an activity done in public for the public, sometimes to clarify, sometimes to intervene, sometimes to generate new perspectives, and always to serve as eyes and ears in our ongoing efforts at understanding the present and deliberating about the future. (Flyvbjerg 2001: 166)

Purpose and Responsibility Defined by MBA Graduates

Each of these notions of professional purpose and responsibility have been conceived from a scholarly perspective. Interestingly, whereas management scholars have thus far not been able to agree on a shared responsibility, MBA graduates of Harvard Business School (Anderson and Escher 2010) have been engaging in efforts to restore professional standards and ethics in management, also in response to Khurana and Nohria's (2008) call discussed in Chapter 1. The initiators of this project studied the Hippocratic Oath in medicine, Thunderbird's Oath of Honor, the Columbia Business School's

Honor Code and other efforts to define a shared sense of professional responsibility (Anderson and Escher 2010). The result is the so-called MBA Oath that is available on the website *mbaoath.org* where it can be signed by all (former) MBA students who are in the final year of their MBA or already hold this degree. The MBA Oath (2015) is as follows:

"As a business leader I recognize my role in society.

- My purpose is to lead people and manage resources to create value that no single individual can create alone.
- My decisions affect the well-being of individuals inside and outside my enterprise, today and tomorrow.

Therefore, I promise that:

- I will manage my enterprise with loyalty and care, and will not advance my personal interests at the expense of my enterprise or society.
- I will understand and uphold, in letter and spirit, the laws and contracts governing my conduct and that of my enterprise.
- I will refrain from corruption, unfair competition, or business practices harmful to society.
- I will protect the human rights and dignity of all people affected by my enterprise, and I will oppose discrimination and exploitation.
- I will protect the right of future generations to advance their standard of living and enjoy a healthy planet.
- I will report the performance and risks of my enterprise accurately and honestly.
- I will invest in developing myself and others, helping the management profession continue to advance and create sustainable and inclusive prosperity.

In exercising my professional duties according to these principles, I recognize that my behavior must set an example of integrity, eliciting trust and esteem from those I serve. I will remain accountable to my peers and to society for my actions and for upholding these standards."

The MBA oath is an appealing code of professional responsibility which is largely tailored to the needs of management practitioners. Evidently, the professionalization of management also depends on the knowledge that management scholars can develop and provide, as well as the educational efforts and systems based on this knowledge.

Academic–Practitioner Collaboration: A Necessary Condition?

The previous section served to outline several notions of professional purpose and responsibility in the area of management practice and scholarship. This raises the question whether these examples can provide a perspective on professional purpose that is likely to be widely embraced. One common thread in these examples appears to be *collaboration between scholars and practitioners*, deemed essential to make management scholarship matter more to society and management practice. Obviously, many management scholars are not likely to acknowledge the importance of active academic–practitioner collaboration (e.g. Donaldson 2003; Kieser and Leiner 2009; George 2014). For example, Kieser and Leiner (2009) question whether truly collaborative research between practitioners and scholars is feasible, in view of the huge communication and language barriers between the worlds of practice and academia as well as fundamental differences in how both sides define and solve problems.

The key problem here is that a notion of professional purpose and responsibility that is exclusively based on academic-practitioner collaboration may be too limited. Bartunek (2007) therefore advocates a relational perspective, implying that academics and practitioners create a broad variety of relationships and connections beyond (only) collaborative research projects. Creating more equal relationships with practitioners is important, says Bartunek, because the knowledge of managers, entrepreneurs and other practitioners often complements that of academics. However, "joint research fosters academic-practitioner collaboration in some instances, but it is not a necessary or sufficient means for developing joint relationships in which academics and practitioners truly learn from each other and share elements of pathos" (Bartunek 2007: 1328). Bartunek (2007) subsequently develops a more broader perspective that fosters positive mutual relationships, discusses the types of difficulties likely to arise in these relationships, and outlines the nature of the boundary spanning efforts and discussion forums that might help develop these relationships.

To become widely accepted among management scholars, a notion of professional responsibility therefore needs to embrace research engagements *without* active contributions from practitioners, such as those drawing on surveys or secondary data to develop and test theoretical models of organizational behavior and performance. This type of research currently prevails in management studies, and has proven to be highly instrumental in explaining practices, systems, processes, and their outcomes in terms of their causal and generative mechanisms (Shapira 2011).

Pragmatism

The last three decades have witnessed a major revival of pragmatism as a philosophical perpective, as a result of work by Richard Bernstein, Hilary Putnam, Richard Rorty, and many others (Ansell 2011; Baert 2005). This revival has also renewed interest in the pioneering work of Charles Peirce and John Dewey on pragmatism. This section explores whether and how pragmatism can inform the search for a shared purpose of management as a profession.

Critique of Foundationalism

In pragmatism, a core idea is the scepticism toward the search for a single, unchangeable foundation of knowledge (Bernstein 1991; Rorty 1982). This kind of search is based on the assumption that some self-justifying beliefs provide the foundation to all knowledge. For example, Dewey was highly skeptical of the "spectator theory of knowledge" (Baert 2005), in which knowledge is assumed to effectively represent the nature of the external world.

Others have extended this critique of the "myth of the scientific method" (Baert 2005) to any other proposed foundation, such as social constructivism or critical realism. For example, Rorty (1979) criticizes the notion of self-evident premises in any foundational approach in two ways. First, he follows Sellars in rejecting the idea that knowledge of what we perceive can be independent of the conceptual processes which result in perception—in other words, that there is a "given" in sensory perception. Second, Rorty draws on Quine's criticism of the distinction between analytic and synthetic sentences (i.e. sentences which are true solely in virtue of what they mean versus those made true by the world). Together, these two critiques of key aspects of foundationalism are, argues Rorty, devastating. Without an unchangeable given in how we perceive our surroundings and with no access to a privileged realm of truths of meaning, what remains is a pragmatist notion of scholarship as well as a notion of knowledge as those beliefs that pay their way.[3]

Regarding the quest for professionalism in management, the critique of foundationalism by Rorty and others serves to make certain questions of method and methodology redundant. That is, it suggests The Quest for Professionalism does not need to be pre-occupied with questions such as "what is the rationale of management research" or "which methodology is intrinsic to management studies" (cf. Baert 2005).

Both Theorizing and Practicing are Human Activities

Another key idea in pragmatism is that both theorizing and practicing can be understood as human activities that engage with and manipulate their environment in practical ways (Zundel and Kokkalis 2010). Following Dewey (1929), there is no question of theory *versus* practice, but rather of intelligent versus uninformed practice.

Moreover, Dewey identified a so-called *philosophical fallacy*, in which scholars take theoretical constructs (e.g. "procedural fairness" or "dynamic capability") for granted, because they do not realize that these are merely nominal concepts invented to help solve specific problems (Boisvert 1998; Dewey 1929; Hildebrand 2003). This fallacy explains why many scholars create accounts of knowledge which project the products of extensive abstraction back onto experience (Hildebrand 2003). As a result, they perceive many observations or experiences as "facts," not realizing that the latter also arise as "artifacts" from one's engagement with the environment.

Notably, a positivist or anti-realist account of knowledge may be highly instrumental for specific research purposes. However, it tends to underappreciate the integrative purpose and function of inquiry (Hildebrand 2003; Martela 2015). So, in our search for a shared purpose of management as a profession, it is important to avoid the foundational fallacy identified earlier.

Pluralism is Essential: The Generative Role of Doubt

The search for a single foundation of research tends to reduce the multitude of perspectives in management research to only one perspective (cf. Baert 2005). For example, it may reduce management research to explanation or interpretation, excluding creation and discovery as alternative lenses, or vice versa.

Instead, the generative potential of, what Peirce called, real *doubt* is central to pragmatism (Warfield 1994). This type of doubt arises from the experience of not-knowing (Locke et al. 2008). More specifically, doubt plays a pivotal role in how we, as human beings, make inferences and thus modify our beliefs. Drawing on Peirce's work, Warfield (1986, 1994) presents two figures to clarify this point.[4] Figure 2.2 depicts the so-called *scale of belief* toward a particular idea or issue. At the left end of this scale is the state of "disbelief," that is, any extreme position against this idea or issue. Moving right, we find "doubt," a tendency toward disbelief and a source of stimulus to inquiry. The position of "neutrality" typically offers no basis for decision-making. The following position, "inclination" toward belief, constitutes the positive side of doubt concerning the idea or issue at hand. And the final position is "belief" that, according to Peirce, is the predecessor of habit or routine (Warfield 1986).

The scale of belief implies two possible scenarios for any (professional) discourse that fails to appreciate and embrace doubt. The first scenario

Figure 2.2. Scale of belief
(Copyright © 1986 IEEE)

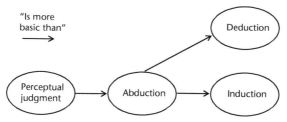

Figure 2.3. Peirce's four types of inference that can modify human belief
(Copyright © 1986 IEEE)

involves minor debates within the right half of the scale in Figure 2.2, where any kind of belief is not fundamentally questioned by those that are neutral or already inclined to adopt the same belief. The other scenario involves largely rhetorical debates and disputes between "believers" and "disbelievers" drawing on highly different worldviews (Walsh et al. 2006). A fundamental professional skill therefore is the ability to expose one self to doubt, the experience of not-knowing.

Figure 2.3 provides an overview of Peirce's four types of inference that might modify human belief (Warfield 1986, 1994). Moving from the left to the right in this figure, each type of inferencing becomes less basic and more academic. *Perceptual judgment* is the most basic form of inferencing, the (almost) instant mental transformation taking place whenever sensory perception is at work. Light or sound signals are converted into mental images, and in turn, these are transformed into interpretations that constitute perceptual judgment. This most basic type of inferencing is least susceptible to analysis, but is also the most fundamental one because it provides "the information foundation for all other forms of inference" (Warfield 1994: 52).

As such, the accumulation of large numbers of perceptual judgments plays a key role in the second type of inference, abduction. *Abduction* is a "mental process whereby theories, conjectures, scientific hypotheses, and explanations are produced involving situations where the outcome has not yet been established as a belief by either induction or deduction" (Warfield 1994: 52). Abduction is much less formal than induction and deduction, but it is the only way to generate new ideas.

Induction involves drawing conclusions from observations, experiments or other data concerning an articulated hypothesis or other statement. Finally, *deduction* starts from a given set of assumptions (not necessarily validated), such as axioms and postulates, and then uses formal reasoning to produce a conclusion with regard to an articulated statement (e.g. initial hypothesis or conjecture). Both induction and deduction serve to displace the initial statement on the scale of belief in Figure 2.2 by validating or invalidating it.

Induction and deduction are fundamentally different from abduction because they operate in terms of "priors," such as theoretical conjectures and empirical observations (in case of induction) and axioms and postulates (in case of deduction). By contrast, abductive reasoning draws on more primitive, not necessarily articulated, priors (Warfield 1986, 1994).

Figures 2.2 and 2.3 together underline the generative and pivotal role of doubt in research, in the sense that it is doubt that makes us engage in inquiry. Without doubt, we would find ourselves in a world of beliefs and disbeliefs, with no access to ways to scrutinize, (in)validate, and adapt them.

Knowledge is (about) Action that Serves Human Purposes

Fundamental to the quest for professionalism in management is Peirce's (1934) "pragmatic maxim," which says an abstract concept is only meaningful when it refers to, or anticipates, some form of experience or action. Peirce's original interpretation of this maxim was that an abstract concept is meaningful when it refers to direct, sensory experiences (cf. Figure 2.3); in other words, the meaning of, for example, a concept or statement arises from its consequences (Warfield 1994). Thus, what ultimately counts from the perspective of pragmatism is the meaningfulness of action, and not merely "what works" (Pfeffer and Sutton 2000; Ansell 2011; Fendt and Kaminska-Labbé 2011; Martela 2015).

While Peirce later developed a number of interpretations of the pragmatic maxim, the key takeaway is that professional knowledge can be conceived as a form of action, rather than being (exclusively) representational or interpretive in nature.[5] Baert (2005: 154) argues "knowledge is action" because any effort to develop knowledge entails questions of aims and, as such, depends at least in part on what the researcher wants to achieve. Similarly, Wicks and Freeman advocate that management scholars draw on a mix of methods to find and develop solutions to practical problems. This allows researchers to move beyond the positivism-constructivism debate and "put this debate to the side and, in the process, develop research that is focused on serving human purposes—i.e., both morally rich and useful to organizations and the communities in which they operate" (Wicks and Freeman 1998: 123).

Evolutionary Learning and Dialogical Encounter

Pragmatism provides a philosophy of evolutionary learning that emphasizes "the ability of both individuals and communities to improve their knowledge and problem solving capacity over time through continuous inquiry, reflection, deliberation, and experimentation" (Ansell 2011: 5). The latter are open-ended processes of developing, evaluating, and refining values and knowledge. As such, pragmatism provides a philosophy that tolerates and facilitates the use of more specific (e.g. critical realist) assumptions at the level of professional action and scholarship, without embracing these assumptions as the foundation of the profession.

In this vein, Rorty (1982) and Bernstein (1991) advocate a dialogical model that promotes conversation amongst a plurality of voices, even when there is hardly any common ground prior to the conversation. In a so-called *dialogical encounter*, researchers and other professionals engage in self-referential knowledge development (e.g. drawing on critical realism or social constructivism), but also regularly expose themselves to fundamentally different views as an opportunity to reconsider their central presuppositions (Bernstein 1991; Baert 2005). Dialogical encounters help scholars and practitioners in learning to see themselves, their personal background, their organizational settings, and their own presuppositions from a different perspective, and in comparing this reinterpretation with alternative ways to engage in their profession (Baert 2005; Avenier and Parmentier Cajaiba 2012).

A culture of dialogical encounters would serve to transform debates between "believers" in highly different worldviews (Walsh et al. 2006) to an ongoing dialogue between professionals. In dialogical encounters, participants draw on different epistemic and theoretical stances but also agree on the need to continually expose themselves to other voices—in the interest of building and sustaining a viable discourse on their profession. At the heart of these encounters is a shared sense of professional responsibility, because professionals (should) always engage in inquiry with ethical ends-in-view (Martela 2015).

Developing Common Ground: A Collaborative Attempt

Pragmatist notions and ideas can possibly constitute key elements of a shared sense of purpose and responsibility in management as an emerging profession.[6] Several years before writing *The Quest for Professionalism*, I teamed up with five other scholars and one practitioner, to collaboratively develop a shared picture of the purpose and responsibility of management as a profession. This group of seven was highly diverse in terms of backgrounds, including people with micro interests (i.e. individual and group behavior) and macro interests (e.g. strategy, culture, operations, design) and epistemic orientations as varied as constructivism, critical realism, and positivism. The size of the group was sufficiently large to include such highly different perspectives, while small enough to work as a team on a significant challenge.

We prepared a collaborative symposium proposal for the British Academy of Management annual conference in 2013, had a lively debate during the symposium in August that year, and afterwards sat down to further discuss and explore the ground we shared and did not share. Our initial symposium at the BAM conference was not entirely focused on professional "purpose" (or lack thereof), but when we decided to start writing a paper, we quickly found out that there was no way we could avoid addressing this challenge. Our readings in the process of writing the paper particularly included the literature on professionalism (discussed in Chapter 1) and pragmatism (discussed earlier in this chapter) as well as other sources. The process of developing common ground primarily took place by collaboratively writing and editing a text, stored and shared in the cloud, as well as some communication via e-mails.

This collaborative effort involved substantial give and take by all seven participants. For example, most participants had to leave their preferred epistemic approach and, in the interest of establishing common ground, adopt a pragmatist lens that could also tolerate and facilitate other epistemic approaches. Moreover, some participants who initially did not believe in professionalizing management (similar to, for example, Barker 2010) changed their position, realizing that the external legitimacy of management research and education entirely depends on the (espoused) quest for professionalism. All of us had to leave our comfort zones.

Our co-writing effort, taking more than a year, served to produce the following proposal for a normative statement of shared purpose and responsibility of management practitioners and scholars (Romme et al. 2015):

- *Management should be(come) a profession* that serves the greater good by bringing people and resources together to create value that no single individual can create alone.

- *Practicing and knowing co-constitute each other.* Practicing and knowing are co-constitutive dialogic processes and management scholars and practitioners alike engage in practicing as well as knowing (possibly in different proportions).

- *Shared interest in outcomes and implications.* Conceptual distinctions such as qualitative–quantitative, positivism–constructivism, and description–prescription provide maps that help scholars and practitioners find their way in the world. A shared interest in outcomes and implications serves to facilitate productive exchange and dialogue across these maps.

- *Learning to see from different perspectives.* Practitioners and scholars learn to see themselves, their personal background, their organizational settings, and their own presuppositions from a range of different perspectives, thus enabling them to engage reflexively with their profession.

- *Pluralism is essential.* Pluralism in philosophical, theoretical and methodical positions is a great asset to the profession. This also implies skepticism toward searching for a single logic of research—be it positivism, constructivism, realism (critical or otherwise) or any other ontology and epistemology. Rather than a single logic of research, what Peirce called "real doubt" is central to management and management scholarship.

- *Dialogical encounter*. In a culture of "dialogical encounter," researchers and other professionals engage in knowledge development by drawing on distinct philosophical assumptions but also regularly expose themselves to fundamentally different views, as an opportunity to reconsider their central presuppositions.

Assessing the Common Ground Proposed

Only time can tell whether this prototyped statement of purpose and responsibility will become widely accepted or not. Therefore, the following assessment is highly speculative in nature, in the spirit of the "veil of ignorance" thought experiment discussed earlier.

For one, the question arises whether a very diverse population of practitioners (Bartunek and Rynes 2014), including those without (much) exposure to management education and thinking, can identify with the proposed statement of purpose and responsibility. In this respect, our proposal for shared purpose and responsibility is entirely consistent with the MBA oath, developed by a group of MBA graduates from a prominent business school (Anderson and Escher 2010) and discussed earlier in the chapter. However, the common ground proposed here is substantially broader than merely a moral code. It also invites MBA graduates to develop a sense of obligation for contributing to a viable discourse on management as profession. Developing this broader sense of purpose and responsibility among young management professionals is critical, because a truly professional culture of dialogical encounter will not come alive without their active contributions. Therefore, with at least 100 thousand MBA students graduating every year (globally), it makes most sense to start developing a shared awareness of professional purpose in our classrooms.[7]

The experiences of those contributing to the prototyped statement of purpose and responsibility, described earlier, suggest many scholars are able to identify themselves with this statement. This is especially the case if they feel the need to develop a shared sense of purpose between otherwise highly different tribes and camps (cf. Gulati 2007; Kessler and Bartunek 2014). Perhaps the most pertinent "test" case is the highly critical position that scholars in *critical management studies* (CMS) have developed toward the idea of professionalism. CMS scholars have been questioning issues of politics, power, and domination that the rise of managerialism incurs (e.g. Deetz 2003), drawing on a variety of sources such as the critical theories developed by Marx, Marcuse, and Habermas and work by Foucault, Derrida, and Deleuze (Alvesson and Willmott 2003).

For example, in a commentary on Rousseau's (2006a) argument about evidence-based management (EBM), Learmonth (2006) argues that management scholars need to avoid a situation in which EBM becomes an expectation, or even requirement, before several fundamental issues are fully debated. He points at two major problems with EBM and the broader professionalization agenda. First, Learmonth argues and illustrates there is no agreement whatsoever in management studies about what is legitimate evidence. This lack of agreement is "particularly difficult for evidence-based management because it cannot be resolved merely by more, or better, evidence; in this case, divergence is a reflection of researchers' contrasting beliefs about the nature of the social world, views held a priori, shaping what they see while conducting research" (Learmonth 2006: 1089). Learmonth's second point is that the rhetoric of science is likely to mask the politics of evidence. That is, any rhetoric on promoting management practices that are validated by evidence "has plausibility only when some evidence gets excluded" (2006: 1090), which in turn is likely to be highly influenced by personal and political considerations, given the lack of consensus on what evidence is.[8]

In her reply to Learmonth's comments, Rousseau calls for a broader professionalization agenda that would serve to energize and integrate better practice, effective teaching, and more influential research: "As a knowledge-sharing venture across multiple communities (scholars, teachers, practitioners), none of which is monolithic, EBM's design and implementation processes would be collective" (Rousseau 2006b: 1092).

Thus, CMS scholars raise fundamental questions about the possibility of reaching some level of agreement about what the nature of professionalism in management is and should be, what would be the "greater good" pursued by professional managers, and so forth. These questions and issues are highly contested, and will also remain disputed in the future. But, as argued earlier, the dialogue about these fundamental issues and challenges is more likely to come alive and be sustained if there is some common ground. In fact, the debate between Rousseau and Learmonth is an excellent example of the kind of dialogical encounter that only can come about if all participants are willing to learn "to see from different perspectives" and to embrace that "pluralism is essential"—as proposed earlier.[9] Only by agreeing on such a basic set of principles, can this type of dialogical encounter become a normal activity rather than an exceptional one.

Future Work

A shared sense of purpose and responsibility will obviously enhance the identity of management as an emerging profession. But a collective effort sustained over a longer period of time is required to develop such a shared sense of purpose. Moreover, given the embryonic stage of the discourse on the purpose and nature of management, any attempt toward closure is not likely to be successful at this stage. In this respect, the statement of professional purpose and responsibility proposed in this chapter is merely a first prototype, intended to revitalize and re-open the debate.

To illustrate the kind of dialogical encounters that might be instrumental in revitalizing and sustaining this discourse, Appendix 1 contains the outline of a symposium that draws on the notion of alpha and beta testing (adopted from the design sciences). A large number of these dialogical encounters might serve to build awareness of the need for a shared professional purpose as well as its key ingredients. Preferably, the results of these dialogical encounters are reported in public media and journals, to facilitate the convergence toward a shared professional purpose. Given the European and North-American bias of these initial attempts to develop normative common ground, future dialogical encounters will also need to include more management scholars and practitioners from, for example, Asian and South-American countries.

Concluding Remarks

This chapter served to explore how a shared sense of professional purpose and responsibility can be developed in the field of management. First, I argued that the plurality of voices in this field needs to be widely embraced and nurtured, but that its fragmented nature is best tackled at the level of (the lack of shared) purpose. With a minimum amount of common ground under our feet, conversations amongst a plurality of voices are much more likely to come alive and be sustained. Subsequently, a set of heuristics for evaluating proposals regarding the purpose and responsibility of management as a profession, suggested by political philosophers, was discussed. I outlined several notions of professional purpose and responsibility, and inferred the contours of a shared sense of purpose and responsibility from pragmatist thinking. Moreover, a prototype of professional purpose and responsibility was collaboratively produced. Finally, the level of support among management scholars and practitioners for this prototype was speculatively assessed.

Notes

1. Ansell (2011) emphasizes the distinction between responsibility and accountability, two notions that management scholars often do not clearly differentiate. Whereas responsibility is an expression of self-restraint and intrinsic obligation, "accountability is an external standard—for instance, someone is held accountable" (Ansell 2011: 134).

2. Chapter 3 will draw more extensively on Aristotle's three intellectual virtues, in the context of the search for a professional body of knowledge.

3. For Rorty (1979), this evolutionary understanding of how knowledge develops is the only worthwhile description of how inquiry actually proceeds. Here, a key source of inspiration for Rorty is Thomas Kuhn's *The Structure of Scientific Revolutions* which suggests a discipline evolves over time, with criteria of relevance and truth being adjusted if not fundamentally transformed after every intellectual crisis and "scientific revolution" (see also: Rorty 1999).

4. Martela (2015) draws on John Dewey's work to develop a similar perspective on the fallible nature of all knowledge, in terms of so-called "warranted assertions."

5. The term "knowledge" is used somewhat loosely here. In Chapter 3, I will more systematically explore the domain of "knowledge," in ways that are fully congruent with the pragmatist idea that knowledge (primarily) serves action.

6. This section draws on: Romme et al. (2015), "Towards common ground and trading zones in management research and practice," *British Journal of Management* 26/3: 544–59.

7. This idea will be further developed in Chapter 8.

8. For a more elaborate critique of evidence-based management: Learmonth and Harding (2006).

9. Interestingly, some critical theorists such as Habermas (1998) have also been embracing the pragmatist ideas of Dewey, Peirce, and others, to shift from a focus on dialogue as being "world-disclosing" to dialogue as a "problem-solving" form of social experimentation (Rorty 1999). Rorty here talks about dialogue as "a way of replacing the task of justifying past custom and tradition by reference to unchanging structure with the task of replacing an unsatisfactory present with a more satisfactory future, thus replacing certainty with hope" (Rorty 1999: 32).

3

Toward a Body of Knowledge

Introduction

The quest for science-based professionalism in management, as a vocational activity that serves the greater good by connecting and coordinating people and resources, implies we need to envision a body of knowledge that management professionals would be able to claim. This chapter therefore explores what constitutes a professional body of knowledge and how it can facilitate a viable discourse on management.

First, the notion of "knowledge" is explored in more depth by drawing on two well-known "maps" of the territory: Aristotle's categorization of knowledge, and the distinction between explicit and tacit knowledge developed by philosophers and sociologists. I then turn to defining and framing a professional body of knowledge in the area of management. A core idea here is that this body of knowledge arises from creative discovery as well as scientific validation. Consequently, both discovery and validation inform the discourse on management practices—in terms of their constituent values, constructs, models, and principles.

Kessler and Bartunek (2014: 241) recently recommended that management scholars "might learn to think like cartographers—sharpening and harmonizing their maps and their boundaries to understand the design of a management landscape more comprehensively." Accordingly, the framework developed here serves to map the landscape, to facilitate dialogical encounters between professionals with widely different backgrounds and perspectives. A key finding arising from this chapter is that most elements of a professional body of knowledge on management are already present in the broader literature, albeit in a scattered and fragmented manner.[1]

What is Knowledge?

There is no commonly accepted definition of "knowledge." For example, Bell (1973: 175) defines knowledge as a "set of organized statements of facts or ideas presenting a reasoned judgement or an experimental result which is transmitted to others through some communication medium in some systematic form." Others have questioned this kind of definition as being too narrow in nature, also in view of the emergent and distributed nature of knowledge (e.g. Hayek 1945; Tsoukas 1996).

For example, Hayek explored the fundamental problem of how knowledge is created and used in society. He argued that knowledge about, for example, the city or society we live in does not exist "in concentrated or integrated form, but solely as the dispersed bits of incomplete and frequently contradictory knowledge which all the separate individuals possess"; accordingly, knowledge is dispersed and uncollectible because it pertains to "the particular circumstances of time and place" (Hayek 1945: 519–21).

However, Hayek did not mean to argue the world is chaotic and random. He acknowledged the existence of institutions like symbols, rules, formulas, habits, and systems of culture, "whose meaning we do not understand and through the use of which we avail ourselves of the assistance of knowledge which individually we do not possess"; these practices and institutions have been developed "by building upon habits and institutions which have proved successful in their own sphere and which have in turn become the foundation of the civilization we have built up" (Hayek 1945: 528).

Hayek's perspective on how knowledge is created and used serves to put the quest for a professional body of knowledge into perspective. It signals the enormous complexity and challenges arising from the notion of a professional body of knowledge and the broader professionalization quest (cf. Tsoukas 1996; Orlikowski 2002; Foss and Klein 2014). Management knowledge, however defined, is widely distributed across millions of individual professionals and their organizations and connections. These individuals create and draw on, for example, apprenticeships, mentoring, business school curricula, social media, popular management books, and many other ways to share, transfer, manipulate, transform, codify, or synthesize some of this knowledge.

I therefore adopt a broader and more inclusive definition of *knowledge* as "a familiarity, awareness or understanding of someone or something, such as information, facts, descriptions, or skills, which is acquired through experience or education by perceiving, discovering, or learning" (Wikipedia 2014). To come to grips with this broad territory, the remainder of this section explores two well-known "maps" of the territory: Aristotle's techne-episteme-phronesis and the distinction between explicit and tacit knowledge.

Aristotle's Map

A classic map of knowledge are the "intellectual virtues" defined by Aristotle (e.g. Flyvbjerg 2001; Van de Ven 2007), that is: techne, episteme, and phronesis. For Aristotle, each of these virtues constituted a form of "wisdom" that we now typically call "knowledge."

TECHNE

Aristotle's *techne* refers to instrumental knowledge, based on a means-ends rationality (Van de Ven 2007). This is the type of knowledge that is essential to all the technology surrounding us, from refrigerators and other home appliances to power plants, and from smart phones to the internet as a global system of interconnected computer networks (Arthur 2009). But it also pertains to the actionable, variable, and context-dependent knowledge that is instrumental in making or managing organizations better (Flyvbjerg 2001)—where "better" is typically defined in terms of the values and goals of those in charge (e.g. executive director) or those to whom they are accountable (e.g. supervisory board). This pragmatic, result-oriented mindset is the kind of intellectual virtue that is strongly developed among executives and other managers as well as their consultants.

EPISTEME

Aristotle's *episteme* draws on universal, invariable, and context-independent knowledge and seeks to uncover universal truths—for example about managing and organizing (Flyvbjerg 2001). As such, it draws on cause–effect rationality, the search for generic causal mechanisms—widely known as "science." Episteme thus thrives on the idea that knowledge represents reality, and as such, on denotative statements regarding the world as-it-is (Lyotard 1984; Romme 2003a). "Episteme" as scientific knowledge is also essential to modern technology, in all its varieties and shapes.

PHRONESIS

Finally, *phronesis* refers to questioning and deliberating about values, with reference to ongoing praxis, that is "to deliberate about 'things that are good or bad for humans' in the words of Aristotle" (Flyvbjerg 2008: 153). Flyvbjerg (2001) argues that a key task of phronetic organization research is providing concrete examples and detailed narratives of the ways in which power and values work in organizations (including their consequences) *and* to suggest how power and values could be changed. In the literature on organizational development, phronesis has also been defined as "dialogical" (e.g. Bushe and Marshak 2009) in nature.

COMPLEMENTARITY

Evidently, these three types of knowledge are complementary. For example, techne and episteme are highly interdependent and synergetic. The conventional view is that fundamental (episteme) knowledge precedes applied (techne) knowledge. However, several authors have questioned this sequential view (Gibbons et al. 1994; Galison 1997; Arthur 2009). For example, Galison (1997) observes that modern physics was created by what, over time, became a highly pluralistic community of theorists, experimentalists, engineers, and mathematicians focused on projects such as the bubble chamber. Therefore, "science forms from technologies: from instruments, methods, experiments, and explanations" (Arthur 2009: 63) as much as technology arises from science.

Techne and phronesis are also complementary. In developing and applying instrumental knowledge, the underlying values are often not (openly) questioned, because the legitimation of this knowledge tends to be incorporated in the method or strategy adopted—think of the CEO explaining that "this organizational turnaround is necessary in view of the dramatic decrease in operating results." Moreover, those in charge typically impose the underlying values, particularly in administrative hierarchies without much external accountability. Phronesis here adds the capability to question how power and values work in organizations, and to raise options as to how power and values could be changed (Flyvbjerg 2001).

A similar complementarity exists between episteme and phronesis. In contrast to techne, episteme draws on an explicit set of values, by assuming that the world "is intrinsically knowable, that it can be probed, that causes can be singled out, that understandings can be gained if phenomena and their implications are explored in highly controlled ways" (Arthur 2009: 64). Thus, Argyris (1993) observes that the emphasis in episteme on descriptive and denotative statements is in itself a normative decision: it means giving priority to describing the reality that people have already created, rather than seeking to improve it or make fundamental changes toward a new reality. Here again, phronetic thinking serves to question the exclusivity, scope, and applicability of episteme-based knowledge (Flyvbjerg 2001).

Aristotle's three forms of knowledge can be rather difficult to disentangle. Any managerial or entrepreneurial activity is explicitly or implicitly based on values and goals, and moreover, can look completely different under varying circumstances; moreover, these values and goals may evolve over time. In these settings, it might not be possible to completely dissociate values and goals from denotative statements regarding the world as-it-is, or from normative statements regarding the world that-should-be (Ackoff and Emery 1973; Simon 1969/1996).

Episteme, techne, and phronesis are also highly complementary in the quest for science-based professionalism.[2] This integral position is also consistent with the pragmatist perspective explored in Chapter 2, which suggests all forms of "knowing" are an outgrowth of ordinary inquiry that starts and ends in experiencing (Martela 2015). Human beings therefore continually alternate between a representational "episteme," an instrumental "techne," and a dialogic "phronesis" mindset. The representational mindset makes us trust that, for example, product labels fairly adequately describe the food we're buying. An instrumental mindset is inevitable when we take a shower, bring our kids to school, get our office work done, and so forth. And the dialogic approach is very helpful in discussions with family members and friends, exploring complex assignments in team meetings, participating in forum discussions, and so forth. If our personal lives can only be comfortable and productive by drawing on representational, instrumental, *and* dialogic forms of knowledge, any professional approach in management also needs to draw on each of them. Therefore, Aristotle's three forms of knowledge are essential and complementary assets in envisioning and crafting management as a professional discipline.

Explicit and Tacit Knowledge

Another way to map the landscape of knowledge is the distinction between explicit and tacit knowledge. Consistent with Hayek's (1945) perspective on knowledge, Polanyi (1958) argued that all knowledge claims draw on personal judgments and commitments, and any "truth" can therefore not be derived mechanically. In *The Tacit Dimension*, Polanyi (1966: 4) argued that "we can know more than we can tell," that is, there is knowledge that cannot be adequately articulated by verbal means. Moreover, he demonstrated that all knowledge is rooted in tacit knowledge. A key example used by Polanyi is that of bicycle riding, which demonstrates we know how to ride a bike without being able to tell anyone how we do this (i.e. the rules and heuristics for bike riding); many children therefore learn how to ride a bike without any explicit guidelines. Our knowledge of the ability to ride a bike is therefore (mostly) tacit.

Other studies have demonstrated that tacit knowledge is also pervasive and critical to science. For example, Collins (2001) shows that detailed experimental protocols in the natural sciences are not sufficient for a research team to replicate a sophisticated experiment that another team had been conducting successfully for many years elsewhere. Some level of personal contact and regular interaction appears to be necessary in order to replicate the experiment at another site. Similarly, in many instances where scientific knowledge is patented, the buyers of these patents are unable to effectively use this codified knowledge without additional help from the inventors, particularly in the form of their tacit knowledge (e.g. Gordon 1991).

Nonaka and Takeuchi (1995) created a broad interest among management scholars in the notion of tacit knowledge, through their study of the process of how Matsushita transformed the craft of bread making into a bread-making machine. They described this process as the transformation of tacit knowledge into the explicit knowledge needed to develop the design of the machine. For example, the baker's ability to twist and stretch the dough was uncovered and explicated by a member of Matsushita's product development team, who worked as an apprentice to a head baker. This "twisting stretch" motion was then mechanized in the context of the bread-making machine, through an elaborate process of experimentation and prototyping. Drawing on this example as well as other cases, Nonaka and Takeuchi (1995) developed the well-known Socialization-Externalization-Combination-Internalization model, a conceptual model of the interaction between explicit and tacit knowledge.

DIFFERENT DEGREES OF TACIT KNOWLEDGE

Collins (2010) explores in more detail why some tacit knowledge cannot be, or is not, explicated. He explores how knowledge becomes explicable, in terms of strings of information elements (e.g. letters of alphabet, 0-1 binary code). In doing so, Collins identifies several meanings of knowledge explication, such as elaboration and transformation. Each of these meanings of knowledge explication can only be realized under certain conditions; for example, elaboration requires a shared language that all agents involved speak and understand (Collins 2010). Collins turns to tacit knowledge, that is, knowledge *which has not or cannot be made explicit*. He identifies weak, medium, and strong degrees of tacit knowledge—referring "to the degree of resistance of the tacit knowledge to being made explicit" (Collins 2010: 85).

The weak form of tacit knowledge is labeled *relational tacit knowledge* (RTK) by Collins. RTK is a matter of how the people involved relate to each other, in terms of their individual propensities or the characteristics of the local social groups to which they belong. In the case of RTK, "both sender and receiver already have enough cultural similarity for a string to afford the intended meaning to the receiver if the string was long enough, but the sender either feels no inclination to make the string long enough or does not know how to make it long enough" (2010: 86). When such conditions prevail, RTK can only be transferred and learned by directly and frequently interacting with, or "hanging around," the person with that RTK. A case in point is the earlier example of sophisticated lab experiments that cannot be replicated elsewhere without personal contact and regular interaction. Similarly, apprenticeships and on-the-job training—often combined with personal mentoring—enable the transfer of RTK from senior practitioners to newcomers in many professions (De Munck et al. 2007). Some of the knowledge transferred by way of, for example, an apprenticeship may actually be explicit in nature, and could therefore also be communicated in written form. However, it is very unlikely this is the case for all knowledge transferred from senior professionals to the apprentice (cf. Collins 2010).

Collins depicts a medium degree of tacit knowledge as *somatic tacit knowledge* (STK) that arises from the properties of individuals' bodies and brains as physical things. This kind of tacit knowledge is similar to that possessed by animals and other living things. Polanyi's case of bike riding, described earlier, is the classic example of an ability that becomes established in our neural pathways and muscles in ways that we cannot adequately explicate in words. One cannot learn to ride a bike from written texts or being told about it, but only from experimentation, demonstration, and guided instruction. Again, close contact with those who already have this STK is the key to learning it. In principle, it is possible to explicate pieces of STK by means of "mechanization" explication efforts (defined earlier), typically by researchers and engineers (Collins 2010). Think of a future robot that can balance and ride on a bike. Fact is that no robot in the world can yet effectively ride a bicycle, and the research and engineering effort required to produce such a robot will be huge.

Collective tacit knowledge (CTK) is the strongest form of tacit knowledge, and as such, it is the "heartland" of the concept of tacit knowledge (Collins 2010). This is the kind of knowledge that we do not know how to make explicit in any of the ways previously defined. CTK is the domain of knowledge that is located in society, arising from the way society is constituted. Collins here returns to the example of riding a bike or driving a car:

> Negotiating traffic is a problem that is *different in kind* to balancing a bike, because it includes understanding social conventions of traffic management and personal interaction. For example, it involves knowing how to make eye contact with drivers at busy junctions in just the way necessary to assure a safe passage and not to invite an unwanted response. And it involves understanding how differently these conventions will be executed in different locations. For example, bike riding in Amsterdam is a different matter than bike riding in London, or Rome, or New York, or Delhi, or Beijing. (Collins 2010: 121)

As such, in these and other settings where CTK is important, a social judgment has to be made about how to balance individual and social responsibility. The right way to balance these different responsibilities in a particular setting (e.g. car driving in New York versus in Beijing) can only be captured through experience in that setting (Collins 2010).

Collins uses the RTK-STK-CTK framework to assess Nonaka and Takeuchi's study of the bread-making machine, and observes it is based on a rather narrow concept of tacit knowledge. Also drawing on observations of the actual process of making bread (Ribeiro and Collins 2007), he argues the tacit knowledge involved in making bread by a professional baker is likely to consist of some RTK, some STK, and some CTK (Collins 2010). In this respect, it is obvious that the articulation of the "twist-stretch" element of breadmaking is an example of RTK becoming explicated, consistent with Nonaka and Takeuchi's assessment. Collins (2010) observes it is also very likely that the actual execution of the twist-stretch by a human baker involves some STK that can be passed on in the context of master–apprenticeship interaction. In the case of developing Matsushita's mechanical bread maker, it took a team of eleven engineers with highly different specializations—working on the project for a year—to identify the appropriate materials and configurations that could perform the baking job (Nonaka and Takeuchi 1995). More importantly, many pieces of CTK are required to bake bread in the real world, knowledge that varies from country to country and setting to setting:

> In the real world bread is made with huge variations of ingredients, in a huge variety of sizes, shapes, colors, and crusts. And bread is made with more or less care according to the anticipated consumer and the expected pattern of consumption. . . . both breadmaking by hand and automated breadmaking are set in their action trees of other kinds of activity. The human bread maker has to know how to purchase and measure ingredients and use the bowls and the ovens, while the user of the mechanical bread maker has to know how to read and follow instructions, purchase ingredients, clean the machine and use it and repair it, or get it repaired, if necessary. (Collins 2010: 143)

In other words, Collins observes there is more to knowledge development than only RTK—especially in the form of STK and CTK. If that idea applies to the ability to ride a bike or make bread, we can readily assume it also applies to knowledge development in the area of management.

The ability to lead a team meeting is an example. In different countries, industries and organizations, there are highly different heuristics, routines, and conventions with regard to how to start the meeting, make or avoid eye contact, use hand gestures when inviting someone to speak, allow for (or avoid) short or longer silences between speakers, and so forth.[3] While some of this knowledge can be made explicit and communicated accordingly, a substantial amount of this knowledge involves RTK, STK, and CTK that can only be acquired through personal observation, close contact, and interaction, and direct experience and experimentation. Box 3.1 provides another example.

Toward a Professional Body of Knowledge

Krippendorff (2006) suggests a professional body of knowledge involves the concepts, terms and activities that make up the incumbent profession and serve to keep the discourse on its practices viable and productive. The literature previously discussed provides guidelines as to how a professional body of

---

Box 3.1 TACIT KNOWLEDGE IN CORPORATE GOVERNANCE

Over the past ten years, I've been on the board of directors of a number of companies and other organizations. Most of these organizations are based in The Netherlands, with an entirely Dutch board. An exceptional personal experience involved a company incorporated as an S.E. (Societas Europaea) in the energy industry, founded by more than 30 companies, institutes, and other investors from all over Europe. I was involved in creating and establishing this enterprise and have been a member of the Supervisory Board since it was formally incorporated. Creating this international corporation, in fact, constitutes a natural experiment (Dunning 2012) in which highly different (national) corporate governance cultures clash and interact.[4]

As such, the newly constituted Board of Directors could not rely on much common (explicit or tacit) knowledge on corporate governance. For example, how to appoint the chairperson of the board? In some European countries, a dominant (group of) share-holder(s) will informally decide this, and then ask the shareholders meeting to formally appoint the chair. The convention in some other countries is that the board members (appointed in the shareholders meeting) elect their own chair. In some European countries, the CEO is an equivalent member of the board, in others she's not. Other contested areas involved the assessment and compensation of the CEO and other executives; whether a board member can also act as shareholder (representative) in the general meeting of shareholders; whether or not corporate strategy is the exclusive domain of the executive team, that is, do shareholders and directors attend strategy workshops with the executive team, or wait until the CEO submits the strategic plan for discussion and approval in the board of directors; and so forth.

Notably, some of the key differences in corporate governance traditions and systems present in Europe have been identified and explicated (e.g. Tricker 2012). In the case of our new corporation, we (gratefully) exploited the explicit knowledge available, because it helped create awareness of the major challenges we were facing. However, both explicit and tacit knowledge constitute any corporate governance practice, and the tacit know-ledge each of us carried into the first Board meetings appeared to be incompatible in many ways. Therefore, together with the corporation's executives and shareholders we engaged in gradually building and adapting a corporate governance system by resolving issues such as CEO compensation in a continuous process of mutual learning and building shared experiences—with, inevitably, many internal conflicts and debates along the way. That is, we had to create a shared history that would be partly explicit in nature, but also partly based on (e.g. relational and collective) tacit knowledge.

---

knowledge can be conceived. Aristotle's map implies that instrumental, representational and (value-oriented) dialogical forms of knowledge are all essential and complementary assets in the pursuit of management as a professional discipline. Whereas any profession will seek to explicate its knowledge base as much as possible, the tacit-explicit map of knowledge suggests that some of the knowledge will remain tacit—in terms of relational, somatic, and collective tacit knowledge. While professional behavior and performance is thus partly based on various forms of tacit knowledge, professional knowledge is by definition explicit in nature. Professionals, unlike for example craftsmen, cannot justify their actions and decisions by referring to any tacit knowledge.

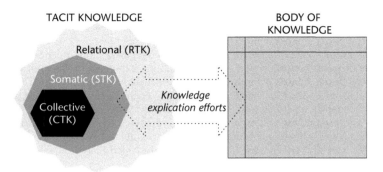

Figure 3.1. A profession draws on a body of explicit knowledge and various kinds of tacit knowledge
Source: Adapted from Collins (2010).

Professionalism and Tacit Knowledge

Figure 3.1 illustrates the key idea that a profession draws on a professional body of knowledge as well as various kinds of tacit knowledge that can only be partly explicated. The area representing tacit knowledge in this figure has three zones. The inner zone of CTK is inaccessible for any attempt to explicate it. The earlier case of chairing a team meeting involves CTK, for example about how one handles the silences in-between, which one can only acquire by being immersed in the local setting and culture for a longer period.

The second zone of tacit knowledge in Figure 3.1 is somatic in nature. This STK is somewhat accessible for knowledge explication, but only a huge effort in this area will lead to explicit knowledge that can be communicated to others. Explicating STK on, for example, hand gestures used by team leaders would require a substantial research program. Such a program would need to include studies of team leaders with different personalities and leadership styles, across a continuum of different kinds of team meetings (e.g. being video-recorded), to codify the exact gestures, develop constructs and measurements of how people respond to particular gestures, and so forth. These studies would have to be conducted in a large number of different national and organizational cultures, in order to explicate the contextual conditions and local routines in hand gesturing during team meetings.

This example illustrates that most STK in the area of management is likely to remain largely tacit, due to the huge effort required to explicate it. In management education and practice, this kind of tacit knowledge is therefore mainly transferred by role modeling, guided instruction, and experimentation (Cameron and Whetten 1983; Chia 1996; Daft 2002). In all instances, the key to getting access to STK is close contact with those who already have it. The "elevator pitch" exercise, widely used in training would-be entrepreneurs

(Gray et al. 2010), is a good example of how role modeling, experimentation, and guided instruction are combined to develop skills that, for seasoned entrepreneurs, are partly somatic in nature.

The zone of RTK is the most accessible one. RTK has some features of human-to-human communication, and therefore differs from the other two zones in which knowledge is tightly coupled to a particular person (Collins 2010). Traineeships and on-the-job training, typically combined with mentoring, enables the transfer of RTK from senior managers to their junior counterparts (Billsberry and Birnik 2010; Kahle-Piasecki 2011; Zepeda 2012). Similarly, in inducting graduate students into particular forms of management scholarship, their supervisors transfer RTK by way of personal mentoring and apprenticeship (cf. Stablein and Frost 2004).

Professional Knowledge is Explicit Knowledge

The remainder of this chapter will be about discovering and validating professional knowledge as an explicit body of knowledge, as Figure 3.1 also implies. Tacit knowledge is pervasive in managerial work and scholarship, as previously illustrated. The pervasiveness of tacit knowledge implies that explicit knowledge—even if it progresses to a highly systematic collection of accounts of management practices and their (codified and theorized) lessons—will never capture all the knowledge professional managers act upon.

In this respect, the domain of management is no different from that of architecture, medicine, engineering, or any other professional domain. Professional work in all these domains partly draws on tacit know-how, developed through years of experience, which cannot be explicated or can only be done by incurring prohibitive costs (Foray and Lundvall 1996; Cowan and Foray 1997; Hansen et al. 1999; Koedinger and Corbett 2006; Barends et al. 2012).

Knowledge Explication: Discovery and Validation

Any attempt to professionalize management requires a unique and explicit body of knowledge (Abbott 1988; Khurana 2007). This explicit body of knowledge is not a substitute for tacit knowledge, but complements and extends it. In this respect, professional knowledge arises from a continuous process of knowledge explication, fueled by an infinite and dynamic reservoir of individual (largely tacit) experiences in millions of organizations being managed and created every day.

Simon (1969/1996) identified two properties of these experiences which make an exclusive focus of knowledge explication on scientific validation inadequate: human intentionality and environmental contingency.[5] These properties create the need for discovery and validation as two distinct but

Table 3.1. Framework for structuring a professional body of knowledge on management

RESEARCH   ACTIVITIES &   METHODS

		DISCOVERY		VALIDATION	
		Creating	Evaluating	Theorizing	Justifying
RESEARCH INPUT/OUTPUT	Values				
	Constructs				
	Models				
	Principles				
	Instantiations				

Source: Adapted from March and Smith (1995).

complementary activities in explicating knowledge. *Discovery* involves creating new knowledge on either established practices or newly emerging ones (Nadler and Hibino 1999; Plsek et al. 2007), but also serves to create knowledge about practices and processes that intentionally "should be" or contingently "might be" (Romme 2003a; Burton and Obel 2011). Once new knowledge has been discovered, *validation* serves to codify, fine-tune, generalize, justify, and (possibly) falsify it.[6] Theoretical constructs and models are the conventional objects of validation in management research, but later in this chapter I will argue that other forms of knowledge also need to be validated.

The complementarity of discovery and validation also arises from the kind of agency involved. Discovery is to a large extent an individual creative act, which reflects Hayek's (1945) conceptualization of knowledge as embodied in individual human beings and pertaining to particular circumstances of time and place. By contrast, validation is essentially an intersubjective act, in which some newly discovered ideas and practices get theorized, justified, and institutionalized, and others do not.[7]

Shaping and Structuring a Professional Body of Knowledge

A framework for shaping and structuring a professional body of knowledge on management is developed in this section, by adapting and extending March and Smith's (1995) categorization. Consistent with the pragmatist perspective outlined in Chapter 2, a key assumption here is that both scholars and practitioners engage with their environments in practical ways, for example by creating, evaluating, using, and interpreting a variety of artifacts.

Table 3.1 provides an overview of the two axes.[8] The vertical axis is about *research input and output*. This is a single axis here because most output can also operate as input (or work-in-progress), because output arising from one research activity frequently acts as a resource to another research effort. For example, constructs are used to develop a model; or an existing model is adapted toward another one. The in- and outputs on this axis are values, constructs, models, principles, and instantiations—each defined and discussed in more detail later. Note that the shortcut "research output" will often be used to refer to both research input and output.

The other axis refers to *research activities*, including (the application of) *research methods*. Research activity here involves any effort to develop professional knowledge with regard to any of the research outputs. A research method is a set of steps—for example, in the form of a procedure or heuristic —which serves to perform a research activity (March and Smith 1995). Evidently, research methods are also outputs from deliberate efforts to create them, and also serve as input to a variety of research activities.

In this respect, research methods could also have been positioned on a third axis.[9] To avoid a three-dimensional representation, the horizontal axis of Table 3.1 includes research activities as well as methods. A single axis for research activities and methods may also serve to identify any differences and gaps between the research activities espoused as (complying with standard) methods and the research procedures and methods actually being used (cf. Argyris et al. 1985). The horizontal axis incorporates four generic research activities: creating, evaluating, theorizing, and justifying (March and Smith 1995). In the previous section, discovery and validation were identified as two fundamental activities in the management profession. Table 3.1 also makes this higher-level categorization visible: creating and evaluating together constitute discovery, whereas validation draws on theorizing and justifying.

Research Inputs and Outputs

VALUES
A value denotes the degree of importance a particular action has for a human agent, and thus serves to determine what kind of action it is best to do (e.g. "right" conduct). Values constitute the normative dimension of any professional community and are a key mechanism for ensuring its capacity to guide professional work (Adler et al. 2008).

Moreover, all inquiry in management research is, implicitly or explicitly, value-laden (Ackoff and Emery 1973; Myers and Thompson 2006). In fact, the prevailing emphasis in management studies on descriptive and explanatory theorizing is in itself a normative, value-based decision. This normative decision gives priority to describing and explaining the instantiated reality that has already been created, rather than seeking to make improvements or fundamental changes in that reality (Argyris 1993).

CONSTRUCTS

Constructs constitute the "key vocabulary" (March and Smith 1995) for describing problems and challenges within a professional domain. Most constructs in management research and practice, such as "output control" or "entrepreneurial opportunity," involve concepts or variables that cannot be directly observed, and therefore need to be operationalized, estimated, or approximated.

Notably, the noun "construct" is closely related to the verb "construct" (i.e. to build, erect, raise), which denotes the human agency in creating and sustaining any construct. The pragmatist perspective adopted in Chapter 2 is also consistent with conceptualizing constructs as the key vocabulary for describing problems and challenges within a professional domain.

MODELS

Where constructs provide the vocabulary, models constitute the "language" of the profession (March and Smith 1995). A model involves a set of propositions or statements expressing relationships among constructs. This broad definition includes conceptual frameworks, mathematical models, and "theories" (as defined by Shapira 2011) and thus captures the variety of narrative, mathematical, and statistical approaches (cf. "language families") used in management research. Notably, the label "theory" is avoided here, because the framework in Table 3.1 implies "theorizing" as a research activity also applies to values, constructs, principles, and instantiations—as will be discussed more extensively later.[10]

Moreover, the definition of model adopted here is broad enough to include explanatory models that provide insight into the causal mechanisms affecting past or current phenomena (e.g. Wareham et al. 2014) as well as intervention-oriented models that serve to describe and develop a future system (e.g. Argyris et al. 1985; Burton and Obel 2011).

PRINCIPLES

Principles, also known as design principles, refer to solution concepts for a certain professional problem or challenge, that is, the "real helps" of managerial thought and action (Sarasvathy and Venkataraman 2011: 130). Principles in the area of management tend to be heuristic in nature, incorporating ambiguity operators in predicate logic format—for example, in context C, outcome pattern O is likely to be generated by means of action A (Baskerville and Pries-Heje 2010).

Constructs and principles are fundamentally different in terms of their functionality as (intermediary) research output: constructs primarily serve analytical purposes, by breaking down complex patterns and phenomena into smaller elements, whereas principles primarily serve to synthesize research findings in the service of practical action and instantiation.[11]

INSTANTIATIONS

An instantiation can be defined as the realization of an artifact in its organizational, entrepreneurial, or managerial context.[12] Accordingly, instantiations serve to operationalize constructs, models, and principles, regardless of whether or not these are (ex ante or retrospectively) defined, codified, or theorized. The emergent and deliberate nature of instantiation is explored in more detail later.

Especially in the Instantiations–Validation cells of Table 3.1, management scholars prefer to talk about instantiations and their immediate or broader settings as *empirical phenomena* (Shapira 2011). Instantiations in an organizational context can be as varied as a work procedure, job description, customer database, operating routine, business proposition, code of conduct, narrative of the organization's history, tool for developing business models, or network of investors. All these instantiations are typically created, embedded and used in ambiguous, fluid, and dynamic settings (Orlikowski 2000; Sandberg and Tsoukas 2011).

Research Activities and Methods

CREATING AND EVALUATING

Before values, constructs, models, and principles can be tried out and realized in instantiations, one first needs to create them (Weick 1989; March and Smith 1995). The largely individual act of creating may also consist of, for example, introducing constructs or other research output from other adjacent literatures and disciplines (e.g. Hodgkinson and Healey 2008). In the context of discovery, the research act of evaluating draws on criteria such as usefulness, novelty, and relevance to assess the (new) research output against those criteria.

THEORIZING AND JUSTIFYING

Obviously, at the heart of mainstream management research today are theorizing and justifying activities. Theorizing involves producing propositions or statements that are generalizable as well as applicable to, or testable on, individual cases (Argyris 1993; Hambrick 2007); accordingly, theory is "simply a way of imposing conceptual order on the empirical complexity of the phenomenal world" (Suddaby 2014: 407). Thus, theorizing may serve to codify a particular value, use constructs and models to explain how or why something has happened (or instantiated), or use principles to brainstorm and speculate about whether an envisioned instantiation is likely to work. Finally, researchers "justify" values, constructs, models, and principles, for example by reviewing the available evidence in the literature, collecting and interpreting data, and statistically testing key causal mechanisms. Successful justification obviously enhances the legitimacy of the research output.

CLARIFYING SOME KEY NOTIONS

This conceptualization of the horizontal axis of Table 3.1 helps to clarify some of the ambiguity around the notions of "theorizing" and "theory." The validation-oriented notion of theorizing prevailing in mainstream management research (e.g. Hambrick 2007; Suddaby 2014) has been questioned by several scholars (Weick 1989; Locke and Golden-Biddle 1997; Zbaracki 2006) because "we cannot improve the theorizing process until we describe it more explicitly, operate it more self-consciously, and decouple it from validation more deliberately" (Weick 1989: 1). This position would actually imply management scholars stop talking about theorizing and theory in the context of the validation segment of Table 3.1, and exclusively "theorize" in the context of the discovery-oriented research activities.

The set of definitions proposed earlier combines key ideas advocated by both sides. First, the terminology introduced here separates constructs and models as research output from the research activities producing this output, as advocated by Weick (1989) and Locke and Golden-Biddle (1997). And second, it retains the "theorizing" notion for the purpose of validation-oriented research, in line with its established usage within management studies (cf. Hambrick 2007; Suddaby 2014), while providing a separate terminology for discovery research.

Moreover, the framework in Table 3.1 serves to accommodate highly different interpretations of the validity notion in the literature. In all "justifying" activities in Table 3.1, research output is primarily assessed in terms of the (e.g. construct or external) validity of the relation between premises and conclusion (Van de Ven 2007). By contrast, in the "evaluating" cells, research output is primarily assessed in terms of what Worren et al. (2002) call "pragmatic validity," the perceived value or utility of the output for an important task: accordingly, the perceived utility of, for example, a model or principle lies in the persuasiveness of the claims that it is effective (cf. March and Smith 1995). Admittedly, this definition of the perceived utility/value of a research output is somewhat ambiguous. Indeed, in the "justifying" column of Table 3.1 the assessment of research output tends to be much more explicit and straightforward. To avoid confusion, I therefore suggest we only talk about validity and validation in the context of the validation segment of Table 3.1, whereas utility, novelty, and relevance are some of the key evaluation criteria in the discovery segment.

Defining a Professional Body of Knowledge

The framework in Table 3.1 implies values, constructs, models, principles, and their instantiations are created and evaluated as well as theorized and justified. This five by four framework has 20 cells, each representing a viable research effort toward a professional body of knowledge. Accordingly, management professionals engage in creating, evaluating, theorizing, and/or justifying any (or a combination) of the five forms of research output.

This framework arises from the idea, advocated in Chapter 2, that (professional) practitioners and scholars share the responsibility to build and sustain a professional body of knowledge on management. In fact, the management discipline initially arose from observational and intervention-oriented studies, by scholar-practitioners such as Taylor and Fayol, which would fit the Principles/Instantiations–Validation cells in Table 3.1. The more systematic development of Constructs and Models did not come about until the pioneering work of Cyert, March, Simon and many others (Wren and Bedeian 2008).

Notably, the development and justification of theoretical knowledge is not the exclusive domain or privilege of management scholars. For example, practitioners theorize in useful ways when they reflect on their experiences with particular instantiations (i.e. Instantiations–Theorizing in Table 3.1) and seek to substantiate their theoretical reflections by consulting peers, internet sources, and so forth (i.e. Instantiations–Justifying). Clearly, these practical insights "often lack a rigorous, systematic basis, but are available as they emanate directly from on-the-spot observation and application" (Poiesz 2014: 23) and therefore need to be scrutinized by means of research activities and outputs in other cells of Table 3.1.

EMERGENT AND DELIBERATE PROCESSES

Creating, evaluating, theorizing, and justifying are equivalent research activities, together enabling a viable discourse on management. As Figure 3.2 illustrates, these four research activities and their products interact in a variety of ways, in which emergent and deliberate patterns can be identified—as observed in similar contexts such as information systems, education, and architecture (Markus et al. 2002; Schön 1983). In general, *emergent* processes start in the bottom-left of this table, with instantiations (e.g. management practices or tools) arising from improvised, on-the-spot try-outs (Weick 1998), reflection-in-action (Schön 1983) and other research strategies resulting in "an

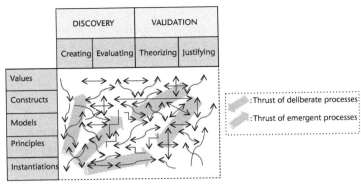

Figure 3.2. Interaction between research activities and methods and research in/output

unfolding story, where data shift as a consequence of intervention and where it is not possible to predict or control what takes place" (Coghlan and Shani 2013: 444).

By contrast, *deliberate* processes tend to start in the top-right corner of Figure 3.2, for example by defining a particular organizational challenge, reviewing the research evidence with regard to values, constructs, and models in this area, and then developing principles that inform the development of strategies or interventions addressing this challenge (Pascal et al. 2013). Regardless of where and how it is initiated, most research tends to evolve iteratively, with emergent and deliberate processes interacting, merging, and materializing in various research outputs over time (Burgoyne and Turnbull James 2006; Bushe 2011; Van Burg et al. 2008).[13]

PROFESSIONAL BODY OF KNOWLEDGE: DEFINITION

The argument thus far suggests that the heart of a professional body of knowledge is the synergy between a variety of research activities and outputs as well as the interaction between deliberate and emergent processes. More specifically, the following definition is proposed here: a *professional body of knowledge* in the area of management is the systematic collection of management activities and outcomes in terms of their values, constructs, models, principles, and instantiations that (a) arises from continuous discovery and validation work by practitioners and scholars and (b) enables a self-reflective growth and reproduction of management as professional activity. This definition informs the argument in the remainder of this chapter.[14]

Examples of Studies Connecting Discovery and Validation

In view of the antagonism between validation and discovery activities as well as the low academic legitimacy of creative discovery, several scholars have argued discovery needs to be *separated* from validation: this would make it easier and more legitimate to engage in developing new ideas and approaches (Locke et al. 2008; Starkey et al. 2009; Weick 1989). While this makes sense from the perspective of individual management scholars, especially those interested in engaging in creative discovery, an institutional separation of validation and discovery efforts would be detrimental to the development of a professional body of knowledge. In the quest for professionalism in management, it is therefore critical to connect creative discovery and scientific validation (Hatchuel and Weil 2009). This section outlines three studies that illustrate how discovery and validation can be connected.

DEVELOPING THE BUSINESS MODEL CANVAS

A business model describes the rationale of how an organization creates, delivers and captures value. In his doctoral thesis, Osterwalder (2004: 2) addressed the question "how can business models be described and represented in order to build the foundation for subsequent concepts and tools, possibly computer based?" Osterwalder's work at the time was largely informed by March and Smith's (1995) methodology.

Osterwalder conducted interviews with business practitioners, analyzed the resulting data, and also systematically reviewed and synthesized the literature. The interviews with business practitioners showed that "the ability to create a transparent big picture of a business and to externalize the relationships and dependencies of business elements seem to interest executives and consultants" and moreover, "business models were perceived as a tool to create a commonly understood language to improve communication and understanding of the fundamental questions of a business" (Osterwalder 2004: 159).

Osterwalder thus argued a more rigid conceptual approach to business models would be necessary to seize the possibilities identified among business practitioners. He then developed, based on a review of existing knowledge in this domain, the so-called "business model ontology" involving four pillars (e.g. product, customer interface) and nine key constructs (e.g. value proposition, target customer, distribution channel) and their relationships. Osterwalder implemented this initial framework in a computer-based tool, and the resulting prototype was tested in a case study of the Montreux Jazz Festival. Osterwalder's (2004) dissertation concluded with an agenda for research with regard to further evaluation and validation of the framework.

After completing his doctoral degree, Osterwalder set out to further develop the business modeling framework, via prototyping processes that involved the active contributions of more than 450 practitioners, resulting into the so-called "business model canvas" (Osterwalder and Pigneur 2010). This large-scale effort to co-create and iteratively develop prototypes of the latter tool may serve as a good example of how academic knowledge can be successfully developed into practical tools by a community of professionals. Moreover, it also demonstrates how design techniques and tools contribute to developing answers to managerial challenges as well as designing strategic management objects such as business models (Osterwalder and Pigneur 2013).

CREATING UNIVERSITY SPINOFFS

In 2005, the senior management of a university of technology in the Netherlands sought to advance the university's capability in creating spin-off firms, that is, business ventures set up to commercialize inventions developed at the university. Several years earlier, the university's president initiated the development of a technology transfer office (TTO) that included business incubation facilities, and hired an experienced TTO professional to set up this office. A few years after the start of the new TTO, a team of management scholars was assigned to develop evidence-based guidelines for spin-off creation, and use these guidelines to evaluate where and how the initial design of the business incubator and its implementation could be changed or improved (Van Burg et al. 2008). As such, the research team could benefit from the initial learning and experiences of the TTO staff. However, it also faced the challenge of transforming an ongoing creative design process into a more deliberate and evidence-based one, as well as the challenge to contextualize generic (evidence-based) guidelines to the local setting. In view of these challenges, an iterative approach was adopted in which principles serve to connect professional practices and research findings (Romme and Endenburg 2006).

Van Burg et al. (2008) developed principles for university spin-off creation in three steps. First, practice-based principles were inferred from the incubation practices (as existing instantiations) within the local TTO, by converting the largely tacit knowledge of key actors into explicit propositions. Second, research-based principles were derived from a systematic review of the literature. Both sets of principles were inferred by means of a careful coding and reduction process from interview data and documents respectively the publications reviewed. Subsequently, the combination and synthesis of these two sets of principles resulted in several principles that were evidence-based as well as contextualized for a (European) university of technology:

> This type of university is likely to build capacity for creating spin-offs by means of the following actions and facilities: "Help starters in obtaining access to resources and developing their social capital by creating a collaborative network organization of investors, managers and advisors. . . . Set clear and supportive rules and procedures that regulate the university spin-off process, enhance fair treatment of the parties involved, and separate spinoff processes from academic research and teaching. . . . Shape a university culture that reinforces academic entrepreneurship by creating norms and exemplars that motivate entrepreneurial behavior." (Van Burg et al. 2008: 123)

These principles were discussed extensively with the TTO manager and his staff members, and then used to improve two existing incubation practices within the TTO. Moreover, the last principle (cited above) served to identify the lack of an entrepreneurial culture at the incumbent university, which led to several new initiatives addressing these cultural issues.

The principles developed by Van Burg et al. (2008) were replicated by Barr et al. (2009) in a study of several US-based universities and extended by Lackéus and Williams Middleton's (2011) study of other venture creation programs in Europe, North America, and Asia-Pacific. Van Burg et al.'s initial study also served to define research gaps and questions informing follow-up studies of transparency and fairness in spin-off creation processes (e.g. Van Burg et al. 2013; Van Burg and Van Oorschot 2013).

DEVELOPING A KNOWLEDGE MANAGEMENT PLATFORM

In the late 1990s, the Sophia Antipolis (SA) technology park in France was facing major challenges. The global economic downturn earlier that decade had led many telecom and IT firms residing on this technology park to downsize their activities, and moreover, many residents were signalling the lack of sufficient synergies with other residents. In 2001, a group of eight leading telecom and IT firms at SA therefore launched the *Knowledge Management Platform* (KMP) project, in order to design and build an interactive map of competencies to enhance knowledge creation through partnerships within SA (Pascal et al. 2013). The project team assigned to the KMP project included all the required expertise (e.g. software engineering, ergonomics) and was led by a management professor, supported by a doctoral student.

The project team adopted a pragmatic and semantic design approach (Warfield 1994; Krippendorff 2006) that combined two complementary perspectives: the development of science-based design principles (e.g. Denyer et al. 2008; Romme and Endenburg 2006) and user-centred, participative, and experience-based design (e.g. Orlikowski 2004). This resulted in a highly iterative process in which a deeper awareness of the design problem is developed, principles are developed and refined, scenarios-of-use are explored to discover user needs from multiple perspectives and embed the (intended) instantiation in work processes, the intended instantiation is (re)designed, prototypes of the instantiation are developed and tried out, and the commitment and support of powerful actors is activated and sustained (Pascal et al. 2013).

Pascal et al. (2013) describe the four iterations through which the KMP project progressed, including detailed reports of the principles for developing an interactive map of competences in a multi-actor cluster of firms, inferred from the literature on knowledge and innovation management. The resulting principles depicted the intended outcomes, mechanisms, and mediators of knowledge creation in collaborative R&D, such as opportunity identification and the ability to anticipate opportunities. These principles informed the initial design of the interactive map of competencies. In the first iteration of the project, a general principle was inferred from the literature, to guide the initial stages of the process. The collective learning that subsequently unfolded served to create and adapt knowledge in response to the particular class of problems at hand. As a result, the principles and prototypes of the knowledge management platform became more specific and elaborate over time. Moreover, the embodiment of principles in tangible instantiations appeared to facilitate the support and acceptance of the platform among users and other stakeholders in SA (Pascal et al. 2013).

This project illustrates that principles can meet the dual requirement of informing the design of a practical solution and responding to a general class of problems. The practical solution in this project was tailor-made for a particular IT cluster of firms in southern France, but can be positioned as a response to a general class of problems pertaining to "knowledge creation in any cluster composed of a large number of actors and a broad scope of technologies" (Pascal et al. 2013: 277).

LEARNINGS AND QUESTIONS ARISING FROM THESE EXAMPLES

Each of these examples draws on some form of academic–practitioner collaboration that serves to "coproduce solutions whose demands exceed the capabilities of either researchers or practitioners by themselves" (Van de Ven and Johnson 2006: 810). The three studies demonstrate one can effectively connect "scientific" knowledge on a general class of problems and challenges to "instrumental" knowledge that applies to local and practical cases, and vice versa. As such, the ability to combine creative and abductive discovery with the inductive and deductive logic of science is critical in connecting the discovery and validation segments outlined in Table 3.1.

In terms of the framework outlined in Table 3.1, the three studies previously reviewed tend to focus on the central cells in this table (i.e. Constructs/Models/Principles–Evaluating/Theorizing). That is, these studies draw on systematic reviews of relevant literature, typically based on elaborate work on justifying (testing) theoretical models, rather than engaging in this type of research themselves. Moreover, practitioners and/or other members of the project team appear to do the most creative work on instantiation. These connections and partnerships illustrate how all the cells in Table 3.1 provide building blocks for a professional body of knowledge, even when specific research projects focus on only a few cells.

Notably, values as a key research in/output are largely underdeveloped and implicit in the three projects. Only in the third study (Pascal et al. 2013), were values such as user-centeredness, pragmatic validity, and scientific validity explicated as premises of the KMP project. This is one of the issues addressed in the next section.

Agenda for Future Work

The argument thus far in this chapter calls for an agenda for renewing the quest for a professional body of knowledge. The agenda developed here serves to demonstrate that many elements of this body of knowledge already exist, but also that many opportunities for connecting them remain untapped. The argument in this section is structured in terms of the five research outputs defined earlier.

To support the agenda for future work developed here, Appendix 2 provides an overview of research methods, categorized in the framework of Table 3.1.

Values

Central to management research and practice is the economic notion of value —such as the financial compensation someone is willing to pay for a product, service, or partnership. The pivotal role of economic value also arises rather naturally from the shared interest of management scholars and practitioners in outcomes and implications (cf. Chapter 2).

Nevertheless, management scholars have become increasingly interested in ethical notions of value. They have been used to explain, for example, the emergence and evolution of corporate social responsibility practices (Joyner and Payne 2002), action patterns in and around organizations as reflections of the core values of their founders, executives, and other organizational members (Berson et al. 2008), the processes whereby values come to be practiced in organizations (Gehman et al. 2013), how emerging organizations augment their initial imprints by using ancillary forms aligned with their organizational values (Perkmann and Spicer 2014), and when and how organizational values affect organizational behavior and performance (Cha and Edmondson 2006; Posner et al. 1985; Maurer et al. 2011). A key finding arising from the latter studies is that clearly articulated ethical values make a significant difference in the lives of employees as well as enhance organizational performance (e.g. Posner et al. 1985; Maurer et al. 2011).

The overall thrust of this literature is validation-oriented, with few studies directly engaging in the creation and evaluation of organizational and other values (e.g. Bushe and Kassam 2005; Cameron and Quinn 2011). Exemplary in the latter category of studies is Flyvbjerg's work on phronesis, also discussed earlier in this chapter. Phronetic research thus seeks to address questions such as: Where are we going with this specific management problem; is this direction desirable; what, if anything, should we do about it? (Flyvbjerg 2001, 2008; Flyvbjerg et al. 2003).[15]

The framework in Table 3.1 implies that all management research is inherently ethical in nature (Myers and Thompson 2006). However, awareness of the ethical dimension is not widespread among management scholars (Wicks and Freeman 1998), which in turn may impede the development of a science-based professional body of knowledge. This is perhaps most conspicuous with regard to values that (ideally) would need to guide "professional" behavior of management scholars and practitioners—particularly in terms of the antagonism between (rigor in) "understanding" and (relevance for) "use." Other professional disciplines such as law, medicine, and engineering have a long history in seeking a balance between the two, conceptually as well as practically (Barends et al. 2012; Warfield 1994).

In the management literature, however, the discourse on the balance between these values mainly draws on conceptual arguments (e.g. Bartunek 2007; Vermeulen 2007; Palmer et al. 2009) rather than empirical and practical work (e.g. Rynes et al. 2001). This may be due to difficulties in measuring "relevance" and other key terms (Worren et al. 2002; Palmer et al. 2009), but also to management scholarship not (yet) being an essential part of a broader community drawing on a shared sense of responsibility—as observed in the previous chapter. In this respect, a broad discourse on key professional values is critical, and the framework developed in this chapter may help advance this debate. In particular, Table 3.1 suggests that, rather than attempting to realize the complementarity of different professional values such as "understanding" and "use" in a single cell in this table, management scholars would be better off by addressing these different values on their own terms. The quest for rigorous understanding can be best exploited in the context of validation, whereas values such as "novelty" and "relevance for use" can be better pursued in discovery-driven work.

Constructs and Models

Most work published in management journals draws on theorizing in terms of constructs and models, using a variety of research designs and methods for collecting and analyzing data (e.g. field studies, case studies, lab experiments, quasi-experiments, historical analysis). In justifying theoretical frameworks and models, scholars primarily attend to issues of validity and reliability (George 2014) and as a result the "managerial implications" in their publications tend to be vaguely scripted (Bartunek and Rynes 2010). Colquitt and George (2011) therefore recommend that management scholars invest more time and resources in discovering and developing constructs, models, and designs that would inform practitioners facing "grand challenges."

In this respect, discovery-oriented work is underdeveloped in management studies (Weick 1989; Alvesson and Karreman 2007), although it enables us to see empirical problems and anomalies and mobilize "our most interesting theorizing" (Locke et al. 2008: 907). Locke and co-authors (2008) recommend the following strategies to *foster the generative potential of doubt* in creative theorizing: developing the ability "to turn toward and embrace not knowing"; nurturing hunches, a hunch being an "undifferentiated sense of something"; and disrupting belief, that is, suppressing the impulse to accept that one already knows how to understand a particular empirical or practical phenomenon (Locke et al. 2008: 912–13). Some of these strategies are employed in appreciative inquiry (e.g. Ludema et al. 2003) and other practice-oriented approaches (e.g. Nadler and Hibino 1999).

Earlier in this chapter, I illustrated how discovery and validation can be more deliberately connected. I am not arguing here that specialized work is no longer legitimate. Most work in management studies has to be somewhat specialized and focused, given the deep knowledge regarding particular research methods, constructs, and models typically required. The key point is that, in addition to scholars and scholar-practitioners focusing on either validation or discovery, we need a discourse that systematically connects them. The next chapter will also address this challenge, in terms of so-called "trading zones."

Principles

Principles connect the descriptive and explanatory thrust of most management research to the normative and situated nature of practical instantiations. The most powerful "action" or "design" principles are those that have been extensively applied and evaluated in real-life settings *and* are extensively validated in research evidence (Van Aken 2004). Drawing on Bunge's (1967) logic of prescription, Merton's (1968) theories of the middle range as well as the notion of social or generative mechanism (Hedström and Swedberg 1996; Pawson 2000; Hedström and Ylikoski 2010), guidelines have been developed for formulating principles in terms of action–outcome effects, the contextual conditions in which these effects are likely to occur, and the generative or social mechanisms explaining these effects (Denyer et al. 2008; Van Burg and Romme 2014).

Principles have only recently been introduced as a distinct form of research output in the management literature, and knowledge on how to develop them is therefore limited. Some recent work in this area draws on a number of methods for developing principles. First, *systematic literature reviews* are instrumental in inferring and synthesizing principles from the available evidence (Tranfield et al. 2003; Briner and Denyer 2012), particularly when a substantial body of research findings has accumulated in other cells of

Table 3.1 (e.g. Dougherty 2008; Van Burg et al. 2008; Pascal et al. 2013). Systematic reviews imply an iterative process of selecting literature, interpreting and codifying each publication, collecting and comparing relevant research findings, and synthesizing these findings in principles—covering the entire row of discovering and validating principles in Table 3.1.

However, when limited evidence on a particular organizational problem or phenomenon is available, systematic literature reviews are less applicable and other approaches such as idealized design are needed. *Idealized design* is a structured process for developing a set of initial principles that "strip away" non-essential aspects of the problem situation and draw on larger purposes and expanded thinking (Ackoff 1999; Ackoff et al. 2006). For example, idealized design is a key element of appreciative inquiry (Cooperrider and Whitney 1999).

Another way to develop principles when there is hardly any research evidence that is directly relevant for the problem at hand, is to *learn from adjacent* areas and literatures. Hodgkinson and Healey (2008) adopt this approach when they draw upon insights from research on social identity, categorization, personality and social psychology to infer and create principles for scenario planning interventions.

Principles can also be *extracted from successful* instantiations and *less successful* ones. For example, Plsek et al. (2007) extracted design principles from successful organizational change programs in the National Health Service in the UK. They applied the following methods: (a) reviewing written documentation of change programs to extract principles; (b) convening groups of change experts and asking them to describe what they do in the form of principles; (c) listening to stories of change efforts told by change leaders, operational managers, and front-line staff, and then extracting principles off-line (via reviewing and coding transcripts/notes); and (d) posing hypothetical scenarios to those experienced in organizational change, by asking them to "think aloud" regarding how they would approach the situation, and then extracting principles off-line. Sarasvathy (2008) also used the last approach, hypothetical scenarios, by extracting a set of principles for entrepreneurial effectuation from "thinking aloud" scenario experiments with highly successful entrepreneurs. Extracting principles from less successful instantiations (e.g. Romme and Endenburg 2006) is rarely done, because these instantiations are more difficult to document and sample. However, work in other disciplines demonstrates that instances of failure and severe underperformance provide essential information for identifying the non-conditions (e.g. in which particular actions do not work) and thereby help to further specify the conditions for successful instantiation (Schön 1983; Warfield 1994). This offers major opportunities for discovery-oriented research in, for example, innovation management, organizational renewal, ecosystem management, and corporate governance.

Overall, principles are an underdeveloped category of research output in management research. Therefore, a key challenge is to rewrite textbooks on research methods and other materials for training new generations of managers and scholars, to provide them with more tools to connect the neat and tidy (analytical) world of scholarship to the fuzzy and embedded (synthetical) world of practice. The ability to distil, infer, or extract principles from a variety of sources may also offer opportunities for new forms of interaction between practitioners and researchers. For example, principles extracted from practical experiences in the field can be compared with those distilled from validated research findings.

Instantiations

As observed earlier in this chapter, the act of instantiation in the area of management is typically left to practitioners. Instead, the last row in Table 3.1 suggests that creating, evaluating, theorizing, and justifying instantiations are essential activities in professionalizing our discipline. Some prominent practitioners provide access to their reflections on these activities, for example by means of biographical reflections on major steps and decisions in their career (e.g. Brandt 2011) or via blogs (e.g. Richard Branson's widely read blog) and other writings in the social media (e.g. at Inc.com). These practical insights on instantiation arise from direct experience and reflection, typically without systematically using constructs, models, and principles developed and codified by management scholars. Nevertheless, this practical discourse around prominent role models plays a key role in introducing and socializing newcomers into the profession, and therefore needs to be analyzed and discussed more deliberately in other cells of Table 3.1.

Another challenge arises from the current emphasis in management scholarship on validating constructs and models of existing instantiations. An example is the literature on experimentation and prototyping, key processes that are at the heart of instantiation in organizational and managerial settings (Myers and Thompson 2006). Studies of experimentation behavior have identified the organizational and industrial conditions enabling respectively inhibiting this type of behavior (e.g. Lee et al. 2004; Massa and Simonov 2009). Others have studied prototypes as "boundary objects" that invite human interaction and participation, particularly in organizational settings involving multiple stakeholders with different interests and backgrounds (Carlile 2002; Boland and Collopy 2004), for example in testing and co-creating new products with customers, distributors, and other stakeholders (Garud et al. 2008; Bogers and Horst 2014).

As such, the current discourse on experimentation and prototyping focuses on theorizing and justifying-testing activity, rather than directly engaging in or contributing to experimentation and protoyping processes themselves. In the early days of management scholarship, these direct engagements in experimentation and prototyping were central to all scholarly work (Wren and Bedeian 2008), but today this type of work (e.g. Schein 1988; Nadler and Hibino 1999; Coughlan and Ponto 2014) has become almost entirely decoupled from validation-oriented research. Evidently, The Quest for Professionalism implies work on creating and evaluating instantiations is as respectable as research in any of the other cells in Table 3.1.

I am not advocating here that every management scholar engages in developing tools and consultancy work. As also argued earlier in this chapter, all professional disciplines draw on a certain degree of specialization and division of labor (cf. Heugens and Mol 2005; Markides 2011). Table 3.1 merely demonstrates that creating and evaluating new instantiations is a core activity in management practice as well as scholarship; without this activity, all other efforts to professionalize management would ultimately be without content and meaning.

Integrated Work

There are few attempts to combine the discovery and validation of instantiations in terms of the underlying values, constructs, models, and principles. A prominent exception is the pioneering work by Argyris and co-authors on learning in groups and organizations (Argyris and Schön 1978; Argyris et al. 1985; Argyris 1993). In this body of literature, different types of learning systems have been discovered, codified, and validated—in terms of the core values enabling, respectively, limiting the learning process, the key constructs explaining whether and how learning occurs, and models of the "limited" and "effective" learning systems that integrate many research findings. Moreover, a portfolio of tools, intervention strategies, and other instantiations has been created, evaluated, and validated in detailed case studies (Argyris et al. 1985; Argyris 1993). While Argyris and co-authors initially covered all cells in Table 3.1, later work on organizational and management learning has become almost entirely decoupled in practical, user-led, and discovery-oriented approaches (e.g. Schwarz 2002) and validation-oriented theoretical and critical approaches (e.g. Rynes and Brown 2011), with a relative decline in publications on the former and a relative increase in publications on the latter type of work—as observed by Turnbull James and Denyer (2009).

The practice-based view offers promising opportunities for connecting discovery and validation, and for scholars to become more appreciative of the "entwinement" logic of practice (Feldman and Orlikowski 2011; Sandberg and Tsoukas 2011). The practice-based literature suggests practitioners tend to experience organizational practices as continuously evolving, fluid, and ambiguous settings. It thus provides a deeper understanding of instantiations such as auditing of financial statements (Pentland 1993), strategy workshops (Hodgkinson et al. 2006), and strategic planning (Spee and Jarzabkowski 2011).

Some recent work in this area also explicitly combines the practice-based lens with a design science perspective (Hodgkinson and Healey 2008; Healey et al. 2014). The framework in Table 3.1 suggests future work in this area should not only seek to understand how management tools and other instantiations are actually used in practice (e.g. Spee and Jarzabkowksi 2011; Jarzabkowksi and Kaplan 2015), but also distill propositions and principles that can proactively inform the design of new instantiations or the adaptation of existing ones (e.g. Dougherty 2008; Hodgkinson and Healey 2008; Healey et al. 2014). This also calls for longitudinal studies of whether and how these principles are actually used, and how evidence-based instantiation processes and outcomes compare to those not informed by evidence.

Complementarity of Phronesis, Episteme, and Techne

To activate and sustain a productive interaction between discovery and validation, a professional body of knowledge covers all cells in Table 3.1. Moreover, active engagement at all levels of research output, including values and instantiations, is likely to enable more substantial theoretical and practical progress, by enhancing productive lines of thinking and weeding out unproductive ones (Starbuck 2006).

Figure 3.3 provides an image of the complementarity of Aristotle's phronesis, episteme, and techne. In this figure, the research input/output axis from Table 3.1 is presented as a cycle of research outputs and inputs; the white arrows reflect the discovery and validation activities conducted horizontally in Table 3.1, and the black arrows refer to research activities conducted vertically or diagonally in this table. This figure serves to again demonstrate that dialogical, representational, and instrumental knowledge are complementary assets in building a professional body of knowledge on management.

Concluding Remarks

The first business schools were established to train a professional class of managers. But when these schools increasingly became "wastelands of vocationalism," they sought to redirect themselves toward "science-based professionalism, as medicine and engineering had been transformed a generation or two earlier" (Simon 1991a: 139). In their quest for academic respectability, most management scholars and business schools have retreated from that goal. Drawing on a pragmatist orientation toward management as a profession

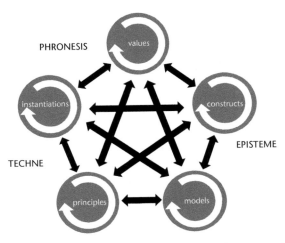

Figure 3.3. The complementarity of phronesis, episteme, and techne

serving the "greater good," the previous chapter called for developing a shared sense of purpose and responsibility.

As a complement to the preceding argument on professional purpose, this chapter serves to envision a professional body of knowledge in which discovery and validation activities inform a productive discourse on instantiated practices—in terms of their constituent values, constructs, models, and principles. Interestingly, most elements of a body of knowledge are already present in the literature, albeit in a scattered and fragmented manner. The framework developed here may facilitate dialogue between theorists from different camps and tribes, and connect creative discovery to scholarly validation in the quest for management as a profession.

The framework of research in/outputs, methods, and activities presented in this chapter may also motivate future work on an evidence-based platform in management, similar to the Cochrane Collaboration in healthcare (www. cochrane.org). The argument here merely constitutes a first step in envisioning such a platform that, ultimately, would enable management professionals to engage with their most pertinent challenges.

Notes

1. In Chapter 1, I argued that professional values and expertise together constitute the body of knowledge claimed by a profession. In this chapter, I will not use the term "expertise," to avoid any confusion with the related notion of knowledge. In the framework for a professional body of knowledge introduced in this chapter and summarized in Table 3.1, the first row refers to the "value" segment and the other rows constitute the "expertise" segment of this body of knowledge.

2. This position differs from the well-known incommensurability thesis (e.g. Czarniawska 1998; Jackson and Carter 1991) implying that episteme, techne, and phronesis draw on starkly contrasting conceptual frameworks whose languages lack sufficiently overlapping meanings.

3. The more generic capability here has also been labeled "emotional intelligence" (Clark et al. 2003; Emmerling and Goleman 2005).

4. This case provides a natural experiment (Dunning 2012) regarding knowledge development as follows. Other startups that grow to a sizable corporation operating internationally tend to start with a rather informal corporate governance approach, and may then gradually evolve toward a more formalized approach. For example, in the first few years, shareholders such as informal investors and (representatives of) venture capital firms meet the entrepreneur frequently to discuss strategy, performance, and other issues, and with each new investment round the company scales up and adopts more formalized accountability and governance systems. This gradual approach provides a learning curve for entrepreneurs, investors, and other stakeholders to develop a company-specific governance culture—partly based on explicit knowledge, partly on various forms of tacit knowledge—aligned with local, sectoral, and (inter)national conventions and guidelines. In the case described here such a gradual approach was not possible because, from the first day this corporation was established, it was accountable to more than 30 shareholders and operated a budget of more than €200 million.

5. Simon (1969/1996) therefore argued business and management research is primarily a science of the artificial, that is, a design discipline in the service of management as a science-based profession (as discussed in Chapter 1). Simon's ideas were later re-introduced in the discourse on the purpose and nature of management and organization studies (Hatchuel 2001a, 2001b; Romme 2003a; Sarasvathy 2003; Van Aken 2004) and subsequently, a "design science" perspective on management research has been emerging (Bate 2007; Jelinek et al. 2008; Hodgkinson and Rousseau 2009; Avenier 2010).

6. The distinction between discovery and validation is similar to the distinction between concept and knowledge space in C-K theory, developed by Hatchuel and Weil. In this respect, C-K theory offers a definition of "design" to make creative thinking and innovation not external to design theory but part of its central core (Hatchuel and Weil 2003, 2009). The knowledge (K) space involves the existing and established knowledge and the concept (C) space contains ideas and other concepts that are unknown or that have not yet been established. By partitioning propositions into these two spaces, "crazy concepts" can be explicitly used to help shape new knowledge. "Crazy concepts" are those concepts that "force the designer to explore new sources of knowledge" (Hatchuel et al. 2013: 154).

7. Collins (2010) also developed a categorization of knowledge explication: elaboration, transformation, mechanization and explanation. These four meanings of knowledge explication arise from his definition of knowledge explication as an operation on strings of information elements (e.g. letters of alphabet). Collins' categorization is a very elegant one, based on "first principles." In this chapter, I use a categorization of research activity as knowledge explication that is more

consistent with widely used terminology in management research: discovery (incl. creation and evaluation) and validation (incl. theorizing and justifying).

8. The main adaptations of the framework of March and Smith (1995), leading to the framework presented in this chapter, were as follows. First, "methods" as a research output were removed from the vertical axis in March and Smith (1995), and incorporated in the definition of the horizontal axis, thereby broadening the latter axis to "research activities & methods." Second, the research activity "building" was relabeled "creating." Third, I added "values" and "principles" as separate research outputs to the vertical axis. Finally, Discovery and Validation were added as higher-level categories to the horizontal axis. Notably, March and Smith talk about design science and natural science as metaphors for the discovery and valid- ation segments in Table 3.1. Instead, I talk about a professional body of knowledge that arises from both discovery and validation activity, consistent with some previ- ous work in this area (e.g. Healey et al. 2014; Romme 2003a; Starkey et al. 2009).

9. Appendix 2 provides an overview of research methods, categorized in terms of the axes used here. This appendix also serves to illustrate the (visual) complexity of a three-dimensional framework.

10. Many authors have tried to define what a (complete) "theory" is (e.g. Shapira 2011; Weick 1989; Whetten 1989). An authority on this topic is Dubin (1978), who also does not distinguish between a model and a theory. In this chapter I talk about models as a category of research outputs, rather than theories, to avoid confusion with "theorizing" as generic research activity.

11. In management research, models are primarily used for analyzing cause–effect relations, but can also serve synthetical purposes (e.g. Mohrman et al. 2001; Burton and Obel 2011; Shapira 2011).

12. This definition is pragmatist in nature and consistent with how instantiation is defined in most dictionaries. In this chapter, I do not take a (strong) theoretical position on instantiation, which is beyond the purpose of the framework devel- oped here.

13. While most work in management research is likely to be emergent as well as deliberate in nature, the emergent dimension is likely to prevail when practitioners run into questions and challenges for which they have no established routines or recipes, and moreover, principles are nonexistent, underdeveloped or unknown (to them). By contrast, the deliberate dimension tends to prevail when change agents have access to principles grounded in a body of evidence (i.e. validated constructs and models).

14. Obviously, this definition depicts an ideal image of a professional body of know- ledge, and does not reflect the current state of the knowledge landscape in the management discipline (cf. Chapter 1). For example, most *discovery-oriented* work by management consultants and scholar-practitioners engaging in instantiation (e.g. developing practical guidelines and tools) tends to be ambiguous, creative and prescriptive in nature, and draws on largely implicit values, constructs and prin- ciples (Visscher and Visscher-Voerman 2010). Academics and practitioners that collaborate to identify and evaluate values, constructs, models, and principles in the context of the instantiations created and/or studied (Cooperrider and Whitney

1999; Nadler and Hibino 1999; Mohrman et al. 2001; Coghlan and Shani 2013) also conduct discovery-oriented projects. By contrast, most management scholars have been focusing on *validation-oriented* activities by theorizing and justifying, particularly in terms of constructs and models (Walsh et al. 2006; Hughes et al. 2011). A typical project here starts from existing constructs and models, or introduces these from adjacent areas, and then prioritizes rigor (e.g. construct validity) above practical usefulness in collecting primary and secondary data, which are analyzed by way of statistical methods or data coding procedures. As such, data collection and analysis becomes confined to existing instantiations (as empirical phenomena), rather than those that might or should be (Burton and Obel 2011). As a result, research output in the form of principles that would inform the creation and development of (e.g. should-be) instantiations, is almost completely absent in this part of the landscape. Discovery and validation have thus become almost entirely decoupled communities, or "tribes that form around rigor and relevance, sequestering themselves into closed loops of scholarship" (Gulati 2007: 775), primarily talk and write to members of their own tribe, and tend to dismiss work done outside their own tribe (e.g. Donaldson 2003; Gulati 2007; Bradbury Huang 2010; Coghlan and Shani 2013). These demarcation lines can be attributed to a variety of conditions, including the ambiguous and fuzzy nature of discovery-oriented engagements that emphasize experiential knowing (Locke et al. 2008), the strong preference of many management scholars for theorizing and testing that may give more academic respectability (Simon 1969/1996), and the academic affiliations of these scholars with business schools and their policies with regard to promotion and tenure (Augier et al. 2005; Walsh et al. 2006; Van de Ven 2007). These social and institutional conditions are reinforced by the philosophical barriers between the two types of work (Tadajewski 2009) which, for example, surface in the form of too simple heuristics and stereotypes determining whether we are either "serious scholars" or "management types" (Gulati 2007: 777). The demarcation lines arising from these social, institutional and philosophical barriers may also serve to explain why Mode 2 research (Bartunek 2011) is not likely to become widely accepted and applied if management scholarship is not pursued as an organic part of a professional discipline.

15. Elements of phronetic research can also be found in studies of the organization of science and technology (e.g. Latour 1999) and power and organizations (e.g. Clegg and Pitsis 2012).

4

Behavior, Expectation, and Trading Zones

Introduction

Assume an ideal world in which all management scholars and practitioners subscribe to a shared professional purpose, for example the one proposed in Chapter 2, and have unrestricted access to a professional body of knowledge (cf. Chapter 3). Even with this common ground under our feet, any effort to set up and develop an ongoing dialogue between management professionals will face major barriers. These remaining barriers arise from, for example, established systems for training and supervising doctoral students, prevailing practices in publishing research findings, and the performance incentives and career tracks offered by business and management schools (e.g. Mohrman et al. 2001; Starbuck 2006; Rynes 2007; Hughes et al. 2011; Rousseau 2012b).

Gulati (2007: 775) observes these behavioral patterns are largely socially constructed "by forces both internal and external to business schools" and are "perpetuated by tribes that form around rigor and relevance, sequestering themselves into closed loops of scholarship and dismissing the work of outsiders on the basis of their inclusion—or exclusion—of theory or of practical applications." This chapter addresses these challenges at the level of behavior and expectation in the framework outlined in Chapter 1.

First, I explore how the tribal nature of management scholarship and practice prevents a culture of dialogical encounter from coming alive. Tribalism may provide another lens on the low level of engagement between management scholars and practitioners (Hodgkinson and Rousseau 2009; Hughes et al. 2011) and the fragmented nature of management scholarship (Whitley 1984; Gulati 2007). Subsequently, the notion of trading zones is adopted to explore how dialogical encounters can be facilitated. Moreover, several examples of trading zones are discussed.

Tribalism

Tribalism is a major barrier in the quest for professionalism, especially when groups of scholars form around rigor and relevance and sequester themselves into "closed loops of scholarship" (Gulati 2007: 775), that primarily talk and write to members of their own tribe and tend to dismiss work done outside their own (group in the) tribe (e.g. Bedeian 1989; Donaldson 2003; Gulati 2007; Bradbury Huang 2010; Coghlan and Shani 2013).

Similarly, management practitioners form tribes around particular corporate ideologies or charismatic leaders. Chapter 1 illustrated how the professional intentions of many executives and other managers may get lost in a one-dimensional focus on maximizing shareholder value, imposed by directors and investor-shareholders. Too often this results in investment debacles, accounting scandals, options-backdating schemes, and other major ethics breaches (Martin 2011). Prominent examples are Nike's abuse of child labor in Pakistan and Cambodia in the 1990s (Boggan 2001), Enron's systematically planned accounting fraud (Fox 2003), and, more recently, the corruption and other ethics breaches in the poor governance and planning of the new Berlin Brandenburg Airport (*Der Spiegel* 2014). The one-dimensional focus on short-term financial gain is, to some extent, the counterpart of the academic publish-or-perish imperative discussed in the remainder of this section.

Publish or Perish

Tribalism among management scholars has given rise to the *publish-or-perish* system prevailing in business schools and other academic settings for management education and scholarship (Starkey and Madan 2001; Starbuck 2006). Publish-or-perish reflects the idea that faculty members' tenure and reputation are primarily a function of their individual success in publishing. For junior faculty members, it "comprises a race against time that typically begins when the faculty member is hired and ends when the tenure decision must be made. . . . Indeed, recruitment, promotion, and tenure appear to be decided primarily based on the number of articles published in a fairly select group of peer-reviewed journals, based on their relative impact, selectivity, and relevance to business school rankings" (De Rond and Miller 2005: 322). Once tenure has been obtained, the reputation of more senior faculty members continues to depend on their productivity in publishing in these so-called "top" peer-reviewed journals.

The publish-or-perish system implies that most scholars emphasize productivity at the expense of innovation and prioritize the theoretical relevance of their research at the expense of its practical relevance (Bouchikhi and Kimberly 2001; Starkey and Madan 2001; Starbuck 2006): "When so much rests on not simply doing the research but, more important, getting it published, the risks of doing something unorthodox, something that might offend strongly held prejudices in a particular field, are great" (Smith 1990: 191).

One symptom of the publish-or-perish culture is that some scholars are under so much pressure to produce and publish papers, that they engage in plagiarism and mischaracterize and manipulate data. In some cases, top journals in the area of management studies have retracted articles because prominent authors evidently mischaracterized data and plagiarized the work of others (e.g. Matlack 2013). A study by Honig and Bedi (2012) suggests these practices are widespread. Honig and Bedi analyzed 279 papers accepted for presentation within one of the divisions of the Academy of Management conference, and found that 25 percent of the sample had some form of plagiarism, and over 13 percent exhibited a significant amount of plagiarism.

Another symptom of the publish-or-perish system involves the behavior of journal editors who want to sustain or increase the position of their journal in rankings based on citation impact scores—to be as attractive as possible for authors who consider submitting papers. These editors sometimes act coercively toward authors whose work is being reviewed for publication in their journals. In this so-called "coercive citation" malpractice, editors exert pressure on authors (of work to be published) to cite as much previous work in their journal as possible. As such, coercive self-citation

> does not refer to the normal citation directions, given during a peer-review process, meant to improve a paper. Coercive self-citation refers to requests that (i) give no indication that the manuscript was lacking in attribution, (ii) make no suggestion as to specific articles, authors, or a body of work requiring review, and (iii) only guide authors to add citations from the editor's journal. (Wilhite and Fong 2012: 542)

To explore the extent and nature of coercive self-citation, Wilhite and Fong (2012) analyzed the survey responses received from more than 6,000 researchers in economics, sociology, psychology, marketing, accounting, management, and several other disciplines, to establish that coercion is rather common and also appears to be practiced by editors quite opportunistically. The analysis of these survey responses as well as other data collected implies that highly-ranked journals are more likely to coerce, and also suggests that marketing and management journals are more likely to engage in coercive self-citation than journals in some of the other disciplines in the sample. These results are unsettling because, when editors "game the system and authors acquiesce, the integrity of academic publications suffers" (Wilhite and Fong 2012: 542).

Genetic Disposition

The most fundamental driver of tribalism may be our genetic disposition. Traditional tribal societies have almost entirely disappeared from our earth, and those that have survived have been pushed to the edges of the western world. But the evolution of the human brain over many hundred thousands of years appears to make it hard-wired toward tribalism (Fromm and Maccoby 1970; Hamilton 1975).

This genetic disposition toward tribalism might also explain why we tend to take the fragmented nature of management scholarship as well as the low level of engagement between scholars and practitioners for granted.[1] Similarly, this disposition toward tribalism helps to understand why Simon's (1967) dream of an ambidextrous orientation of business schools toward both professional practice and fundamental research has not materialized. In this respect, most business schools have ended up misappropriating Simon's idea of an intellectually robust and relevant research agenda, resulting in the intellectual stasis that currently characterizes management scholarship and its capacity to inform and guide management practice (Khurana and Spender 2012).

The notion of tribalism therefore invites the perspective of "trading zone," rather than calling for major institutional reforms and changes as Simon and others have done. In the history of the human species, trading posts and zones have time and again been arising as places where different tribes and communities meet and exchange. Before engaging with the literature on trading zones, I turn to the role of public expectations.

Public Expectations

The multi-level framework of professionalization introduced in Chapter 1 implies that a high level of professionalism at the level of shared purpose, knowledge, and behavior is likely to raise high expectations of external stakeholders. In turn, professionals tend to internalize these expectations as their own ambitions and intentions, which inspire and guide them to perform and deliver their best.

Professionalization is often equated with conditions and regulations for entry to the profession as well as sanctions and penalties regarding unprofessional conduct. However, these regulations and sanctions may have counterproductive effects on professional conduct—especially when they cause the intrinsic commitment to professional standards to transform into an extrinsic one (Deci 1980). In fact, one reason why many management professors have come to dislike the more bureaucratic aspects of their educational work is that management education has become highly regulated by accreditation bodies such as AACSB and EQUIS (Mintzberg 2004; Spender 2007; Somers et al. 2014). As a result, professors approach their undergraduate and MBA students as consumers of course contents, rather than as apprentices in a profession.

In Chapter 1, I observed that mechanisms to control and regulate entry to the profession as well as behavior by its members should not be considered as fundamental to the idea of professionalization. Rather, these regulatory and institutional mechanisms are outcomes of "successful" professionalization trajectories (Abbott 1988); "success" here refers to contesting and winning the battle for claims on a body of knowledge and professional work conducted on the basis of that knowledge (Khurana 2007). The history of professions such as law and medicine demonstrates that certain groups within these occupations first had to contest and claim a unique body of knowledge in competition with other groups, typically with a major role of research and education at universities, before regulatory mechanisms could be developed and implemented (Abbott 1988).

High expectations from internal and external stakeholders are therefore also essential to the quest for science-based professionalism in management. Evidently, these expectations have actually become very low. Misconduct, mismanagement, and other forms of unprofessionalism have become so widespread that the public media only pays attention to the most extreme and dramatic cases. Employees and other internal stakeholders in many organizations often do not feel safe enough to speak up and signal such problems (Milliken et al. 2003) and in some cases are intimidated and silenced by their bosses (e.g. Beer 2009). Moreover, management scholars and their business schools have stakeholders with expectations that often are competing and ambiguous in nature (Rasche and Gilbert 2015). For example, many MBA students and graduates are calling for more efforts to restore professional standards and ethics in management (e.g. Anderson and Escher 2010), while the corporate sponsors of business schools are demanding more attention to management knowledge and skills which help them improve their bottom line.

Purpose-Knowledge-Behavior-Expectation

An initial assessment of the level of professionalism in management was given in Chapter 1. At this stage of the argument in The Quest for Professionalism, the findings arising from Chapters 2 and 3 as well as this chapter provide the basis for the following, more informed assessment of the nature of professionalization processes in management. Overall, the argument thus far suggests that the underdeveloped layers of professional purpose, knowledge, and behavior affect the expectation layer as follows (cf. Figure 1.2 in Chapter 1):

- there is hardly any shared sense of professional purpose and responsibility in the management discipline (Chapter 2);

- the academic body of knowledge is highly fragmented and only loosely connected to practical knowledge and experience (Chapter 3);

- at the behavioral level, both management practitioners and scholars—as all other human beings—are hard-wired toward tribalism (earlier this chapter);

- as a result, the lack of shared purpose and knowledge as well as our genetic disposition toward tribalism are so great that nonprofessionalism is ubiquitous and widely accepted as normal and unavoidable, and both insiders and outsiders to the management discipline have lowered their expectations accordingly (cf. Elias and Scotson 1994).

The previous two chapters explored ways to enhance a shared sense of professional purpose and responsibility and develop a professional body of knowledge. In the remainder of this chapter, I discuss how we can get out of the deadlock at the behavior-expectation levels in ways that respect our genetic disposition toward tribalism.

Trading Zones

The notion of trading zone serves to explore ways to address these challenges.[2] In a *trading zone*, communities with disparate meanings and logics collaborate despite their differences (Galison 1997). The notion of a trading zone can help to address often overlooked, yet deep-seated, problems related to the process of knowledge integration—such as the need for forms of social interaction and communication that enable collaboration and engagement between disparate academic communities as well as between academic and practitioner communities. Such trading zones might therefore facilitate the professionalization of management practice and scholarship.

Sociologists of science and technology (Collins et al. 2007; Galison 1997; Gorman 2002) have introduced the trading zone notion to capture the idea of a space where knowledge is integrated among scientific communities that face a challenge of communicating across (partly incommensurable) paradigms. For example, Galison (1997) observed how theorists, experimenters, and instrument makers in physics come together to focus their respective knowledge and skills on addressing, through a process of trading, major challenges in their discipline. Modern physics was thus created by what, over time, became a highly pluralistic community of theorists, experimentalists, engineers, and mathematicians focused on projects such as the bubble chamber.[3] Accordingly, Galison (1997: 844) presents a picture of "the disorder" of any scientific community, arguing that "it is the *dis*unification of science—the intercalation of *different* patterns of argument—that is responsible for its strength and coherence."

Most work on trading zones is about multidisciplinary interactions among highly diverse communities in the context of large-scale science and technology programs. Interestingly, management research does not have a tradition of large collaborative projects or programs, bringing together scholars from differing subfields, with alternative theoretical traditions and complementary methodological expertise. In this respect, almost all management research is individualistic or, at best, a small group exercise, with knowledge integration achieved mostly by carefully balanced theoretical bricolage (Boxenbaum and Rouleau 2011).

However, evidence-based and actionable knowledge in management arises from purposeful collaboration. Collaborative projects that integrate knowledge across theoretical and methodological traditions can act as effective trading zones, in which integration is facilitated and managed to create impact on management practice. The shortage of trading zones in our field is not a result of management scholars' inability or unwillingness to create them. Rather, it is predominantly a consequence of the primacy of individual scholarship and the inability of all key stakeholders (including journal editors, deans of business schools, and research funding agencies) to value and reward efforts to develop and integrate knowledge through collaborative research.

Moreover, these collaborative efforts will remain incomplete if they do not involve practitioners in co-producing knowledge (Van de Ven 2007). The orientation toward practice has to go beyond translating research findings into more practitioner-friendly formats, such as the *Harvard Business Review* or *Sloan Management Review*. The latter type of translation might help to disseminate research, but is insufficient in the context of more structural collaboration that serves to jointly identify research topics and continually engage throughout research programs and projects (Avenier and Parmentier Cajaiba 2012). University–industry collaboration in science and engineering tends to draw on a shared sense of purpose and responsibility as well as an institutional setting that fosters such collaboration (Perkmann et al. 2013). But these conditions do not yet exist in the management discipline; the current state of affairs thus inhibits sustained and productive interactions between management practitioners and researchers.

While academic–practitioner collaboration is widespread in science and engineering as well as in professional disciplines such as architecture and medicine, collaborative projects in the domain of management involve, at best, a small number of reflective practitioners or, more typically, resourceful academics undertaking consultancy assignments, in exchange for empirical evidence to be used in academic publications. One of the few exceptions in the field of management is the Evidence-Based Management collaborative, set up by Denise Rousseau, which involves a large group of scholars and practitioners with highly diverse backgrounds and orientations (Rousseau 2012a).

Notably, exchange in a trading zone can happen even if the interacting groups ascribe utterly different significance to the knowledge being exchanged, or even disagree on the meaning of the exchange process itself (Collins et al. 2007). These so-called *fractionated* trading zones involve spaces where disparate constituencies collaborate without creating a shared meaning (Kellogg et al. 2006). In this type of trading zone, a productive collaboration around "boundary objects" such as prototypes, conferences, workshops, and documentary programs for YouTube and TV can be accomplished without the need for any of the constituencies to change its core values and practices.

Characteristics of Trading Zones in Management

A trading zone can provide the "mortar" (Galison 1997) that connects the different camps and tribes in the quest for professionalism. For example, dialogical encounters in these trading zones may be of great value in identifying key professional problems and challenges. However, to successfully contribute to the professionalization quest in management, a trading zone will need to go beyond an entirely fractionated one. A successful trading zone in this context is likely to have the following characteristics: action and goal orientation, durability, psychological safety, and informed consent.

ACTION AND GOAL ORIENTATION
First, a trading zone is explicitly *action* and *goal* oriented, involving a commitment from all participants to contribute to advances in scholarly knowledge as well as management practice (Simon 1967). Purposefully designed events such as conferences (Lampel and Meyer 2008) may provide the space where scholars and practitioners can explore common ground, but they are not sufficient for the kind of trading zone promoting the professionalization of management. A trading zone requires collaborative action and research to accomplish a goal that motivates participation of different constituencies. A trading zone is a space not only for dialogical encounter (such as between Rousseau and Learmonth, discussed in Chapter 2), but also for initiating and guiding collaborative efforts to advance the practice of management.

DURABILITY
A trading zone enabling collaboration among diverse communities has to be *durable*. This durability is especially important when two or more of the communities involved initially expect highly different speeds. In this respect, the speed expected by CEOs and public policy makers almost by definition

exceeds the speed of scientific consensus formation (Collins and Evans 2007). In setting up and starting a trading zone, then, it is critical to mediate between disparate expectations regarding the time horizon and speed of delivering key results (cf. O'Mahony and Bechky 2008) and explicitly agree on a time horizon. A trading zone also becomes more durable if it can make the collaboration visible and tangible in terms of "shared" people, office space, virtual platforms, and the like (Carlile 2002). The most durable trading zones are thus likely to be embedded in the context of industry-sponsored projects, large publicly funded research programs, or research institutes established and governed collaboratively by the different constituencies involved (Boisot et al. 2011; Leten et al. 2013; Van de Ven and Zahra 2015).

PSYCHOLOGICAL SAFETY AND INFORMED CONSENT
Any trading zone in the area of management research and practice will, almost by definition, be highly political in nature.[4] Whereas trading zones would ideally facilitate "domination-free" encounters and interactions (Rorty 1989: 62), in practice they often begin as a research program encouraged or coerced by a powerful actor, subsequently allowing collaborators to develop interactional expertise over time, strenghten engagement, and enhance knowledge sharing (Collins et al. 2007). Issues of domination and coercion are, of course, highly problematic for a genuine dialogical encounter about the research agenda and other questions to be collaboratively addressed (Bernstein 1994; Burrell 1994).

Critical theorists such as Habermas (1984) have uncovered the self-seeking and power asymmetry barriers that inhibit a genuine dialogue. Habermas argues that achieving genuine dialogue requires transcending these barriers by establishing social and political conditions that are highly similar to what management scholars have labeled psychological safety and informed consent. A high level of *psychological safety* involves any setting that all participants perceive to be safe for interpersonal risk taking, such as feeling free to speak up about any issue, including highly sensitive ones (Edmondson 1999). As a decision rule, *informed consent* implies a decision is taken when all participants, based on their understanding and appreciation of the relevant facts, implications and consequences, accept the proposed course of action (Romme and Endenburg 2006).

Similarly, Gadamer (2004) offers an hermeneutic elaboration of what constitutes ideal conversations in which participants seek to overcome their differences and develop common ground. He discusses this in terms of a commitment to confronting one's "horizon of understanding" by learning from others.

Of course, most if not all attempts to create ideal conditions for dialogue actually fail to do so. As such, it is a matter of aiming at the best approximation of these ideal conditions possible in the given circumstances. A similar approach is adopted by Rorty (1999) and Ansell (2011), in the form of a pragmatic and experimentational approach to consent-based dialogue and collaboration.

DBA Programs, Incubators, and Management Labs

DBA PROGRAMS

An example of a trading zone that may have at least some of these characteristics is the Doctor of Business Administration (DBA) program offered by a growing number of leading business schools, such as Harvard Business School, Cranfield School of Management, Manchester Business School, and IE Business School. The DBA program requires coursework and research beyond the masters degree, resulting in a dissertation. In contrast to PhD programs in management research, DBA programs are deliberately set up to facilitate practice-oriented research by management professionals supervised by management scholars. In terms of the characteristics of a trading zone discussed earlier, DBA programs may not be very durable at the individual project level (with DBA students leaving after 2 to 3 years) as well as offer far-from-ideal conditions for dialogue—for example, with both the student and supervisors pressing for completion of the degree. Some of my own observations and experiences in DBA programs also suggest that faculty focused on publishing in top journals tend to avoid the supervision of DBA students. This obviously undermines the effectiveness of DBA programs as trading zones between management practice and scholarship.

NEW BUSINESS INCUBATORS

The new business incubation facilities that many universities and their business schools have been creating might also constitute a trading zone. Some of these incubators have been founded as relatively autonomous units or companies (owned by the university), others have been embedded in so-called Technology Transfer Offices (TTO). Collaborative work between scholars, technology transfer officers, and other practitioners in these incubation environments has produced a coherent and actionable body of knowledge on technology entrepreneurship, technology transfer, and university spinoff creation (e.g. Shane 2004; Vohora et al. 2004; Clarysse et al. 2005; Wright et al. 2007; Van Burg et al. 2008; Szopa et al. 2013; Shane et al. 2015).

As trading zones, new business incubators can also enable and promote collaboration between scholars and (nascent) entrepreneurs and their stakeholders. In this respect, entrepreneurs and managers of new firms and ventures tend to have more discretion to experiment with new management perspectives and approaches than their counterparts in established organizational settings. However, the relationship between university and nascent entrepreneur, especially in the context of negotiations about the distribution of equity and the transfer of intellectual property, can be highly asymmetric. This asymmetry might cause unfairness perceptions that undermine the psychological safety and other conditions for genuine dialogical encounters between entrepreneurs and scholars (cf. Van Burg et al. 2013).

MANAGEMENT LABS

Another example of a potential trading zone are management "labs" for (re) designing, prototyping, developing, and testing management processes, tools, and practices—perhaps along the lines of the partnership between the UK Design Council and Warwick Business School (www.behaviouraldesignlab. org). There is no evidence yet as to whether these labs can deliver on their promise, but this type of initiative toward more design-oriented and experimentation-driven research may generate substantial learning effects, with considerable potential to advance management scholarship and practice.

As trading zones, management labs will only be viable and durable if they become embedded in institutional and cultural settings that promote long-term collaborative ties and intensive collaboration between management practitioners and scholars. Notably, many academically trained management scholars lack skills in problem-driven collaborative work with practitioners, as a result of how they were trained as doctoral students. Consequently, initiatives such as management labs should address the problem of capacity building, by equipping present and future generations of doctoral students with relevant research skills (outlined in Chapter 3) as well as offering training programs that address the needs of established management scholars who wish to meet these highly demanding challenges.

HOW TO ENGAGE PRACTITIONERS?

The characteristics of a trading zone outlined and illustrated thus far raise the question whether and how practitioners can be motivated to actively engage in trading zones. Given the enormous heterogeneity of the population of management practitioners (Bartunek and Rynes 2014), the very notion of a trading zone suggests one needs to turn this question around: how do we better facilitate the engagement of those practitioners that actively seek collaboration with management scholars? In other words, attempts to convince a larger group of practitioners to engage in a trading zone can be avoided, when a small but highly motivated group of practitioners is already highly interested in trading and working with us (e.g. Amabile et al. 2001; Mohrman et al. 2001; Romme and Endenburg 2006).

Management Consulting

Management consulting firms have traditionally been operating at the inter-face of management scholarship and practice, and can therefore be considered as potential trading zones in the quest for professionalism in management (cf. McKenna 2006).

Evidently, management consultants are action and goal oriented: they analyze organizational problems, develop strategies and plans for improve-ment, and assist in managing organizational change (Scott 1998; Heusinkveld and Benders 2002; Visscher and Visscher-Voerman 2010). In developing recommendations and interventions for their clients, however, many man-agement consulting firms draw on their own proprietary knowledge, in the form of codified methods and tools, while some firms also extensively draw on (e.g. relational) tacit knowledge that is transferred and shared between col-leagues collaborating closely with each other (Hansen et al. 1999). Manage-ment consulting firms therefore tend to be very protective of their proprietary and tacit knowledge assets, which are often pivotal to their business model. As a result, there are few examples of durable partnerships between management consultants and scholars, in which both participants feel psychologically safe enough to engage in a genuine dialogue, collaboratively develop knowledge, and publish the results (e.g. Brown and Eisenhardt 1998; Coughlan and Ponto 2014).

In fact, the most productive "trading zones" around consultancy and inter-vention work are initiated by management scholars who have embraced this type of work as critical to their scholarly endeavors (e.g. Argyris et al. 1985; Schein 1988; Prahalad and Hamel 1990; Cooperrider and Whitney 1999; Goold and Campbell 2002; Burton and Obel 2004; Weggeman 2007; Johns and Gratton 2013; Jeannet and Schreuder 2015). For example, Schein (1987) believes one cannot understand a human system without trying to change it. Without actually intervening in such a system, he argues, backstage realities that should inform research are not brought into the academic debate. A similar perspective was developed in Chapter 3, implying that creative work is complementary to scholarly validation in the quest for professionalism.

Evidently, this type of trading zone tends to involve at least one scholar-consultant who integrates and embodies both sides of the spectrum. Espe-cially when the primary interest of this scholar-consultant is in scholarship, and consulting work is therefore instrumental in pursuing key scholarly tar-gets, the resulting trading zone will not raise any substantial barriers and issues in the area of proprietary knowledge and dialogical encounters. This appears to be case for Andrew Campbell, David Cooperrider, Lynda Gratton, Robert Kaplan, Ed Schein, and many other exemplary scholar-consultants. Overall, this suggests management consulting firms do not provide the conditions and characteristics of a successful trading zone, whereas scholar-consultants out-side these firms are not curtailed by the proprietary and bottom-line issues typically faced by management consulting firms.

Moreover, consulting firms are not likely to invest in the professionalization of the management discipline. While the management consulting industry in most Western countries does engage in professionalizing their own work (e.g. Van der Arend et al. 2013), it clearly has no interest whatsoever in developing advanced management approaches and technologies—especially those that make their client organizations more robust and resilient and therefore less dependent on external help and support from consultants.[5] Chapter 5 refers to cases in which companies in crisis situations come up with turnaround strategies and interventions that no management consultant would ever have recommended, because consulting firms lack the capability to go beyond the conventional wisdom on (crisis) management and cannot risk going beyond the boundaries of the client assignment.

More broadly speaking, the rise and growth of the management consulting industry has made many large corporations structurally dependent on its services, and vice versa. This structural *co-dependency* implies these corporations again and again enlist the help and support of consultants in case of any major challenge in the area of strategy and organizational change, rather than investing in any structural dynamic capability that would make them independent of management consultants. This co-dependency also implies management consultants do not "rock the boat" by recommending such investments, to increase the likelihood that their clients will continue to use and "buy" their services in the future. The only realistic way for a management consulting firm "to be coveted is to be a high-class whore," as observed by Scott (1998: 29).

Trading zones centered around scholar-consultants are therefore more promising and productive in the quest for professional management than those centered around management consulting firms. Consequently, trading zones such as DBA programs and new business incubators will greatly benefit from this type of scholarship.

Implications

More and better trading zones are needed in view of the tribal nature of management scholarship and practice.[6] These trading zones appear to be critical to the quest for professionalism in disciplines such as medicine, engineering, and management, but also in scientific domains not closely linked to a profession. They may especially provide a platform for aligning subcultures, interests, and voices that are all-too-frequently isolated from each other.

Similarly, Kessler and Bartunek (2014: 237) argue that "understanding of reality assesses a theory's merit based on outcome utility, not dicta or dogma." Reviewing the work of the eminent physicist Stephen Hawking (Hawking and Mlodinow 2010), they observe that in physics

> the philosophy of pragmatism rules the day....A theory is useful if it provides prescriptions for action that, if followed, offer elucidating perspectives and sensible guidance. This is also true in professional fields such as management, which are inexorably embedded in practice and the success of which is eventually calibrated by the degree to which their lessons are reflectively applied toward improving the quality of actions and outcomes. (Kessler and Bartunek 2014: 237)

To be effective, trading zones must therefore enable actors to overcome the dead weight of dogma as well as their predisposition toward tribalism.

Scale is Not Critical

There are few examples of successful trading zones in management research. Examples such as professional degree programs and new business incubators, previously discussed, do not (yet) meet all the requirements of an ideal trading zone.

An entirely different example is the Atlas program at the Large Hadron Collider (LHC) in CERN (Geneva), involving several management research projects in areas such as the knowledge architecture, information systems, and HRM processes of large-scale multidisciplinary science programs (Boisot et al. 2011). This type of project illustrates the contribution management scholars can make to big scientific challenges.

Osterwalder's design science program on business modelling, outlined in Chapter 3, is another example. In his doctoral thesis, Osterwalder (2004) systematically reviewed the literature as well as collected interview data on business model development, resulting in an initial framework. This framework was subsequently developed, together with hundreds of practitioners from many different countries, into what is now widely known as the "business model canvas" (Osterwalder and Pigneur 2010, 2013). More generally, the design science perspective has increasingly been used to connect descriptive-explanatory and normative-interventionist research in management (e.g. Denyer et al. 2008; Dougherty 2008; Hodgkinson and Healey 2008; Van Burg et al. 2008; Avenier and Parmentier Cajaiba 2012; Pascal et al. 2013; Healey et al. 2014).

These examples suggest it is not the scale of the trading zone that is critical to its success. Osterwalder's platform for business model development arose from a single doctoral dissertation, whereas LHC is one of the largest scientific programs ever, including thousands of scholars of which a small number has a background in management studies. Indeed, small and large scale programs may be complementary. Smaller programs can generate trading zones in which specific and/or novel practical problems and challenges are explored at a faster pace than is possible in large-scale programs. Large-scale ventures can, however, capitalize on large amounts of resources, practitioners, companies, scholars, and doctoral students being brought together to address major professional challenges in the area of management and entrepreneurship.

Institutional Context is Changing

Establishing trading zones requires institutional entrepreneurship from prominent scholars, deans of business schools, and others in influential leadership positions that orchestrate the governance and funding of the business and management field. If management scholars are able to demonstrate that collaborative work in trading zones, such as the one pioneered by Rousseau (2012a), has a lasting impact on the professionalization of management practice, then more and better trading zones are likely to arise and become increasingly legitimate.

Recent changes in the policies of research funding bodies are likely to reinforce the momentum toward more impactful research and dialogue across the academia–practice interface. For example, research funding bodies in the UK have developed an agenda to encourage economic and social impact from research, through its "pathways to impact" initiative (Research Councils UK 2015). Furthermore, the UK Higher Education Funding body has made the assessment of research impact an integral part of its Research Excellence Framework. Similarly, the EU has been developing its Horizon 2020 agenda to stimulate research focusing on grand societal challenges. These policy changes in Europe and elsewhere may stimulate management scholars to engage in research that serves to advance management as a profession.

Professional Societies and Associations

Academic and professional societies such as Academy of Management (AoM), BAM, and EURAM, and professional bodies and associations such as the All India Management Association (AIMA), Canadian Institute of Management (CIM), and Chartered Management Institute (CMI) can play a key role in creating and sustaining the trading zones needed to further professionalize management.[7] However, there is hardly any research addressing the role of these societies and associations in developing and growing the level of professionalism in management—in contrast to, for example, accounting (e.g. Lee 1995; Suddaby et al. 2009).

One obvious difference with other disciplines such as accounting, law, and medicine is that there are no professional bodies in management that effectively operate across the academic–practitioner divide. The membership of academic societies such as AoM and BAM is primarily academic in nature, and as a result, all their elected representatives and leaders are management scholars. Similarly, professional bodies such as CIM and CMI are almost entirely focused on practice, which is also reflected in the way these bodies are managed; for example, the CMI presidential team of ten currently includes nine practitioners (CMI 2015). This also means the forums, meetings, and online social networks initiated and orchestrated by these organizations are highly skewed toward either the academic or the practitioner world.

Any attempt to create a trading zone that promotes and sustains genuine dialogical encounters would therefore have to be supported and sponsored by two or more established associations (e.g. a shared platform of BAM and CMI), or alternatively, as trading zones developed from scratch (e.g. IAOIP 2015). Evidently, any initiatives in this area can learn from the experiences and attempts in other disciplines to develop more civic forms of professionalism and (re)build the incumbent profession's status and reputation in society (e.g. Sullivan 2000; Adler et al. 2008; Suddaby et al. 2009; Barends et al. 2012). One insight arising from other disciplines is that participants in successful trading zones accept that any philosophical stance is precarious and there are no rights or wrongs, as also argued in Chapter 2.

Distributed Experimentation

The professionalization of management is one of the grand challenges of our time, as also argued in Chapter 1. Drawing on pragmatism and the concept of robust action, Ferraro et al. (2015) characterize a grand challenge as a societal problem that involves many interactions and nonlinear dynamics, has highly uncertain dimensions and consequences, and cuts across jurisdictional boundaries implying multiple evaluation criteria. Accordingly, grand challenges such as climate change and professionalizing management require a collective response that draws on three elements. First, a participatory architecture is needed, that is, a setting with rules of engagement allowing diverse and heterogeneous actors to interact constructively over prolonged timespans (Ferraro et al. 2015). This is highly similar to the idea of a *trading zone* defined and illustrated in this chapter.

Second, the collective response to any grand challenge should draw on "multivocal inscription," the "discursive and material activity that sustains different interpretations among various audiences with different evaluative criteria, in a manner that promotes coordination without requiring explicit consensus" (Ferraro et al. 2015: 373). This reflects the need for *dialogical encounters* between a plurality of voices, framed by a *professional body of knowledge*, advocated in Chapters 2 and 3.

Third, Ferraro and his co-authors call for *distributed experimentation*, because any grand challenge potentially has many solutions and therefore "there is no way of knowing in advance how best to proceed"; multiple distributed experiments will then be instrumental in finding out what works and what does not (Ferraro et al. 2015: 376). In this respect, the professionalization quest in management is still at such an early stage that, at this point in time, distributed experimentation in many different trading zones is the best strategy toward progress and success in this quest.

Concluding Remarks

Despite the phenomenal growth in the number of business schools and the volume of research produced by their faculty, the body of academic knowledge on management is highly fragmented and the level of interaction between management scholars and management practitioners is generally poor.

In this chapter, I argued these behavioral patterns in management scholarship and practice essentially arise from the evolution of the human brain over many thousands of years, which has made it hard-wired toward tribalism. The notion of trading zones was adopted to explore how common ground between different tribes in the management discipline can be developed and sustained. Several examples of trading zones were discussed. Management labs, new business incubators and professional degree programs appear to offer promising (albeit imperfect) trading zones that enable meaningful dialogues between tribes with highly different voices and interests.

Moreover, scholar-consultants are more productive contributors to this type of trading zone than management consulting firms. Finally, several other implications were discussed, including the need for distributed experimentation in many different trading zones at this early stage of the quest for professionalism.

Notes

1. Related perspectives that can serve to describe and explain the tribal nature of behavior of scholars and practitioners are theories of autopoiesis and self-referentialism (e.g. Luhmann 1990) and defensive behavioral routines (e.g. Argyris et al. 1985). Consistent with the idea of a genetic disposition toward tribalism, these

theories can be used to specify the cognitive and behavioral mechanisms arising from tribalism in more detail.

2. This section is adapted and extended from Romme et al. (2015), "Towards common ground and trading zones in management research and practice," *British Journal of Management* 26/3: 544–59.

3. Galison (1997) distances himself philosophically from both logical positivism and anti-positivism (or realism and anti-realism) in arguing that physics is neither unified nor entirely fragmented, but rather *poly-cultural* and *intercalated*: "many traditions coordinate with one another without homogenization. Different traditions of theorizing, experimenting, instrument making, and engineering meet— even transform one another—but for all that, they do not lose their separate identities and practice" (Galison 1997: 782–3). Galison's view of science "as an intercalated set of subcultures bound together through a complex of hard-won locally shared meaning fits awkwardly into the debate over relativism" (p. 840), it fits rather well with the plea for more common ground in and around management scholarship, in the form of trading zones thriving on diversity and dissent but also drawing on a shared sense of purpose (such as proposed in Chapter 2).

4. Some have advocated that management scholars need to scrutinize the political and power constellations in and around organizations in more detail, also in terms of how these affect how research outcomes are framed as well as which particular types of evidence are incorporated and which ones are ignored or rejected (Hodgkinson 2012). These concerns are important because research findings may challenge the legitimacy of existing practices of those in charge within organizations (Bartlett 2011; Denzin 2011). As such, I believe management scholars should become more (self-)conscious and explicit about the managerial and organizational values they would like to question, scrutinize, or exploit in their research. My own experiences suggest that by being more self-aware and outspoken regarding the values I pursue in research, I'm also more in control of the political dimensions of collaborative research.

5. There is hardly any (self-)critical work on management consulting. An exception is the assessment by Strikwerda (2013), who questions whether management consultants are truly indispensable and whether the management consulting industry is suffering from its own dominant logic.

6. This section is adapted from Romme et al. (2015), "Towards common ground and trading zones in management research and practice", *British Journal of Management* 26/3: 544–59.

7. An example is the vision and mission of the Academy of Management (AoM), the world's largest association of management scholars. The AoM (2015) intends to "inspire and enable a better world" through scholarship and teaching about management and organizations, and seeks to do this by building "a vibrant and supportive community of scholars by markedly expanding opportunities to connect and explore ideas." In this mission, the AoM is guided by a set of values such as providing "a dynamic and supportive community for all of our members, embracing the full diversity of our backgrounds and experiences" and respecting "each of our members' voices."

5

Discovering Circular Organizing

Introduction

Highly dissatisfied with the conventional wisdom and body of knowledge on management, several entrepreneurs have been discovering and creating "circular" models and instantiations of organizing.[1] This is highly interesting because entirely new territory may need to be explored in the quest for professionalism, given the low levels of professionalism prevailing in management practice (as observed in Chapter 1). I explored and discussed ways to revitalize this quest in the more familiar terrority of purpose, knowledge, and behavior in the three preceding chapters.

By contrast, this chapter turns to a management approach that challenges the conventional wisdom about management and as such might provide a better understanding of aspects of the professionalization quest that would otherwise remain undetected. As circular organizing serves to fundamentally redistribute power and leadership throughout the organization, it resonates well with Hayek's (1945) conception of knowledge as dispersed among many individuals as well as highly contextualized to particular times and places.

Notably, the abuse and rationalization of power in organizational, administrative, and many other settings may be one of the most important problems of our time (Foucault 1978; Habermas 1998; Flyvbjerg 2001). In the Introduction, I referred to several examples of the abuse of power and authority by managers. This chapter will explore how power can be constructively shaped and controlled in organizational settings, in the interest of the professionalization agenda. The argument in this chapter and the next one may also help to demistify the notion of power, by extending work by Flyvbjerg (1998) and others that has demonstrated how power defines and shapes reality. The argument is organized as follows. First, I describe how and why circular organizing has been creatively discovered. Subsequently, circular organizing is explored in terms of its key constructs, principles, and instantiations.

The Discovery of Circular Organizing

Sociocratic Values and Engineering Education

Gerard Endenburg was born in 1933 in Rotterdam.[2] As a young boy, he witnessed the turmoil and suffering that World War II caused for many people, including his parents. Gerard's parents emerged very disappointed from the war period, but had nonetheless retained their idealism. They argued that the business owner's "side of the line" was the power source where most social and economic structures were shaped, and from which most problems arose. In 1950, Gerard Endenburg's parents founded Endenburg Elektrotechniek to pioneer new forms of entrepreneurship and business ownership. Gerard attended a Quaker boarding school, where he was influenced by Kees Boeke and his wife Betty Cadbury, in particular by their ideas about sociocracy (Quarter 2000). Subsequently, he studied electrotechnical engineering and, after graduation, worked for a short period at Philips.

In 1968, Gerard Endenburg took over the position of general manager of Endenburg Elektrotechniek from his father.[3] As a condition of accepting this position at the time, Gerard requested he be allowed to experiment, both technically and organizationally. In the early 1970s, he therefore decided to halt the company's growth in order to give more attention to organizational renewal.[4]

Also drawing on his training as an engineer, Gerard Endenburg started experimenting with the idea of sociocracy in the late 1960s and early 1970s, which resulted in the sociocratic circular approach (Endenburg 1988, 1998), also known as "sociocracy." The word *sociocracy* is derived from the Latin "socius" (companion, peer, or colleague) and Greek "kratein" (to govern). Sociocracy thus refers to the governing and managing of an organization by people who regularly interact with each other and have a common aim. The French philosopher Auguste Comte first coined the notion of "sociocratie" in 1851. The idea of sociocracy was later adopted by the American sociologist Lester Ward (1892). Ward believed a highly educated public is essential if a country is to be governed effectively, and he argued democracy would eventually have to evolve into more advanced forms of deliberation and government, such as sociocracy.[5]

Endenburg initially developed the notions of sociocracy and circularity to enhance employee participation within Endenburg Elektrotechniek. In the early 1970s, the company was grappling with the implementation of a works council, a consultative body required by Dutch law on organizational democracy. In the first years of operating this council in combination with a conventional administrative hierarchy, participants grew increasingly dissatisfied. Instead of providing genuine consultation between management and employee representatives, it frequently produced conflict. Endenburg therefore

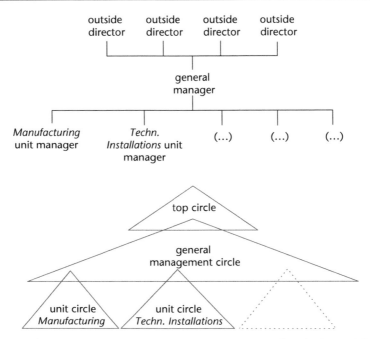

Figure 5.1. Administrative hierarchy and circular structure of Endenburg Elektrotechniek in 1980s

Source: Adapted from Romme (1999).

decided to completely redesign this consultative system (Endenburg 1998; Romme and Endenburg 2006).

Endenburg initially inferred several key constructs from cybernetics, which then served to develop preliminary guidelines for making policy decisions in units by informed consent, double linking between units, and electing managers and representatives. These initial principles were tried out, adapted, and developed in Endenburg Elektrotechniek, and later also applied in many other organizations. Figure 5.1 shows the implications for the company's structure, involving an administrative hierarchy (for "getting work done") that co-exists with the circular structure (for making policy decisions at all levels).

Critical Experiences: The First Test

Before exploring some of the conceptual thinking behind the circular model, I describe the first "test" that the initial design of the circular approach was exposed to. This test was critical to the entire evolution of circular organizing. If the circular management approach initially conceived by Endenburg had not survived this major test, the development of circular organizing would most likely have been abandoned and Endenburg Elektrotechniek (EE) would have long ago gone out of business.

This major test involved a crisis situation that EE ran into in 1976. The unusual chain of events which subsequently occurred can be reconstructed as follows (Romme 1999). A Rotterdam-based shipyard, accounting for more than one-third of EE's business, suddenly shut down. As general manager, Gerard Endenburg saw no other solution but to layoff 60 workers, most of whom worked in the Technical Installations unit, and thus he decided to start a layoff-procedure for these employees; this decision fell within the mandate he had as general manager, the functional leader of the general (management) circle.

In the same period, the top circle was called together to discuss the crisis situation. The top circle at that time included two representatives from the general circle, the general manager (Endenburg), and four external members (or outside directors). During the meeting, two external members expressed serious concerns with the operation of the circular model in a crisis. They argued that an adequate response requires a major re-organization effort without the circular system, perhaps by means of a turnaround manager. The representatives from the general circle refused to go along with this proposal, because they believed this was precisely the kind of situation where the circular system had to prove itself. As a consequence, these two outside directors decided to resign from the top circle.

The day after Gerard Endenburg (on behalf of the general management circle) had announced the decision to lay off 60 employees, Jan De Groot asked the secretary of his circle to set up a meeting as quickly as possible. De Groot was an employee in the Manufacturing unit, who wanted to discuss an idea he had for handling the crisis situation. The circle secretary arranged a meeting the next day, where De Groot put forward a proposal about delaying the layoff for a few weeks and shifting everyone who was to be laid off into a concentrated marketing effort. The circle decided to support the proposal and appointed De Groot as a temporary representative to the general management circle.

De Groot subsequently requested a special meeting of the general circle to discuss his proposal. In this meeting, which lasted two hours, the general circle decided to support the initiative of Jan De Groot. All "spare" employees would spend most, if not all of their time acquiring new projects. A final decision could not be made because the general circle was not authorized to use the company's (limited) financial reserves for this purpose; such a decision fell within the policy domain of the top circle. Jan De Groot was therefore also elected as a temporary representative of the general circle in the top circle. A few days later, the top circle decided to support De Groot's proposal to spend part of the company's financial reserves on his turnaround strategy, which allowed the general manager to launch the plan.

Within several weeks, a sufficient volume of new projects had been acquired to justify further postponement of the layoff. Only a few workers were actually laid off during this period. The Technical Installations unit was sized down, but the accelerated growth of several other units led to a much more diversified customer base. This major test therefore appeared to demonstrate that the circular model enhances EE's performance and viability. But the chain of events at EE in 1976 also served to practically demonstrate the notion of circularity of power, that is, how power can flow from the operational level to the top circle, in interaction with the (usual) top-down flow of information and decisions.[6]

Constructs and Principles of Circularity

This section first outlines several key constructs that have informed the creation of circular organizing.[7] Subsequently, several management principles such as informed consent and double linking are introduced and explained.

Endenburg inferred most of these constructs and principles from cybernetics, but his earlier exposure to Quaker ideas and values (cf. Louis 1994) was also a major source of inspiration. Endenburg's creative discovery of circular organizing therefore initially was highly abductive in nature, and he then used cybernetics to deductively and inductively shape his initial ideas.[8] In the next few pages, the example of cycling (or biking) provides a rather simple and straightforward context for "managing" processes (as in Chapter 3). I deliberately use the case of biking, because it serves to emphasize the generative nature of these principles. Notably, these principles can also be illustrated with any other venture—such as launching and flying a rocket to another planet, or starting and growing a new business venture.

Key Constructs and Principles Inferred from Cybernetics

When Gerard Endenburg took over his parents' firm in the electrotechnical industry, he had the mandate to run it as both a profitable business and a real-time laboratory for experimenting with new management ideas. Cybernetics, as the science of steering and control (e.g. Beer 1959; Mayr 1970), served at the time as an important framework for organizational design. Drawing on the cybernetic notion of circularity, Endenburg conceived a different kind of organization in which equivalence and (psychological) safety in decision making would be guaranteed, while maintaining a hierarchical system of different accountability levels.

Endenburg first developed a number of key constructs that would have to apply to any kind of system "capable of maintaining a state of dynamic equilibrium" (Endenburg 1998: 65). In this respect, cybernetics implied that the purpose of any circular process "is to detect the disturbance of a dynamic equilibrium and to take steps to restore it. It is a process which is unnecessary in a static equilibrium, because the factors influencing a static equilibrium are not variable" (Endenburg 1998: 65). As such, the following ideas and constructs for building a self-regulating system were crafted (Endenburg 1974):

- *Searching and adapting ("weaving") must be possible.* Any biker riding from A to B follows a certain track. While cycling, she must be able to continually search and correct course to keep her bike on track. Let's assume the steer of the bike has been mechanically locked, while all other functions of the bike are still active. The biker will then not be able to continually correct course, and as a result will lose her balance—unless she is a fairground artist. To realize any objective, therefore, search and adaptation must be possible.

- *We have to deviate (or: make mistakes).* To realize an objective or reach a destination, we have to deviate from the "optimal" route. That is, we can only reach a destination if the direction in which we travel is—most of the time—at variance to the desired direction. In other words, to be able to realize an objective, one must continually deviate from the ideal or planned route. Figure 5.2 illustrates the continual process of search and adaptation, in the most simple case of a completely linear route (the dotted line) from A to B, as it arises from the first two principles. That is, to get from A to B, we need (a) the managerial capability to continually search and adapt and (b) to actually draw on this capability by continually deviating from the ideal course.

- *Enabling search by means of the circular process of leading–operating–measuring.* The bike riding example seems fairly obvious, but it is actually far more complex. The biker has to engage in several different steering and feedback processes simultaneously, so-called circular processes. A circular process consists of three basic activities: operating, measuring, and leading. The biker's feet and hands do the operational work; measuring is done by the biker's sensory organs (i.e. the eyes as part of a larger nervous system) taking in signals that the brain converts into mental images; and

Figure 5.2. To get from A to B, weaving must be possible
Source: Adapted from Romme and Endenburg (2006).

leading involves another part of the brain that compares images and may issue "instructions" to correct the direction and speed level controlled by the biker's hands and feet. If, for example, bikers shut their eyes for a longer period, the circular process is broken and it will be impossible to avoid an accident and reach the destination.

- *Exploring and setting boundaries.* If we conceive of biking as a managerial challenge, there apparently is no such thing as the "right" or "optimal" route. Instead, bikers and other managers can define their route approximately, that is, "more or less." That is, they can explore and set acceptable boundaries within which one moves toward the destination, by answering questions such as: within what boundaries can we effectively weave from side to side? How much space to maneuver do we need and how much space is actually available? Which other external (e.g. speed) limits, legal and otherwise, have already been set? What influence do we have over those boundaries and how do we exercise that influence?

- *In the case of collaboration, agree on acceptable boundaries.* If two or more people agree to pull a trailer on their bikes together toward a particular destination, the situation shown in Figure 5.3 arises. To maintain balance, each biker will have to weave from side to side. But, if both bikers are to pull the trailer, this "oscillation" must not be so great that one of them is forced to let go of the trailer. Moreover, varying degrees of tension (or conflict) will arise; for example, when one biker is deviating somewhat to

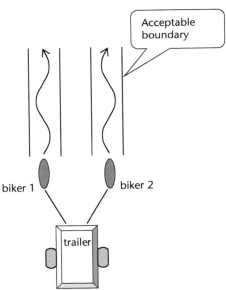

Figure 5.3. Agreeing on acceptable boundaries in the context of collaboration
Source: Adapted from Romme and Endenburg (2006).

the left, while the other is pulling more to the right. The bikers will therefore have to collaborate in ways that serve to keep their balance, keep hold of the trailer, and reach the destination. That is, they will have to maintain all tensions and deviations within boundaries that are acceptable for each participant.

- *Create an unambiguous hierarchical sequence of accountability levels (in larger organizations).* If the trailer is very large and heavy, many bikers will be needed to pull it. Some form of hierarchy is then required to organize and direct the collective effort. While it is still important that the boundaries under which each individual biker operates are acceptable to him/her, there is also an immediate need to clarify who will decide on adapting the course and speed of the collective venture in the event of major potholes on the road ahead, when and where to stop to take a break, and so forth. In other words, a clear and unambiguous hierarchy is necessary, in terms of different levels of accountability. This hierarchy serves to filter, select, assess, and act upon a variety of signals and data—for example about the physical condition of individual bikers, weather conditions, other traffic on the road, or potholes ahead—perceived by at least one of the bikers pulling the trailer.[9]

In sum, this suggests any organizational system is able to search and find its way toward a target, if:

- it is sufficiently capable of searching and adapting, and thus can deviate from its intended course; in turn, this capability for search and adaptation draws on the (unbroken) circular process of leading–operating–measuring;
- it continually explores and sets boundaries for (those contributing to) the search effort, in ways that ensure the participants can effectively work within these boundaries;
- it draws on an unambiguous hierarchical sequence of accountability levels.

Informed Consent

The constructs and ideas outlined thus far serve to create several generic principles for managing and organizing. A key principle involves *informed consent*, or "no argued objection" in Endenburg's (1974) initial definition. For decision making, the principle of informed consent implies that a policy decision is taken when there are no remaining "paramount" objections to the proposed decision. By giving informed consent to a proposed course of action, one is essentially saying: "I do not object to it, based on my understanding of the relevant facts, implications, and consequences."

The decision principle of informed consent has a strong basis in the literature on the Pareto criterion and unanimity rule (e.g. Chichilnisky and Heal 1983; Sen 1995; Sobel and Holcombe 2001). Already in the early 1960s, Buchanan and Tullock (1962: 250) argued that "political theorists have perhaps shrugged off the unanimity requirement too early in their thinking." They observed that economic and political theorists focus on "false" alternatives for unanimity rule, such as majority, minority, or authoritarian decision rules—false in the sense that these rules can never produce Pareto optimality. As a result, the attainment of unanimity is now widely viewed to be infeasible or impossible, particularly in large groups.[10]

Circular organizing responds to this challenge in several ways, some of which are discussed later. One way in which the notion of "informed consent" avoids the problem of a single person (or minority) blocking a proposal is by using a fundamentally broader interpretation of unanimity. Informed consent is therefore fundamentally different to consensus. Whereas a consensus decision demands an unqualified "yes" with regard to the proposed course of action, informed consent merely requires the absence of an argued objection.[11] Informed consent thus invites participants to express and discuss their arguments, integrate all input, and take an informed decision—which makes it less likely that an individual or a minority blocks a proposed decision.[12] In other words, the principle of informed consent "is not about the right of veto but about the right to argue" (Buck and Villines 2007: 70).

A straightforward illustration of the informed consent principle is a heating or cooling (aircon) system:

> Assume a simple circular process composed of three components: directing, operating, and measuring. For example, a heating or cooling system has a thermostat that regulates temperature, an operational device for heating or cooling the air, and a sensor device for measuring the actual temperature. These components must be designed and linked to one another such that the system as a whole functions properly. The three components must "decide" together whether they are able to maintain the set temperature, given their acceptable limits. As a matter of principle, a single component or a majority of components cannot "take" this decision. If, for example, the temperature is set to 100 degrees Celsius (or 210 Fahrenheit) and the thermostat instructs the boiler to raise its water temperature to that level, the boiler will be destroyed. Thus, even a simple technical system can only function properly if it is directed in such a way that *none* of the components has a "reasoned" (or informed) objection to proposed changes. By consequence, the rule of informed consent must also apply to organizations in which, at each level of the hierarchy, the circular process of operating-measuring-directing is essential to performance. (Romme and Endenburg 2006: 291)

This example also demonstrates that informed consent as the primary decision rule does not imply all decisions are taken by consent. As long as you use the thermostat to heat your apartment within the boundaries that the boiler and radiator can handle, no consent is required from the latter. Of course, the entire heating system and especially its thermostat are likely to be designed in ways that prevent any conflict between preferred and realizable temperatures.

Accordingly, in circular organizing only decisions about *policy* (e.g. the boundaries in Figure 5.3) are taken by informed consent. All actions and decisions taken by team leaders, department heads, general managers, and other functional leaders do no require any consent from others, as long as they operate within the policy boundaries that have been set. In some instances, the distinction between policy (boundaries) and managerial discretion and implementation may become blurred, as in the crisis situation in Endenburg Elektrotechniek discussed earlier in this chapter. If that is the case, circular organizing truly comes alive, by people throughout the organization being engaged in re-assessing and adapting earlier policy decisions or developing entirely new policies and strategies.[13]

Circles as Units of People with a Common Objective

The second key principle developed by Endenburg is about circles and circular processes. Earlier in this chapter, I introduced the construct of a *circular process*, involving an unbroken cycle of leading, operating, and measuring activity.[14] Obviously, such a circular management process can only come about if people have a common objective, such as acquiring and completing projects for a particular group of customers. Figure 5.4 visualizes this management cycle arising from a common objective.

For organizations applying the circular approach, the implication is that every organizational member belongs to at least one circle. A *circle* is a functional work unit, involving a group of people with a common work objective. These people meet as a circle to discuss topics and problems relevant to its work processes, and decide on policy issues that are within the domain it is accountable for.

The idea here is to create organizational settings in which people feel safe enough to participate in decision making, while maintaining a hierarchical

Figure 5.4. The circular process of leading, operating, and measuring
Source: Adapted from Endenburg (1998).

system of different accountability levels (Endenburg 1974). Endenburg did not precisely define the notion of safety, but later work by Edmondson (1999) serves to make this notion explicit. Accordingly, a high level of *psychological safety* involves a group setting that all participants perceive to be safe for interpersonal risk taking, such as feeling free to speak up about any issue, including highly sensitive ones (Edmondson 1999).[15]

To create psychological safety, Endenburg argued, each individual member of the organization should be able to raise issues and voice opinions on matters relevant to his/her work and work setting. This opportunity needs to be structural, and not selective—such as the rare opportunity to join a works council or a committee established by the boss. In circular organizing, this structural opportunity will also not be lost when a particular employee decides not to attend any circle meetings. The crisis situation at Endenburg Elektrotechniek, described earlier, in fact provides an excellent illustration. Recall Jan De Groot, the employee who initiated and pioneered a solution that prevented many colleagues being fired: before this crisis situation, Jan had not attended any meeting of his unit circle for several years. Later, he reflected about his initiative as follows: "For me it was a kind of physical experience, involving co-workers who were about to be fired. I have tried to fight back using the channels which were available" (Romme 1999: 813). Therefore, participation in circle meetings is voluntary, and the opportunity to participate is a structural one—as Piet Slieker, who succeeded Gerard Endenburg as general manager of Endenburg Elektrotechniek, also emphasizes:

> If we have an excellent mechanic who says "I only come here to work, and I'm not interested in those circle meetings", this should be possible. Nevertheless, he should have a place in the circular structure, so he can participate whenever he feels like it. In terms of promotion opportunities, he can easily become a senior-mechanic, but he will never be promoted to the position of unit manager, because in that case he also shares a responsibility for the sociocratic circular method in his unit. (Romme 1999: 818)

Overall, circles and their circular processes serve to increase the governance and management capacity of the incumbent organization, by facilitating and promoting search, continually exploring and setting policy boundaries, and monitoring the implementation of policy.

Double Linking Between Circles

A single leading–operating–measuring process is no longer adequate when the organization becomes larger. Moreover, with an increasing number of people in the organization, it is also increasingly difficult—if not impossible—to collectively take policy decisions by consent. Circular organizing responds to these challenges by *decomposing* the system for policy making in multiple units. In this respect, Simon (2002: 587) observed that, to be resilient and responsive to environmental turbulence, all multi-celled organisms and organizations "consist of a hierarchy of components, such that, at any level of the hierarchy, the rates of interaction within components at that level are much higher than the rates of interaction between different components." He called such systems "nearly decomposable."

In circular organizing, the notion of near-decomposability is applied by decomposing the decision-making system into small units or circles (e.g. < 25 people) that are double linked. *Double linking* involves a circle being linked to the next higher circle by means of a representative chosen at the lower level and a functional leader chosen at the higher level. Figure 5.5 shows two circles that are hierarchically ordered. Each circle is responsible for leading, operating, and measuring its activities, but also maintains a circular flow of information and power with the other circle.

Double linking therefore involves two linkages. The first link, the functional leader, connects one of the operating activities in the upper circle with the leadership activity in the lower circle; the higher circle appoints this leader, by informed consent of all its participants. As such, this link is very similar to Likert's (1961) famous "linking pin."[16] The second link, the delegate, serves as the feedback connection between the lower circle as a whole and the measuring process in the higher circle; the lower circle appoints the delegate(s) by consent. In this way, the double linking principle differentiates Likert's single linking pin into two linkages. Moreover, linking both pins to the same two circles avoids the problem of creating two separate communication channels.

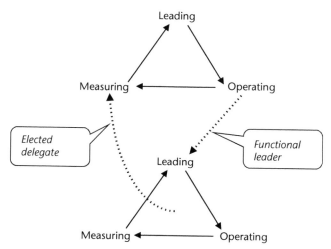

Figure 5.5. Double linking between circles
Source: Adapted from Romme and Endenburg (2006).

Double linking provides representation upward, without undermining or eroding the authority of the functional leader, and as such tends to promote both downward and upward communication between groups, units, and hierarchical levels.[17] Decomposing the system into double-linked units facilitates dialogue and policy decisions by informed consent, by avoiding the need for plenary discussions and decisions in very large groups. Moreover, it also offers the opportunity to delegate or mandate a decision to another level—either a lower or a higher unit in the circular hierarchy.

Instantiations of Circular Organizing

The principles of circular organizing have been applied in more than a hundred organizations worldwide. These organizations are as diverse as industrial and agribusiness firms, IT firms, consulting and accounting firms, and educational and health care organizations. Most of these organizations are small or medium-sized (Romme and Endenburg 2006); the majority are Dutch. In addition, a variety of organizations in Canada, the United States, Germany, and Brazil have implemented circular organizing.

Examples of companies that have embraced circular organizing include *Fabrique*, an award-winning design agency with offices in Amsterdam, Delft, and Rotterdam (employing about 100 people), which has pioneered the introduction of agile methods and practices in the Dutch design sector; *MyWheels*, a care-sharing service in the Netherlands that has been applying circular organizing from its very beginning as a start-up in 2003; the Brazilian agribusiness firm *Terra Viva Group* that used circular organizing to facilitate and spur its growth from a small family-owned business to a medium-sized company (currently employing about 1,300 people); and *Schmuckatelier Becker*, a small jewelry fabricator in Hamburg (Germany), that has been using the circular structure to empower employees and transform all its operations. Other organizations applying the circular approach are, for example, *IVT Thuiszorg*, a Dutch organization of about 350 employees offering a broad portfolio of homecare services; *In Zwang*, a partnership of more than 30 midwives and gynecologists in the Gouda region (Netherlands) which uses circular organizing to provide client-oriented care, based on well-structured collaboration between (otherwise) independent professionals; several so-called *democratic schools* in the Netherlands that provide primary and secondary school education to children from age 4 to 18, based on principles of self-organization; and several *cohousing communities* in the US, for example Champlain Valley Cohousing and Burlington Cohousing East Village, which use circular organizing as a practical tool for self-governance and community development.[18]

The reasons for adopting the circular approach vary substantially: many firms and other organizations apply circular organizing to improve productivity, customer service, employee engagement, or communication throughout the organization; other firms faced bankruptcy and used circular organizing to recover their performance—with almost immediate results.[19] These rather successful instantiations of circular organizing as well as less successful attempts to apply circular principles have been generating a variety of learning outcomes, some of which will be discussed in this section.

Learning about Implementation

One learning outcome is about how to explore and implement circular organizing. A case-in-point is a medium-sized American firm, a manufacturing company in the high-tech sector, whose CEO in the late 1980s decided to introduce the circular design to get his employees more involved in the decision-making process. The CEO strongly preferred to implement the design himself, contrary to how circular organizing had previously been introduced elsewhere. This implementation strategy was to some extent inevitable, in the absence of consultants with relevant expertise on the American continent (at the time). Accordingly, the CEO introduced circular organizing in different units and tried to teach his employees how he believed the method should work. During the start-up period of each new circle, he acted as chair and subsequently asked the functional leaders of each circle to take over. After one year, each circle was given the opportunity to elect its own chair. The CEO, however, continued to attend circle meetings at all levels in the organization.

After two years, however, circular organizing in this high-tech firm did not appear to work. Employees felt "forced" to have circle meetings, and many therefore no longer attended these meetings, and those who did tended to remain silent. In 1993, the American economy moved into a crisis and the firm started to face some severe financial performance issues. The CEO redirected his attention to these problems. Without the CEO's direct involvement, circle meetings were gradually dissolved and around 1997, circular organizing was no longer practiced in this firm.

The attempt to introduce circular organizing in this company mainly failed as a result of the "hit and run" strategy adopted by the CEO as well as his strong need to be in control. As a result, the CEO personally facilitated and guided the implementation process, in which middle managers and employees were not offered much space for participative management and engagement and therefore did not learn some of the key skills and routines of circular organizing (e.g. preparing, participating in, and chairing meetings; raising questions about policy issues; formulating and monitoring policy). In terms of his actual behavior, the CEO appeared exclusively to "own" the implementation strategy, although he repeatedly expressed his intent to involve others in directing and controlling processes. In 2004 the CEO therefore decided to reintroduce the circular design, but now with substantial support and involvement of external experts.

Another example is the application of circular organizing in a multinational corporation, Royal Dutch Shell (Romme and Damen 2007). In this case, the manager of the security unit of a large oil refinery facility within Shell decided to introduce the circular approach within his unit to provide an opportunity for employees to voice opinions and share experiences, as well as decide on policy issues by informed consent; the unit manager also expected to transform and improve communication and interaction with division and other senior management levels. (This manager had sufficient managerial discretion and authority within Shell's administrative hierarchy to initiate such an organizational change.) With support from external consultants, the circular approach was successfully introduced throughout the unit.[20] It resulted in an internal culture of participation, engagement, transparency, and mutual learning that significantly differed from the past (Romme and Damen 2007; Van der Meché 1999).

However, the unit manager was not able to get his superiors interested and engaged, and circular organizing was therefore not adopted in any other units or at other management levels within Shell. Although senior managers at the plant and division levels acknowledged the successful introduction of a new managerial practice in the security unit, they avoided any further (including personal) exposure to this management innovation.[21] This also meant that the policy boundaries of the security unit continued to be defined rather strictly and without any interaction with higher management levels. One illustrative example of this boundary at work can be seen in a required investment in new fire-fighting equipment. Since the unit manager did not have any decision-making authority or budget in this area, he had to submit investment proposals to the division management, without being able to affect decision making at the higher level. This resulted in substantial delays in purchasing and obtaining new equipment, but also in a lack of understanding of how and why the final decision was taken. The security unit's domain for decision making on policy remained limited to minor operational matters. As a result, this local unit in a large multinational company successfully applied circular principles to managing its daily operations, but any diffusion of circular management beyond the unit did not come about (Romme and Damen 2007).

More generally speaking, these two cases as well as similar experiences elsewhere suggest implementation processes are not obvious and self-evident. This calls for an explicit definition of the implementation approach, as a key component of the circular organizing approach. Romme and Endenburg (2006) outline such an implementation strategy as follows:

- Obtain top management's commitment early in the process, by raising the "how" as well as "why" question regarding the choice of a circular design.
- Set up a project team that coordinates and monitors the implementation and experimentation process. Connect this project team directly with the top team: that is, the project team should include at least one top manager (preferably the CEO or managing director of the organization).
- Invite external experts to help the project team, if not all relevant expertise is available in the organization.
- Draw on experimentation to design the entire process, including at least one pilot:
  (i) Each pilot involves a unit of people who will be trained in the skills and rights linked to the circular system and processes (including decision making by informed consent).
  (ii) The pilots are embedded in ongoing operational and management processes.
  (iii) After completing the pilots, top management (including the Board of Directors, if any) takes a go/no-go decision regarding organization-wide implementation, based on a proposal submitted by the project team.
- Create statutory safeguards for the circular organization design to make it sustainable over time.[22]

An implementation strategy of this form serves to avoid the pitfalls encountered in the two cases discussed in this section. For one, it respects and uses the hierarchical structure that currently prevails in the organization, by giving the CEO and other executives a key enabling role. While the initiative to explore circular organizing can still come from anywhere in the organization, this implementation strategy requires top management to come on board early on in the process. Moreover, this strategy tells the CEO and other executives that they need to avoid a central (e.g. coaching) role in trying out and applying circular management principles in the organization, other than testing and applying them in their own boardroom.

Learning about Ownership and Authority

Circular organizing has key implications for the notions of ownership and authority. The vast majority of external owners of corporations, such as institutional investors, are not interested in any other commitment than their share of the corporation's equity, as observed in Chapter 1. But the case of an entrepreneur-manager owning the company, the situation in which Gerard Endenburg took over the company from his parents, can also undermine circular organizing—as he observed at the time:

> The traditional ownership situation is a threat to the circular nature of Endenburg Elektrotechniek, because it allows outside meddling based on financial ownership only. Consent decision-making presupposes that the nature of one's function in the organization, and not the amount of shares held, determines what a person gets to consent to. (Romme 1999: 815)

To address this problem, Endenburg Elektrotechniek developed a profit and compensation system in the 1970s. This system separated financial interests from power in the company by (a) subjecting external shareholders to decision making by informed consent in the top circle, which includes a shareholder representative, and (b) offering employees opportunities for financial participation, in addition to participation in circles making policy decisions.

In the 1980s, it became evident that Dutch corporate law would not adequately support these principles, because all existing legal forms were based on the concept of *external ownership* (Hansmann 1996). A practical solution was therefore created in the form of two conventional legal forms, the corporation and foundation. In this legal structure, the foundation owns all equity in the corporation, and as such controls the company from a financial perspective. The articles of incorporation of the company draw on the same circular principles as the statutory articles of the foundation (i.e. policy is decided by informed consent in circles that are double linked). Moreover, the statutory articles of both legal entities are connected, by having the top circle of the corporation also act as the top circle of the foundation. The foundation, as the legal owner of the corporation and its assets, can sell certificates to, for example, managers, employees, or outside investors. These certificates are essentially a form of economic ownership on the basis of which one receives a share of the organization's net earnings.[23]

This hybrid legal entity implies that, so to speak, the *company owns itself*. It safeguards the company from external intervention on the basis of financial interests only, and in several instances has proved to be an effective shield against hostile takeover attempts. The Dutch government formally accepted this legal construction around 1985. Shortly thereafter it was implemented in Endenburg Elektrotechniek and also, later, in other Dutch companies.[24] For example, when Henry Mentink pioneered the cooperative care-sharing service MyWheels in the Netherlands, he decided to adopt the corporation-foundation entity to prevent conflicts between the company and its many member-shareholders as well as to increase the efficiency of decision making:

> In typical cooperatives, only a small number of members show up for a general meeting, which is why decisions cannot be sustained. The sociocratic approach enables us to make sustained decisions in every circle.[25]

Outside the Netherlands, the Terra Viva Group adopted a similar configuration, using an association instead of a foundation. The Terra Viva Group is a large agribusiness company that arose from a fast-growing farm in Brazil owned by a family with 11 children. The current CEO of Terra Viva, Frans Schoenmaker, reflected as follows:

> My parents founded Terra Viva in 1959. In the early 1980s we adopted the circular approach, to deal with the hick-ups and dilemmas of participatory decision-making and growing the business. At a later stage, we also decided to neutralize the detrimental effects of legal ownership and inheritance issues arising in any family-owned company. We created an association to which each shareholder-owner transferred a major part of his or her shares in Terra Viva.... This association today holds 51% of all shares. Members of the Schoenmaker family, as owners of certificates in the association, receive dividend payments. But due to the association owning 51% of the company, Terra Viva largely 'owns itself', as Gerard Endenburg recommended at the time. This contributes to the continuity of the company, and prevents that capital investments stop when one or more shareholders leave the company. Over time, Terra Viva has developed its own interpretation of the sociocratic circular approach, but key principles such as making decisions by consent and sociocratic elections continue to be used throughout the company.[26]

Interestingly, Russell Ackoff developed a similar notion of ownership and authority in the context of circular organizing. For example, he argued that all units and boards in the company need to operate by consensus: "Boards should prepare their own operating procedures, but most of them operate in much the same way. Most, for example, operate by consensus rather than majority rule. The advantages of consensus over split decisions are apparent. The principal advantage is that it removes the possibility of a tyranny of the majority, the type of tyranny most frequently encountered" (Ackoff 1994: 133). Ackoff's (1994) concept of circular organizing entails a "democratic hierarchy" that would have three characteristics:

(i) the absence of an ultimate authority;

(ii) the ability of each member to participate directly or through representation in all decisions affecting him or her directly; and

(iii) the ability to make and implement decisions that affect no one other than the decision makers.[27]

These three characteristics resonate very well with the notion of circular organizing pioneered by Endenburg—the main difference being the distinction between informed consent and Ackoff's consensus.

Learning about how to Sustain Circular Organizing

Earlier in this chapter, we observed that participation in circle meetings is voluntary in nature, at least for those employees who do not have a specific role such as chairing the circle or representing their circle in the next higher one.[28] Several examples discussed earlier also suggest the circular structure—especially when compared to a regular administrative hierarchy (cf. Figure 5.1)—at times appears to be an almost dormant system that is activated in response to exceptional conditions such as crisis situations or other major policy problems and challenges. This raises questions about how one sustains the circular capability for learning, monitoring, and policy making at all organizational levels.

First, circles have to meet at least once or twice a year, to create basic conditions for the process of leading–operating–measuring. For example, a circle has to appoint a chair as well as a secretary (note taker) from its participants, in order to be able to function properly. Moreover, the three principles of circular organizing defined earlier—decide on policy by informed consent, organize in circles, and double link these circles—imply that functional leaders as well as delegates at all levels are elected and appointed by informed consent.[29] Circle members therefore have to meet to evaluate their current delegate in the higher circle and (any) functional leaders it has appointed in lower circles. This assessment is typically done at the end of their (e.g. two-year) term as delegate or leader, but can also be done annually; moreover, in cases of major performance issues, any circle member can initiate a (interim) discussion on the performance of its delegate in the higher circle or any of the leaders appointed in lower circles. When the term of a delegate or leader expires, the circle appoints a new person or re-appoints the current one for another term.[30]

Moreover, the praxis of electing and appointing managers and delegates by consent, after an open discussion, appears to enhance both the transparency of and trust in "decisions about people." The frictions and tensions arising from how managers are typically selected and appointed in companies, and from how delegates are chosen by way of anonymous voting in democratic elections in the public sector, have been widely documented (Kets de Vries 1989; Ackoff 1994; Collins 1997; Flyvbjerg 1998; Ansell 2011). In this respect, electing people by consent after an open discussion "builds a strong sense of trust and assures that people who assume jobs know they have the support of their peers. Circle members are more likely to trust someone whom they have elected. It also makes day-to-day leadership and decision-making much easier because it reduces the friction that results in both autocratic and democratic people selection processes" (Buck and Villines 2007: 149).

Another way to sustain the circular approach is to annually draw up a (circular) accountancy report. Such a report commissioned by the top circle provides data on the circular infrastructure and processes—similar to how a chartered accountant assesses the financial systems, processes, and results of the organization. An assessment of circular practices draws on unobtrusive and quantifiable measurements, so that every circle and any external bodies can assess whether the circular system is actually functioning (Endenburg 1998). A circular accountancy report will therefore include an assessment of, for example:

- Whether there is a place for every employee in the circle (regardless of whether s/he actually participates in the circle's meetings); that is, is each employee directly invited for meetings of his circle, even when he's been absent from many previous meetings?

- Do the participants feel psychologically safe in circle meetings (e.g. do they feel free to speak up about any issue)?

- How are policy decisions made? After an open discussion? Are decisions taken by informed consent, and if not, what other decision rules are used?

- Double linking: are the functional leaders and delegates appointed; is this done after an open discussion; are they periodically assessed?

- Is the process of leading–operating–measuring used, and how?

Notably, a circular accountancy process is not meant to suffocate the organization. The key purpose of circular accountancy is to inform the top and general circle (cf. supervisory board and general management), and give them the opportunity to correct "any attrition or deformity that may occur" and to tackle "abuse, manipulation, or deception" (Endenburg 1998: 169).

Circularity and Pragmatism in Public Administration

In some organizational settings it may be almost impossible to rewire the system toward circular organizing, in the absence of a single (group of) agent (s) that can authorize such a fundamental transformation. This may seem paradoxical, but there is no way to get around it: to systemically transform any organization into a circular one, an ultimate authority must first enable and start this transformation. An exemplary case is the context of public administration, where some circular principles outlined earlier cannot be directly used. National laws and governmental regulations determine and prescribe how a public governance system operates.

Nevertheless, elected politicians and administrators of public bodies at the local, regional and national level are facing huge challenges arising from decreasing budgets and resources, increasing demands on public services, and low trust in political institutions (Bovens and Wille 2008; Hendriks 2009; Ansell 2011; Citrin et al. 2014).

The opportunity to experiment with circular organizing in public administration arose when the mayor of Utrechtse Heuvelrug invited a group of citizens to investigate options for more effective local governance.[31] Utrechtse Heuvelrug is a Dutch municipality with about 50,000 citizens, which was created in 2006 from the integration of five smaller villages. In the first few years of this newly created municipality, the city council's decision to build a new city hall caused growing distrust in local politics among many citizens. Despite almost 6,000 citizens signing a collective letter of protest as well as public exposure in a national television program, the city council decided to pursue the new city hall. One of the alderman stepped down and public distrust grew to an all-time high.

In early 2012, the mayor of Utrechtse Heuvelrug invited a group of citizens to investigate options for more effective local governance and ways to restore trust, with the objective of improving the interaction between citizens and the local administration. All citizens were invited to volunteer to participate. As a result, a group of 15 citizens was formed. One of the citizens in this group was an expert in circular organizing.

This group arranged meetings with other citizens as well as with civil servants, city councillors, and aldermen to investigate the needs of these stakeholders. It also studied and discussed several reports and best practices in other cities, to define key guidelines for citizen participation in public governance.[32] Several workshops were then conducted, in which civil servants, councillors and aldermen jointly developed a new approach that would draw on the principle of informed consent.

In April 2013 the group of 15 citizens presented its conclusions and recommendations to the city council. Key recommendations for strengthening the connection between citizens and the municipal administration were as follows:

- Decide early on about the level of citizen participation that will be used for a specific policy issue.
- The city council should set and define the boundaries (e.g. budget constraints, delivery time, and other conditions) for any process involving citizen participation.
- Subsequently, the city council assigns a project group to investigate the topic and decide by informed consent on a solution within the boundaries set by the city council.
- Every citizen who is interested can join this project group, in which representatives of interest groups and other stakeholders can also participate.
- Once the project group has presented its solution, the city council merely assesses if the solution proposed meets the boundaries defined earlier. If this is the case, the city council validates the solution. Any other contribution from the city councillors must be in the form of participating in and/or providing information to the project group.
- If the project group does agree on a solution within the boundaries set, the city council again has the exclusive authority to decide on this policy issue.

In a special meeting, the city council discussed these recommendations. In addition to all city councillors, one of the aldermen, representatives of the civil servants, and the group of 15 citizens participated in this meeting. Before the meeting, it was agreed and communicated that decision making would be based on the informed consent principle, to create a setting that was acceptable and sufficiently secure for all participants.[33] An external expert in circular organizing chaired the meeting. At the end of this meeting, the participants decided by consent to launch a pilot project based on the recommended approach, and thereby to build more practical experience.

Over time, this pilot project has been evolving into a praxis of collaborative governance and learning. Several specific results have been obtained. First, the terminology of "consent" is now widely used in political discourse in Utrechtse Heuvelrug. It has become a symbol of the culture of dialogue and collaborative problem solving, which increasingly prevails over the culture of political polarization this city previously suffered. For example, after the elections for a new city council in March 2014, all newly appointed city councillors agreed by informed consent (in April 2014) on a new policy program for the council—including plans for major budget cuts.[34] Such a collaborative consent-based approach is highly different from what is usual in municipalities in Europe, North America, and elsewhere. Standard practice is that a majority coalition of parties exclusively defines the new policy program and also selects the aldermen; and then has the (majority of the) city council validate the results.

The Utrechtse Heuvelrug case also illustrates that, in many instances in democratic governance, the "real" experts and stakeholders with regard to a particular policy domain or issue are not part of the city council.[35] Citizens with a particular expertise typically only want to contribute in a transient manner, focused on a specific policy challenge. This requires more flexible arrangements for citizen participation in developing policy proposals. The approach developed in the city of Utrechtse Heuvelrug appears to enable these flexible arrangements, with the city council increasingly claiming a role as *orchestrator* of civic participation in public policy making. Overall, the city council and administration of Utrechtse Heuvelrug have embraced the idea of citizen participation in developing proposals for major policy decisions. In doing so, they have adopted a mindset of collaborative learning, which serves to try out new methods and continually improve decision making and other processes.[36]

This case illustrates there are ample opportunities for applying the circular approach in public administration and local democracy, even when existing laws and regulations suggest otherwise.[37] This also reflects the pragmatist mindset explored in Chapter 2. For example, when a principle such as "double linking between circles" cannot be directly applied, the challenge is to creatively work with the given conditions and resources. This can be done in two ways. One can identify and use only those principles that can be applied (e.g. informed consent in this case). In addition, by reflecting on the underlying constructs, the principles can be adapted to make them work in the incumbent setting: for example, given the relative inertia of the city council's legal position, how can we create a structural capability for searching and learning (arising from opportunities to weave and deviate) around the city council?

What counts in pragmatism is not merely "what works" but the meaningfulness of action, says Ansell (2011: 11): "Actions take on enhanced meaning through the cultivation of an emergent sense of purpose." The circular organizing approach enables this pragmatist mindset, by providing a set of key constructs as well as several more specific management principles.[38] The key constructs can inform the creative application and adaptation of principles in settings that cannot be straightforwardly transformed toward circularity. And when managers and other change agents find they cannot use basic principles such as "weaving must be possible" and "circularity of leading–operating–measuring," they can decide to adopt any other set of principles.

Holacracy as an Outgrowth of Circular Organizing

Circular organizing as previously discussed has inspired the development of what is now known as *holacracy*. Brian Robertson, an American software engineer and founder of Ternary Software, inferred holacracy as an organizational system from principles of circularity, self-organization, requisite organization, agile software development, and other sources (Robertson 2007).

Koestler time coined the term "holarchy" in 1968 in his book *The Ghost in the Machine*. A holarchy is composed of holons, units that are autonomous and self-organizing but also depend on the greater whole of which they are part. Thus, a holarchy is a hierarchy of self-regulating holons that operate both as autonomous wholes and as interdependent parts (Koestler 1968). In applying the idea of holarchy to organizational design and governance, Robertson (2007) renamed it "holacracy," inspired by Endenburg's work on circularity.

In several ways, holacracy entails a vocabulary that has differentiated away from Endenburg's vocabulary. For example, in Robertson's (2007, 2015) holacracy, the building blocks of organizational structure are *roles*, which serve to clearly distinguish between roles and the people who "energize" them by using certain capacities and talents, perform certain functions, and achieve results for the organization. A system of self-organizing circles serves to structure the various roles. Each circle uses a well-defined governance process to create its own roles and policies, drawing on "integrative decision making" that (similar to informed consent) goes beyond a consensus-based approach (Robertson 2007; Ulieru 2014).

An important extension of circular organizing arises from how Robertson draws on the notion of *requisite organization* developed by Jaques (1996). This notion in particular serves to answer a series of questions that are often raised when all the basic elements of circular organizing are in place:

> How do you know what specific circles an organization should have, and how many levels these should be organized into? And how do you know what specific accountabilities should exist within the organization, which role should own which accountabilities, and which circle should own which role? Does it matter? The answer is a strong yes, it definitely does—this is an issue in any organization, with or without Holacracy, but with Holacracy in place the ability to both find and harness an effective structure seems to increase significantly.
>
> Holacracy suggests that, at any given point in time, an organization has a naturally ideal or "requisite" circle structure, which "wants" to emerge. And within that circle structure there seem to be requisite roles and accountabilities. In other words, the organization is a natural holarchy that has emerged over time and will evolve with time. This requisite structure is not an arbitrary choice. Finding it is detective work, not creative work—the answer already exists, it just needs to be uncovered. This discovery process feels a lot less like explicit design and a lot more like listening and attuning with what reality is already trying to tell you—what naturally wants to emerge.
>
> The benefits of doing this listening are significant. The closer our explicit structures mirror these natural structures, the more effective and trust-inducing the organization becomes. As we align with the requisite structure, the organization feels increasingly "natural", and self-organization becomes easier. Circles feel more cohesive—they have healthier autonomy and clearer identity, and more clear-cut interplay with other circles. Each circle more easily performs its own leading, doing, and measuring, with its super-circle able to more comfortably focus on specific inputs and outputs rather than the details of the processing going on within. Roles and accountabilities become more clear and explicit, and it becomes easier to match accountability to control. Aligning with requisite structure dramatically eases and enhances everything Holacracy already aims for. (Robertson 2007: 13)

Next to Ternary Software, organizations as varied as David Allen Company, Zappos, Boulder Center for Conscious Community, Precision Nutrition, and Medium have recently been adopting holacratic principles and practices.[39] For example, the CEO of Zappos (part of Amazon), Tony Hsieh, is using holacracy to replace Zappos' traditional management structure to confront some of the plagues he observed at many large companies—including employee disenchantment and inability to take risks (Monarth 2014). He thus wants "Zappos to function more like a city and less like a top-down bureaucratic organization" (Groth 2015). Notably, Hsieh and other tech entrepreneurs are attracted to holacratic circular organizing because it is in many ways a tool to get companies to operate more like software. Robertson uses engineering terminology and likens Holacracy to Apple's iOS operating system. The system, largely misunderstood as non-hierarchical or flat, actually creates a new hierarchy around work rather than titles. (Groth 2015)

Moreover, CEOs and entrepreneurs expect holacratic circular organizing to be highly effective in facilitating high growth rates, by propagating leadership throughout the organization.[40] Obviously, this also implies that entrepreneurs and CEOs have to learn to let go and step back (Groth 2015; Mays 2013). Phil Caravaggio of the Toronto-based company Precision Nutrition reflects on this as follows:

It sounds trivial because it's something that I think you'd imagine every organization has to face as it grows. But in some organizations, they really don't face it. There's a sense that only the people at the very top have the final word on everything. That's very different in Holacracy. There really isn't a top. There are different perspectives, and they're not necessarily hierarchical. I can't say "I'm a founder of the organization, so no matter what part of the organization we're talking about, I'm the final word on it. I get to decide." That's not the way it works. That is a fundamental difference in Holacracy. This is an opportunity for people in every area of the organization to have not just lip-service authority, but genuine authority. That took a commitment from me. I think the hardest thing to do is make this mental shift. Other people are going to have genuine authority. They will be the authority, not me, on X, Y or Z. I will be subservient to them in these various functions.[41]

As in the instantiations of circular organizing discussed earlier, holacracy appears to offer a fundamentally different "operating system" for organizations—one that might revolutionize how they are structured, how decisions are made, how authority is distributed, and how power flows (Ulieru 2014). As an outgrowth of circular organizing, the holacratic approach draws on a somewhat different set of terms, but has started to demonstrate a similar potential as a professional management approach as the circular system pioneered by Endenburg.

Consolidation and Codification

In 1978, Gerard Endenburg founded the Sociocratic Center in Rotterdam to promote the growth and diffusion of sociocracy. Over the years, this Center has been training and educating experts who in turn have set up similar centers in Canada, the US, the UK, France, Austria, Germany, Australia, and other countries. More recently, the creation of *The Sociocracy Group* (TSG) has served to consolidate this global network of pioneers and expertise centers. TSG is organized and managed using the principles of circular organizing discussed earlier.[42] The Sociocratic Center at the time also started building a codified body of knowledge, resulting in the so-called "sociocratic norm," a document available from TSG. This codified norm is regularly updated, like the Holacracy Constitution. Unlike the latter, however, the sociocratic norm for circular organizing is not yet available as an open source document.

In 2007, Brian Robertson and Tom Thomison co-founded the partnership *HolacracyOne* to support holacracy's growth and package it for use by other organizations. By developing and offering training and implementation services, HolacracyOne has been helping other organizations to learn and apply holacratic principles and practices. In 2009, HolacracyOne formalized the method into the first Holacracy Constitution, a document that lays out the core principles and practices of the system. This document has been developed into new versions since then, like an operating system in software development.[43]

In view of their mission to grow the level of professionalism in management practices, both TSG and HolacracyOne are facing the challenge of developing a business model that avoids the co-dependency problem discussed in Chapter 4. This co-dependency between management consulting firms and their clients implies the capability for strategic and organizational change of many (large) corporations has become almost entirely dependent on external management consultants. TSG and HolacracyOne are deliberately seeking to build professional management practices, based on circular organizing principles, which would make the incumbent organizations structurally independent from external help and support.

This will require TSG and HolacracyOne to develop a business model that sustains their capability to provide initial support and coaching services, without the need for their clients to call upon TSG or HolacracyOne again and again. The business model currently used by TSG and HolacracyOne appears to rely primarily on providing certification to individuals who have developed and demonstrated professional skills in training and implementing the sociocratic or holacratic circular method. This would enable any client organization to build its own internal capability for circular organizing, by having a number of its staff members trained and certified in circular organizing. It is not clear yet whether this truly is a sustainable business model in the longer run for TSG and HolacracyOne.

Concluding Remarks

"The only true voyage of discovery . . . would be not to visit strange lands but to possess other eyes, to behold the universe through the eyes of another, of a hundred others, to behold the hundred universes that each of them beholds, that each of them is" (Proust 1929: 348–9). This quote from Marcel Proust suggests the true merit of discovery is the opportunity to develop alternative ways of looking at the world. The discovery of circular organizing might offer a novel perspective on the world of management and entrepreneurship. In this respect, the constructs, principles, and instantiations of circular organizing suggest that "power" in general, and circularity of power in particular, is a promising construct. The next chapter serves to more extensively theorize about circular organizing, particularly in terms of power, ownership, hierarchy, and related constructs.

Circular organizing has been pioneered in the periphery of mainstream corporate and managerial practice. Indeed, it is very unlikely that mainstream management thinking could have provided the basis for creating circular organizing or any other management model that systematically redistributes authority and power throughout the organization. The conventional wisdom about management therefore appears to marginalize major opportunities for professionalizing management. A higher level of engagement of both management practitioners and scholars in (re)discovering—newly emerging as well as established—general management practices may serve to break the silence and revitalize the quest for professionalism.

Notes

1. This chapter partly draws on ideas and arguments previously published in: A. G. L. Romme (1999), "Domination, self-determination and circular organizing," *Organization Studies* 20: 801–32; and A. G. L. Romme and G. Endenburg (2006), "Construction principles and design rules in the case of circular design," *Organization Science* 17: 287–97.
2. This section is largely based on Romme (1999), "Domination, self-determination and circular organizing," *Organization Studies* 20: 801–32. The latter article also provides detailed information about data collection and analysis.
3. Endenburg Elektrotechniek was, and still is, a company that designs, produces, installs, and renovates electrotechnical installations, control systems, switching boards, and other electronic instruments. The company at the time employed about 130 employees, primarily with a technical background, either working on projects at the customer's site or involved in design and development work in the company's own facilities. The most important customers of Endenburg Elektrotechniek in the early 1970s were companies in the manufacturing, ship building, and offshore industries.
4. Many years later, looking back at the decision in the early 1970s to stop further growth, Endenburg observed this was a key decision because "when your predominant commitment is to pursue growth in turnover and profitability, all time and energy required for organizational renewal is depleted" (Romme 1999: 810).

5. Buck and Villines (2007) provide a detailed overview of the history of the notion of sociocracy.

6. A more detailed narrative of the incubation and initial development of circular organizing at Endenburg Elektrotechniek is given in Romme (1999). The latter study also describes the critical role of educating and training employees and managers in the area of making policy decisions, chairing circle meetings, and so forth.

7. This section largely draws on Romme and Endenburg (2006) "Construction principles and design rules in the case of circular design," *Organization Science* 17: 287–97, where we talked about construction principles and design rules. This chapter draws on the terminology of values, constructs, principles, models, and instantiations (as defined in Chapter 3).

8. For details, I refer to Endenburg (1974, 1998), Romme (1999), and Buck and Villines (2007).

9. Interestingly, this construction principle was only uncovered at a later stage, in the context of several attempts to apply circular organizing in large organizations that did not have an unambiguous hierarchical structure. The initial set of successful applications of circular organizing thus apparently involved organizations where there was such a administrative hierarchy. Romme and Endenburg (2006) describe the practical experiences that were instrumental in uncovering a (previously implicitly used) principle regarding hierarchy: "Several attempts to introduce the circular design in organizations structured as an association uncovered the, until then implicit, role of hierarchy. For example, one of these projects was done in a cooperative association of a large number of agribusiness firms. The delegates of these firms participated in a general membership meeting constituting the ultimate (formal) authority in the organization. This general membership meeting appointed a board charged with running the activities of the association. The ambiguous nature of the relationship between members and the board created a major governance problem: members were formally in charge but in practice unable to act collectively, whereas the board was formally subordinate to the members but actually governed the organization. Thus, interpersonal relationships between the members were generally rather poor and highly dependent on the board as intermediate agent. This type of problem caused several associations to explore the circular design. However, all attempts to add a circular organization to these organizations failed as a result of the absence of a clear hierarchy (as a sequence of accountability levels). Moreover, in all these cases there was in fact no one authorized to repair this fundamental problem, in order to create the conditions for developing a circular organization for policy making. These experiences suggested an additional construction principle that defines the importance of hierarchy. This principle had apparently been implicit in previous implementation projects. In this respect, the existing organizational structure in previous cases involved a clear administrative hierarchy" (Romme and Endenburg 2006: 294). The notion of hierarchy as an unambiguous sequence of levels of accountability is well known in the literature (e.g. Jaques 1990). For example, Simon (1973: 23–4) described the crucial role of hierarchic structure for the synthesis and survival of

large self-regulating systems as follows: "By virtue of hierarchic structure, the functional efficacy of the higher-level structures, their stability, can be made relatively independent of the detail of their microscopic components. By virtue of hierarchy, the several components on any given level can preserve a measure of independence to adapt to their special aspects of the environment without destroying their usefulness to the system."

10. For example: Sen (1979) and Nurmi (1999). Sen (1979: 25) criticizes the unanimity rule as being one of supreme conservatism because even a single person can block change altogether no matter what everybody else wants: "Marie Antionette's opposition to the First Republic would have saved the monarchy in France, and the world would have seen very little change. Clearly there is something grotesquely unsatisfactory about a social decision rule like this." In a study that draws on simulation modeling, I indeed demonstrated that the larger a group is, the more likely it is that unanimous decision-making breaks down (Romme 2004).

11. I'm here referring to the formal (dictionary) meaning of "consensus," rather than how this notion is often applied in practice. In fact, most practical applications of consensus decision making tend to be more in line with the "informed consent" notion (e.g. Hartnett 2011) than the formal meaning of consensus, as unanimity regarding a proposed course of action. This underscores the idea that informed consent (i.e. no one has an argued objection) is a highly useful decision rule in any professional context, whereas "full agreement" (i.e. everyone says yes to the proposal) is not.

12. As such, the "veto" problem does not exist in organizations using the circular approach. In this respect, a basic course in (sociocratic) circular organizing serves to teach anyone chairing a meeting in which policy decisions are taken by consent to approach all arguments and objections raised by participants as opportunities to improve the proposed action or decision. Thus, the chair first invites everyone to raise any argued objections and thus promotes divergence in opinions and positions. Subsequently, the chair directs the dialogue toward a decision by consent, and in doing so, may invite those have any remaining objections to help solve the problem, for example: "John, can you provide more background to your objection to the proposed decision, and then tell us how you think the proposed decision needs to be adapted."

13. For other cases and examples: Romme and Reijmer (1997); Romme (1998); Romme and Van Witteloostuijn (1999); Romme and Endenburg (2006).

14. In the management literature, many similar management methods and cycles are available, all derived from the cybernetic control literature. One of the most prominent ones is the Plan-Do-Check-Act (PDCA) iterative method, widely used in business organizations for the control and continuous improvement of processes and products (Deming 1986). Another example is the DMAIC cycle used in Six Sigma projects (Tennant 2001). The leading-operating-measuring cycle is perhaps the most basic version of this management method, that as such may also be more widely applicable—that is, it can be applied at any level in the organization (from operational teams to the supervisory board level) and by small ventures and enterprises as well as big companies and organizations in a variety of sectors.

15. Many studies have demonstrated that psychological safety in team and other meetings enhances group and organizational learning and thus organizational performance (e.g. Edmondson 1999; Detert and Trevino 2008).

16. In order to reduce the dysfunctionalities of hierarchical organizing, Likert (1961, 1976) introduced the famous principle of the linking pin, a manager or supervisor that leads a unit (e.g. department) as well as participates in decisions at the next higher hierarchical level (e.g. management team), in order to support top-down as well as upward communication. Two related assumptions are crucial to the linking pin. First, the single linking pin is based on the idea that power flows from top to bottom. This assumption is correct in many organizational constellations, but less so in the case of circularity of power. The second critical assumption made by Likert (1976) is that a balance between downward and upward communication can be achieved by managers who are appointed by the next higher level in order to serve as the linking pin with the subordinate unit. This assumption has never been truly questioned, but a number of studies conclude that upward versus downward communication requires different personalities and skills (Manz and Sims 1987; Mueller 1994; Flood et al. 1996).

17. As observed by Van Vlissingen (1991) and Mueller (1994). Throughout this chapter, the term "authority" is used to refer to the ability, right, and/or justification to exercise power (Simon 1976). This ability, right or justification may originate from governmental rules and laws (e.g. in the case of police officers), established customs and habits (e.g. monarchs), academic knowledge and status (e.g. professors), corporate constitution (e.g. shareholders or boards of directors), or other sources. This chapter obviously focuses on authority in corporate and other organizational settings.

18. With regard to Fabrique (www.fabrique.nl/en/): "De fun factor bij Fabrique" retrieved via http://www.sociocratie.nl/resultaten-en-praktijkervaringen/praktijkervaringen/ January 14, 2015; for MyWheels, see its website (https://mywheels.nl); Terra Viva Group's website (english version: www.terraviva.agr.br/?lang=eng); www.tbschmuck.de is the website of Schmuckatelier Becker; www.ivtthuiszorg.nl with regard to *IVT Thuiszorg*; the experiences of *In Zwang* are described in "Samenwerken en autonomie behouden, bij In Zwang," retrieved via http://www.sociocratie.nl/resultaten-en-praktijkervaringen/ praktijkervaringen/ March 17, 2015; http://deruimtesoest.nl/ regarding the democratic school *De Ruimte* in Soest; regarding the two *cohousing communities* in the US, I refer to www.champlainvalleycohousing.org and www.sociocracy.info/burlington-cohousing--east-village/ (both retrieved February 28, 2015). Please note that, in the US, sociocratic circular organizing is also known as "dynamic governance."

19. Many of the learning outcomes arising from circular organizing are beyond the scope of this book. For example, several other cases (e.g. Romme 1998; Romme and Endenburg 2006) served to establish the applicability and responsiveness of circular organizing in crisis situations, as illustrated in the Endenburg Elektrotechniek case discussed earlier in this chapter. The learning arising from these experiences is that participative decision making generated and bounded by the structure of a circular organization can be very effective—as it also can be in a crisis situation requiring bold and immediate action. This was, and still is, not in line with the

conventional wisdom about crisis management that suggests a top down approach with few opportunities for participation by employees (cf. Lalonde 2004). On a more fundamental level, the introduction of the circular design appears to enhance connectivity by bringing people, information, and knowledge together to solve problems and make policy decisions (Romme 1999).

20. The key challenge in this case arose from the fact that almost all employees in this security unit work in shifts around the clock, implying that circles had to be composed on the basis of participation in shifts rather than team membership (Romme and Damen 2007).

21. This non-engagement of senior managers in this particular case can be (hypothetically) explained in many ways: for example, the personality traits (e.g. locus of control) of these managers, the discomfort arising from "bottom up" innovation in an administrative hierarchy that thrives on top-down communication and information flows, or perhaps the results achieved with circular organizing in the security unit were simply not good enough. Regardless of which explanation is valid, I focus here on developing a strategy for exploring and implementing circular organizing which serves to avoid such a stalemate.

22. The key role of statutory safeguards will be explained and discussed later in this chapter.

23. Source: Romme and Endenburg (2002). This hybrid corporation-foundation entity is a pragmatic solution within the constraints of the existing framework of (Dutch) corporate law. The ideal solution would involve a new legal entity, a corporate entity with so-called consent-shares (Romme and Endenburg 2001, 2002). In this type of corporation, a share (in the corporation's equity) provides the right to participate in corporate governance processes, but in an *inclusive* rather than exclusive manner. That is, the shareholders' meeting chooses a representative in the top circle that also includes other stakeholders and makes policy decisions by informed consent.

24. In this respect, in the 1970s the Dutch government created a legal requirement for all companies and organizations with more than 100 employees to establish a works council. Since 1985, the Dutch government has exempted companies from this requirement when they can demonstrate having implemented the circular method, including the corporation-foundation structure outlined earlier. In fact, this exemption implies that Dutch corporate law since the 1980s formally acknowledges the circular corporation-foundation structure in which the corporation owns itself, as a viable alternative to other legal entities such as the cooperative corporation and investor-owned corporation. Generally speaking, the investor-owned corporation has two legal forms in most market economies: the privately traded and publicly traded corporation. Both are characterized by a formal structure in which the investors/owners constitute the final authority in all matters—through the shareholders meeting and their representatives in the Board of Directors (Hansmann 1996). However, the separation between ownership and control in publicly traded corporations makes the authority dimension in these organizations more complex, as we will explore in more detail in the next chapter.

25. K. Flanagan, "MyWheels cooperative car sharing," November 18, 2014. Retrieved via http://blog.p2pfoundation.net/mywheels-cooperative-car-sharing/2014/11/18 March 10, 2015.

26. Terra Viva adopted an ownership configuration in the form of an association-corporation legal structure whereby all shares in the company are held by an association (or an "associação" in Brazil). Source of the quote: interview with Frans Schoenmakers, conducted April 17, 2015.

27. Ackoff's (1981) work was initially triggered by his search for an organizational design that supports interactive planning processes. He therefore proposed all people with authority in organizations, from the chief executive to the supervisor, should have boards made up of their immediate superiors and subordinates to create a circularity of responsibility and accountability. The board at any given level is responsible for planning and coordinating the work for which that person is responsible, and also for reviewing and evaluating his or her performance. Ackoff (1989) reported that companies such as Kodak, Alcoa, Anheuser-Busch, and A&P Supermarkets have applied these ideas, but did not provide any further information.

28. This is also reflected in the statistics of presence/absence during circle meetings in most organizations using the circular approach. For example, Romme (1999) collected data of meeting frequency and attendance rates over a period of six years in Endenburg Elektrotechniek. The top circle of this company met on a regular basis once every two months (6 meetings per year), the general circle held an average of 20 meetings per year, and most unit circles met 4 or 5 times per year. The average attendance rates of the circle's membership were: 89 percent for the top circle, 68 percent for the general circle, and 65 percent for the unit circles (Romme 1999).

29. In fact, the exact implications of the three design principles for appointing leaders and delegates was so unclear in the initial try-outs of working in circles, that Endenburg at the time introduced a fourth principle that explicitly says that all people are elected by consent after open discussion (Endenburg 1974, 1998). Buck and Villines (2007) provide an excellent set of guidelines for decision making by consent, in general as well as specifically for electing people.

30. This also implies that most functional leaders—be they operational supervisors and leaders, department managers, or general managers and CEOs—come from the current population of staff members of the organization. Only in exceptional situations, for example when no suitable internal candidate for the CEO position is available, will an external candidate be recruited and appointed.

31. The description of this case is based on Van der Eyden et al. (2015).

32. The search for a more effective public governance is obviously not new. Many municipalities in the Netherlands and elsewhere have been experimenting with different forms of participation and decision making. A key conclusion of the WRR (2012) report "Trust in Citizens" ("Vertrouwen in Burgers") is that a variety of approaches toward public governance need to be explored and evaluated. The same report also emphasizes there are no quick fixes or standard solutions for restoring trust in political institutions, and that a new facilitator-oriented role of government is required (WRR 2012).

33. To ensure the connection with the city councillors who were not participating, these formed a "second ring" that could be consulted by the "first ring" city councillors during the meeting (Van der Eyden et al. 2015).

34. For the press release (in Dutch) regarding this decision taken by consent from all new city councillors: www.heuvelrug.nl/actueel/nieuwsberichten_44515/item/ge-meenteraad-geeft-consent-op-raadsprogramma_61000.html#titel61000.

35. In this respect, democratic governance has much to learn from the notion of "open innovation." Open innovation implies that in a world of widely distributed knowledge, companies cannot afford to rely entirely on their own experts and knowledge, but should instead leverage a network of internal and external contributors to develop and commercialize new technologies, products, and services (Chesbrough 2003).

36. The high level of transparency in how the city council orchestrates civic participation may also make a variety of moral issues—arising from, for example, potential conflicts of interests or lobbying to influence policy decisions—more manageable. The participative approach in Utrechtse Heuvelrug will not eliminate such issues, but does make them more controllable and transparent for the city council, citizens, and the public media. For example, a local group of enterprises may have multiple citizens (e.g. employees) join a project group to represent their interests and voice their concerns. However, these participants are not likely to direct the project group toward a solution that only serves their interests, because other participants are free to voice other interests and concerns that cannot be overruled when a collective decision needs to be taken by informed consent. Moreover, the proceedings of any project group are public, which reduces the chance that such power plays will go unnoticed.

37. The circular approach to civic participation in municipal politics might also serve to generate policy outcomes that are broadly accepted (cf. Romme 1999; Romme and Endenburg 2006). In this respect, the acceptance of policy decisions taken by the city council has increased substantially among the citizenship of Utrechtse Heuvelrug (Van der Eyden et al. 2015). However, given that the mayor of this city initiated change in a situation in which the level of acceptance of local politics was at an all time low, one can argue that any kind of attention or intervention would have improved the situation (the so-called Hawthorne effect). At a more theoretical level, the case study in this chapter suggests that efforts to renew public governance are more likely to succeed if they exploit the strong desire of many citizens to engage in other forms of "expressive" behavior (Copeland and Laband 2002) than merely participating in local elections once every four years. Notably, most citizens only want to actively engage and participate with regard to topics and issues they are (highly) interested in. In other words, they do not want to express their opinions on a broad range of issues, but merely on policy issues that energize and activate them to join the discussion. In all other topics, they trust (the expertise and opinions of) "others" to create effective policy solutions. The key challenge for democratic governance is how expertise and political interest, unevenly distributed across many citizens and policy issues, can be effectively exploited to the benefit of policy development and decisions.

38. We used a similar pragmatist and outcome-oriented approach when applying circular principles in a variety of educational settings (Romme and Eltink 2002; Romme 2003b; Romme and Putzel 2003). For example, in developing and managing an undergraduate Business Studies program at Tilburg University, a circular structure served to connect student teams to the next higher circle with a single linking pin. The decision rule of informed consent could be used throughout this system, but we had to develop a practical solution in the area of double linking. Rather than applying the principle of double linking directly, we created a circular flow of information, learning, and power by means of a single link (i.e. team leader) who was nominated by the team but appointed by the next higher circle (Romme and Eltink 2002).

39. Sources: Mays (2013) with regard to David Allen Company; Groth (2015) with regard to Zappos; www.consciousboulder.com/content/holacracy retrieved February 25, 2015; "How Medium is building a new kind of company with no managers," retrieved March 11, 2015 from http://firstround.com/review/How-Medium-is-building-a-new-kind-of-company-with-no-managers/.

40. For example, Phil Caravaggio, co-founder of Precision Nutrition:

> When we first started toying with the idea of adopting Holacracy, we were 25 people and millions of dollars in sales. We've grown, in both people and revenue, somewhere between 25% and 50% every year since our inception. Then something just felt like it wasn't going to work anymore, like there were things duct-taped together. The burden was too high for me, and for our other co-founders, and for all the people who were in the organization at that time. Holacracy has propagated leadership throughout the organization, not in the managerial sense, like you're the manager so now you technically lead a group of people. It's given people a say in the governance and tactical meetings, and just in general knowing who does what and having a framework for resolving tensions.

Source: "Case Study: Precision Nutrition, retrieved from http://holacracy.org/case-studies/case-study-precision-nutrition March 12, 2015.

41. Source: "Case study: Precision Nutrition," retrieved from: http://holacracy.org/-case-studies/case-study-precision-nutrition March 12, 2015.

42. TSG has also adopted a legal construction that makes the organization own itself, as explained earlier in this chapter. The contractual relations between TSG global and its divisions (e.g. in the US, Germany, or Australia) are based on franchising agreements; the circular structure with informed consent as decision rule for policy making and double linking between circles prevents the relationship between franchisor (TSG global) and franchisee (division) from becoming asymmetric. An independent arm of TSG provides certification to practitioners, to assure users and other external stakeholders about the capacities of experts that draw on this body of knowledge (TSG 2012). This certificate can be obtained by anyone who has finished practical training in the application of sociocratic circular organizing, to a degree that assures their competences in implementing, teaching or facilitating it in their professional environment (source: www.sociocracy.com).

43. Source: "The Holacracy Backstory," retrieved from http://holacracy.org/backstory March 30, 2015. The website http://holacracy.org provides the most recent version of the Holacracy Constitution as well as many other resources regarding holacracy.

6

Validating Circular Organizing

Introduction

Circular organizing has initially developed outside mainstream management thought.[1] This raises questions about how mainstream theorizing can be applied to validate circular organizing. Given the limited theorizing in this area, this chapter will also seek to develop a model of circular organizing as a system for distributed management and learning.

Bertrand Russell once argued that the most fundamental concept in social science "is Power, in the same sense in which Energy is the fundamental concept in physics. . . . power, like energy, must be regarded as continually passing from any one of its forms into any other, and it should be the business of social science to seek the laws of such transformations" (Russell 1938: 12–14). The notion of "power" may therefore be one of the most fundamental constructs in management studies (cf. Pfeffer 2013). This chapter serves to theorize about circular organizing in terms of power and related constructs such as ownership, authority, and hierarchy. Generally speaking, the professional use of "power," in all its forms and varieties, might be what ignites and sustains virtuous interactions between the purpose, knowledge, behavior, and expectation levels in management practice and scholarship. While pioneers in circular organizing have been developing and trying out responses to fundamental challenges in the area of power, the conventional wisdom about management appears to marginalize any opportunity for professionalizing management in the critical area of power, authority, and ownership.

A related finding arising from this chapter is that the professionalization quest calls for a deeper understanding of management as a body of instrumental knowledge (Aristotle's techne) as a missing link in the current academic body of knowledge in this area. In this respect, the case of circular organizing illustrates how dialogical, representational, and instrumental knowledge complement each other.

Theorizing about Circular Organizing

Circular organizing has developed relatively independently from mainstream management theorizing. This section outlines findings from several studies conducted to theoretically validate the circular organizing approach.

Hierarchy and Circularity

One of my first attempts to theoretically come to grips with circular organizing, published in Romme (1996), was crafted as a contribution to the debate between authors blaming administrative hierarchy for many problems in organizations and those defending hierarchies as indispensable, especially in managing large organizations.[2]

In this respect, Tom Peters, Peter Senge, and others have criticized hierarchy as being a major obstacle to the kind of learning processes that seem better supported by team-like, non-hierarchical structures (Peters 1987; Mills 1991; Iannello 1992; Senge 2006). By contrast, others argue that hierarchy itself is not the problem, but the way it is used as an organizational system (Carley 1992; Manz and Sims 1987; Jaques 1990). Jaques (1990) even praised hierarchy as the only effective organizational form for employing large numbers of people and yet preserving unambiguous accountability for the work they do.

HIERARCHIES AND TEAMS AS INFORMATION SYSTEMS

The two positions in this debate can be synthesized as follows. First, hierarchies and teams can be conceived as ideal-typical "information systems," human systems that process, transform, and create information; these systems therefore not only process and manipulate data (like computers) but also attribute meaning to these data.[3] This conceptualization serves to define teams as ideal-typical *horizontal*, or heterarchical, information systems in which free and creative exploration of complex and subtle issues is possible. By contrast, a hierarchical structure is the ideal-typical *vertical* information system that enables large organizations to filter environmental noise and information into chunks that they can effectively handle (Simon 1973; Jaques 1996; Ethiraj and Levinthal 2004).

This conceptualization of team and hierarchy as highly different but complementary information systems implies teamwork does not crowd out hierarchy. For any organization that is larger than a single team (say ≤ 8 people), both hierarchy and teams are therefore essential. Team learning serves to absorb and generate novel information, whereas hierarchy provides opportunities to filter, process, store, and exploit important learning results. In terms of the tacit–explicit knowledge dimension discussed in Chapter 3, one can also argue that hierarchies largely operate on explicit knowledge, whereas teams are better equipped to deal with various kinds of tacit knowledge.

CIRCULARITY

This conceptualization of hierarchy and team as ideal-typical information systems raises the question how they can co-exist and mutually reinforce each other. Here, *circularity* involves the capacity to switch between hierarchy and teamwork as complementary information systems. Ackoff (1981) and Nonaka (1994) have coined similar notions of circularity. For example, Nonaka (1994) talks about "middle-up-down" management involving circular processes that operate as a "hypertext organization" which allows users to search for large quantities of text, data, and graphics by means of user-friendly interfaces. The core feature of the hypertext organization is the ability to switch between the various contexts of information, each context having its own distinctive way of organizing processes. Thus, self-organizing activities of teams are indispensable for generating new information as well as acquiring "deep" knowledge through intensive, focused search. On the other hand, hierarchy is more efficient and effective for exploiting and accumulating information. According to Nonaka (1994), the circular hypertext organization therefore combines the efficiency and stability of a hierarchical organization with the dynamism of the flat team organization.[4]

HIERARCHY

A key insight arising from circular organizing is that the "hierarchy" construct can be used and applied in multiple ways (cf. Van Olffen and Romme 1995). Hierarchy is traditionally defined in terms of a vertical sequence of authority, status, and/or power (Pfeffer 1992), in other words, a chain of command in which leaders can impose their will on people at lower levels. This definition provides an easy target for those criticizing hierarchical structures. The contradiction between vertical-hierarchical and horizontal-heterarchical structures can be overcome by reframing *hierarchy* as a sequence of layers of accountability. This sequence involves different degrees of abstraction, through which knowledge and information are filtered, transformed, and communicated (Jaques 1990; Nonaka 1994). This construct of hierarchy is used in circular organizing, but can be generalized to many other settings (e.g. Simon 1973; Ethiraj and Levinthal 2004).

Bounded Rationality and Circular Organizing

The management and governance systems of any large organization needs to be (nearly) decomposed into relatively small units of people. Simon's notion of near-decomposability (discussed in Chapter 5) is closely linked to the more fundamental idea of *bounded rationality* that he developed to understand how individual people deal with the limitations of both knowledge and cognitive capacity. Simon argued that the rationality of individual decision-making is limited (or bounded) by the information available, the limitations of individual cognition, and the time available to decide. Decision makers can therefore only seek a satisfactory solution, because they lack the ability and resources to arrive at the optimal one (Simon 1955, 1991b).

The idea of bounded rationality has generated an abundance of studies in the area of organizational learning, incremental and local search, decision-making heuristics, and related organizational and managerial phenomena (e.g. Cyert and March 1963; Tversky and Kahneman 1981; Levitt and March 1988; Stuart and Podolny 1996; Tisdell 1996; Rubinstein 1998; Gigerenzer et al. 2011). Moreover, several scholars have sought to develop the implications of bounded rationality for organizational architecture and design (e.g. Ethiraj and Levinthal 2004; Grant 1996). In line with Simon (1973), these studies have identified the pivotal role of hierarchies in coordinating the actions of many individuals, while also deliberately moving away from hierarchies of *authority* that reflect

> the organizational antecedents of business corporations: churches existed to impose the authority of God, government departments to impose the authority of the monarch or (in democracies) the people, while the effectiveness of armies and navies required the authority to send men to their deaths. (Grant 1996: 117)

This calls for organizational hierarchies that permit near-decomposability (Simon 2002), enhance resilience (Välikangas 2010), promote self-management and empowerment (Stewart and Manz 1995), and facilitate a fundamental redistribution of decision authority (Buchanan and Tullock 1962; Grant 1996). While many entrepreneurs and other pioneers have experimented with solutions to this major challenge (e.g. Ackoff 1994; Quarter 2000; Nayar 2010; Erickson 2014; Laloux 2014), the emergence of circular organizing might be offering the first systematic solution that is well-codified as well as applied in a growing number of organizations.

Circular organizing draws on a circular hierarchy without an ultimate authority, which is nearly decomposed into relatively small units of people (with the double links preventing the system from becoming completely decomposable) that collaborate and decide by informed consent. The circular nature of this organizational architecture is firmly grounded in the notion of search, as demonstrated in the previous chapter. As such, it accommodates local search in the proximity of the current expertise and knowledge of the incumbent circle (Simon 1955; Stuart and Podolny 1996), while connecting each circle's search to other circles in ways that exploit all benefits of a hierarchical structure without its usual downside in the form of the abuse of authority and power (cf. Grant 1996).

There is not yet a robust body of evidence regarding the performance and resilience of circular organizations compared to their non-circular counterparts, but the available data suggest the principles and instantiations of circular organizing are very promising. Overall, circular organizing may provide an organizational design and system that respects and exploits bounded rationality, rather than being crippled by it.

Power and Circularity

Many social scientists have called for a deeper understanding of how power can be shaped and controlled in organizational settings (e.g. Foucault 1978; Habermas 1998; Flyvbjerg 2001).[5] The case of circular organizing can be used to respond to this call, by developing the notion of circularity of power in the context of the broader literature on control, power, and related constructs. The analysis in the remainder of this section also extends the earlier argument on the complementarity of teams and hierarchy.

CONVENTIONAL FORMS OF CONTROL

Established forms of control, such as direct supervision and performance control, play a central role in administrative theory and practice (Tannenbaum 1967; Ouchi 1979; Daft and Macintosh 1984). Conventional control practices draw on vertical communications, permanent constellations of people (e.g. departments, units), and hierarchical structures (Hedlund 1994). Conventional control may be necessary and inevitable for organizing large numbers of people and preserving unambiguous accountability (Jaques 1990).

However, this approach is also subject to significant difficulties. Important information from lower levels, which could prevent a bad decision from being made by top management, is easily excluded from consideration (Ouchi 1981). Other implications or side-effects of traditional control may involve, for example, employees becoming demoralized, less cooperative, less satisfied, less productive, alienated from their work, and harassed and terrorized (O'Connell Davidson 1994; Leymann 1996; Vartia 1996; Van Fleet and Van Fleet 2014). Other unintended effects are whistleblowing employees, middle and top managers becoming indifferent to the fate of others in the organization, and top managers feeling isolated and lonely at the top (Kets de Vries 1989; Miceli and Near 1989; Rothschild and Miethe 1994; Jackall 2010; De Janasz and Peipert 2015).

SELF-ORGANIZING FORMS OF CONTROL

A variety of managerial innovations have led to other forms of organizational control that may be fundamentally different from traditional ones. These alternative forms of control include, for example, autonomous work groups

(Emery and Thorsrud 1976; Emery 1980), self-designing organizations (Hedberg et al. 1976), self-managing teams (Manz and Sims 1987) and cluster organizing (Mills 1991). In contrast to their traditional counterparts, these forms of control emphasize lateral rather than vertical communications, temporary rather than permanent constellations of people, and heterarchical rather than hierarchical structures (Hedberg et al. 1976; Hedlund 1994).

These forms of control are to a large extent self-organizing because they rely on spontaneous communication and informal cooperation, and the formation of consensus on and commitment to group objectives (Stacey 1995). However, self-organizing control is also subject to substantial difficulties because the nature of self-organizing processes tends to inhibit external control efforts (Vaughan 1983); external leadership of self-organizing units is therefore particularly problematic, in the sense that leaders are expected to lead others to (learn to) lead themselves (Stewart and Manz 1995).

Self-organizing and traditional forms of control are widely believed to be inconsistent and incompatible (e.g. Mulder 1971; Manz and Sims 1987; Dahl 1989; Hedlund 1994; Böhm et al. 2010). As a result, self-organizing control has shown greater diffusion at the level of rhetoric than of practice, in a world in which traditional control continues to prevail (Stewart and Manz 1995; Loorbach 2010).

DOMINATION AND SELF-DETERMINATION

The circularity notion introduced earlier provides the opportunity to explore how and when traditional and self-organizing types of control can co-exist. Building on the definition developed earlier, *circularity* involves the co-existence and integration of hierarchical and self-organizing control, based on the capacity to switch between these two modes of control. This is obviously a highly academic definition. I will therefore develop this definition further, by drawing on domination and self-determination as two archetypical notions of control and power. The key idea here is that the antagonism between traditional and self-organizing control arises from the fundamental difference between domination and self-determination as notions of power.

Traditional forms of control are based on *domination*, that is the capacity (or power) of one actor to carry out his own will despite the resistance of other people, for example, to get these people to do things they would not otherwise do (Perrow 1986; Clegg 1989; Pfeffer 1992). By contrast, self-organizing control, such as in the case of self-managing teams, is based on a different concept of power, the idea of *self-determination*. In general, self-determination involves the capacity to act autonomously. On an individual level, this involves utilizing one's capacity to choose how to satisfy one's needs (Deci 1980). On a collective level, people are self-determining when they have the capacity to negotiate, decide, and act together voluntarily (Dahl 1989; Emery 1980). Many empirical studies show that self-determination has important motivating properties, and that being denied the opportunity for self-determination is likely to result in feelings of insecurity as well as loss of motivation and well-being (Atchison 1991; Hartley et al. 1991; Lai 2011).

In an organizational context, the difference between these two concepts of power also reflects a difference in contractual notions. In this respect, the concept of domination is reflected in employment contracts, which can be individual or collective in nature, and either tacit or written in form. As such, the employment contract implies an unequal division of authority: the employee sells (the right to decide over) his or her labor power to the employer who in exchange agrees to compensate the employee by way of certain monetary or non-monetary rewards (Knudsen 1995). In this respect, there is a clearly defined ultimate authority which is based on, or derived from, the legal ownership of the organization (Hansmann 1996). By contrast, the concept of self-determination is linked to the idea of a partnership contract, which can be either tacit or written in form. Partnership arrangements imply an equal division of authority, and thus the division between "employer" and "employee" ceases to exist (Hansmann 1996). A single ultimate authority is absent, because the partners share ownership of the organization.[6]

Generally speaking, both self-determination and domination are universal and archetypical human concerns. In this respect, expressions such as "it's up to you" and "get in control" (e.g. of your life, mood, kids, or dog) are almost as common as phrases such as "good morning" in most cultures and societies (Argyris and Schön 1978; Deci 1980; Clegg 1989; Hofstede and Hofstede 2005). Self-determination is essential for individual people as well as relatively small groups dealing with open-ended, dynamic situations in which new problems and issues frequently emerge. And domination is inevitable as the more effective control strategy in large groups facing rather predictable or stable situations (Stacey 1995). Therefore, effective governance and control systems will incorporate both domination and self-determination as fundamental concerns. Table 6.1 summarizes some of the key differences and implications between domination and self-determination as archetypical notions of power.

CIRCULARITY OF POWER

In turn, the notions of domination and self-determination now serve to define, and more deeply understand, what *circularity of power* is. Instantiations of circular organizing, reviewed in the previous chapter, suggest circularity of power manifests itself as power flowing upward as easily as downward in the organization. But the argument thus far in this section implies this circularity

Table 6.1. Domination, self-determination, and circularity of power

	Domination	Self-determination	Circularity of power
Definition	Capacity of one participant to carry out his/her own will despite resistance of other people involved	Capacity to act autonomously (as an individual or as a group)	The extent to which power flows both upward and downward in the organization, which in turn is determined by the capacity to continually switch between domination and self-determination
Contractual notion	Employment	Partnership	Each employee/partner is member of at least one circle
Authority and ownership	Ultimate authority is clearly defined and based on, or derived from, legal ownership	There is no ultimate authority, because ownership is shared among participants/ partners	Each circle member can participate directly or through representation in all policy decisions that affect him/her; the ability to make and implement decisions that affect no one other than the decision makers; organization owns itself; the top circle includes representatives of all key stakeholders
Organizational Structure	Hierarchical: vertical sequence of layers of accountability	Heterarchical: cooperation based on equivalence and mutual adjustment	Hierarchy is used to define levels of accountability and manage operations; heterarchy prevails within each circle when making policy
Control	Top down control	Collective self-regulation	Collective self-organization in circles is the main mode of control (safeguarded by informed consent as decision rule); clear accountability is main mode of control for operational processes delegated to functional leaders
Communication	Vertical communication is strongly preferred	Horizontal communication is strongly preferred	Vertical/lateral communication takes place between/within circles connected by double links
Context	Large number of people (in permanent constellations) in a predictable, rather stable context	Relatively small number of people (in temporary constellations) in open-ended, dynamic context	Circularity supports switching between (responses to) predictable/stable and open-ended/dynamic settings

Source: Adapted from Romme (1999).

arises from the capacity to continually switch between domination and self-determination as fundamental organizational and human concerns. Table 6.1 demonstrates how circularity of power synthesizes aspects of domination and self-determination. Some of the most salient dimensions are discussed here.

For example, the notions of employment and partnership can be synthesized as follows. Each employee or manager has a (tenured or untenured) employment contract, which gives him or her direct access to at least one circle's policy-making process in which all circle members participate as equivalent partners. Each circle has its own decision domain, which includes the decision authority to untie existing employment relationships.[7] This suggests that the circular model goes beyond the contractual notions of employment and partnership (see Table 6.1). The employment contract as an essential element of any market economy is used throughout the company, while the notion of partnership is realized to a large extent in circles in which equivalence in decision making is safeguarded by the decision rule of informed consent and the double linkages between circles.

The implications of circular organizing for the construct of ownership and the legal form of the organization were explored in Chapter 5. An important function of organizational and corporate law is to allow for the creation of a juridical person, or legal entity, that can serve as the signatory to contracts (Hansmann 1996). Almost all juridical persons available by national law in Europe, the Americas, and elsewhere are based on an exclusive (group of) owner(s) who formally has the ultimate authority to exercise discretion over the organization's assets, funds and employees: the patrons in the case of a partnership, the investors in the case of a business corporation, the producers or consumers in the case of a cooperative corporation, and so forth (Hansmann 1996).

The idea of ownership is less clearly defined in the foundation and similar legal entities (e.g. nonprofit corporation): those controlling a foundation act as its owner, or ultimate authority, but only as long as no profits are distributed to the controlling persons. In this respect, the "nondistribution constraint" in a typical foundation's constitution requires the owners to have a strictly non-financial interest in the organization. In any case, entrepreneurs, investors, and other stakeholders cannot shape their commercial venture as a foundation. As a result, the portfolio of legal entities available in the Western world does not include a legal entity that naturally supports circularity of power and control among investors, directors, managers, employees, and other stakeholders. As observed in the previous chapter, circular organizations therefore adopt a hybrid legal solution; this type of solution is, of course, not likely to facilitate the adoption and diffusion of circular forms of organizing.

Reflexivity, Whistleblowing, and Resistance to Change

Circularity of power may provide the structural reflexivity that is missing in many organizations. Management and control systems in these organizations are essentially domination-based, with the idea and spirit of partnership merely cultivated in small pockets of the organization, such as board rooms and project teams. Earlier in this chapter, I observed that top managers in these organizations easily become prisoners of their leadership positions, employees cannot blow the whistle in a legitimate manner, and so forth. By creating a system of interconnected circles, both bosses and employees can affect policy decision making, while different levels of accountability and responsibility are respected.

As such, the notion of circularity of power raises fundamental questions about widely used constructs such as "whistleblowing" and "resistance to change." These two theoretical constructs only make sense when power is explicitly or implicitly conceived from the perspective of domination, as defined earlier. In organizational settings where circularity prevails, both constructs lose the negative connotation they tend to have in mainstream management thinking. By making power flow circularly, whistleblowers and opponents of change become redefined in constructive roles that are contingent on the particular context: agents of change, innovators, idea champions, rescuers, and so forth.

Notions such as resistance to change and whistleblowing therefore become largely irrelevant in the case of circular organizing because any opposition becomes, and is perceived as, an essential and legitimate component of the dialogical processes of diverging and converging toward informed consent. In a system where the power of argument prevails over the power of rank and position, opposition and counter-argumentation are key mechanisms in improving the quality of policy decisions and thereby enhancing the viability of the entire system.

More generally speaking, the case of circular organizing raises fundamental questions about widely used constructs, or jargon, in management. Pragmatism as the philosophical basis of any profession, discussed in Chapter 2, implies all management vocabulary is created and sustained by professionals dealing with particular challenges or problems. The case of circular organizing illustrates that management scholars and practitioners, as members of an emerging profession, should not take constructs such as whistleblowing for granted.

Ambiguous versus Unambiguous Instantiations of Authority and Power

Circular organizing has not yet been successfully introduced in publicly traded corporations or large established cooperative firms, as observed in

Chapter 5. One intuitive explanation might be that these organizations simply resist a fundamental redistribution of power and authority. However, the successful implementation of circular organizing in fast-growing technology start-ups and cooperative start-ups like MyWheels suggests otherwise. These cases suggest it is not so much the lack of vision and leadership that inhibits any transformation toward circularity, but rather the highly ambiguous instantiations of authority and power created. In the latter setting, it may be almost impossible to rewire the system toward circular organizing, simply because a single (group of) agent(s) with proper decision-making authority must explicitly support and enable such a fundamental transformation. This point can be elaborated by distinguishing two initial situations in the case of an investor-owned corporation: the initial setting where authority and power are unambiguous, and one where authority and power are highly ambiguous.

UNAMBIGUOUS AUTHORITY AND POWER

In the first setting, the shareholders formally and informally constitute the final authority of the organization: this is the case for most privately owned corporations, which can involve companies owned by a single entrepreneur, several entrepreneurs as business partners, a small number of external investors, or a combination of these. In all these instances, the initial setting is clear: the shareholders have the ultimate authority to decide whether or not to engage in a transformation toward a circular structure. While this may be a major challenge for some shareholders, Endenburg Elektrotechniek and several other companies have made this transformation successfully; in these cases, the implementation strategy outlined in the previous chapter has been instrumental in getting shareholders and directors actively engaged and committed to this transformation.[8]

AMBIGUOUS AUTHORITY AND POWER

In this initial setting, shareholders legally constitute the final authority, but in practice their authority and influence is severely restrained. This is the case in many publicly owned and traded corporations. The corporate constitution formally implies that shareholders appoint directors and can then hold them accountable via the general meeting of shareholders. However, the same constitution and especially many by-laws serve to severely restrict shareholders' authority, and instead empower directors (who appoint executives) to actually run the corporation.[9] This separation of legal ownership and actual control of the corporation creates a highly complex and unclear distribution of power between shareholders, directors, and executives, in which typically the directors and executives in charge have a lot of discretion to pursue their own interests (Jensen and Meckling 1976). In this highly ambiguous setting, shareholders can only use their authority incidentally, for example to replace directors when financial performance is far below their expectations. However, no one has the authority to decide on the transformation toward a circular structure; moreover, no executive, director, or shareholder will ever feel compelled to call for a transformation that is very likely to fail.[10]

IMPLICATIONS

The analysis of these two initial settings suggest that any bottom-up initiatives toward circular organizing, such as in the case of Royal Dutch Shell, are not likely to be taken up and adopted elsewhere in the organization. In this respect, directors and executives of publicly traded corporations appear to share a reservoir of collective (tacit) knowledge that essentially tells everyone "not to rock the boat" by questioning the distribution of power between shareholders, directors, executives, and other stakeholders such as employees.[11] Of course, the highly ambiguous distribution of power and authority in many public corporations does not only demotivate initiatives toward circular organizing, but also any other kind of organizational transformation that will fundamentally redistribute power and authority (e.g. Ridley-Duff and Bull 2014). Any senior staff member or executive who, against the odds, openly questions these highly "delicate" issues, will—almost by definition—end up with only one option: to leave the organization.[12]

The observation that publicly traded corporations are too often unable to transform themselves and adapt to new challenges is not new. Economic and legal experts alike have argued that the publicly held corporation has outlived its usefulness in many sectors of the economy (e.g. Jensen 1989; Bratton and Wachter 2010). The literature on property rights and ownership has also long acknowledged the need to reassess the role of (investor) owners in the publicly traded corporation. A key idea here is that financial or economic ownership should not imply exclusive ownership of the corporation (Munzer 1990; Donaldson and Preston 1995). The circular organizing approach illustrates how financial ownership can be embedded in a configuration in which the corporation legally owns itself, authority and power is distributed throughout the organization, and representatives of shareholders therefore participate in its governance based on informed consent.

Toward a Model of Circular Organizing

Based on the findings arising from the discovery and validation of circular organizing in the previous and this chapter, a theoretical model can now be developed. Central in this model are the causal conditions that create and sustain the capacity for distributing management and learning throughout the organization, which in turn promotes the organization's viability and performance. Figure 6.1 pictures this model.

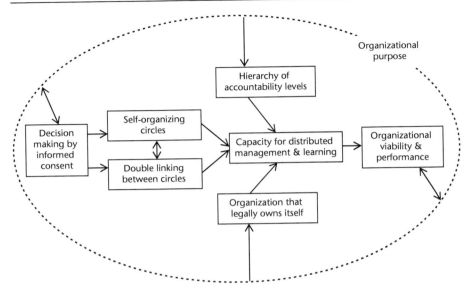

Figure 6.1. Model of circular organizing

Overall, the model in this figure assumes there is a clear organizational purpose (e.g. mission and long-term objectives), regardless of whether it is commercial or not in nature. A clear statement of purpose talks about what kind of value it seeks to create for a particular group of clients, customers, end-users, or other key stakeholders. This purpose infuses a system that distributes management and learning, and therefore authority and power, throughout the organization. The top circle defines and, if necessary, adapts the formal statement of the organization's purpose. In turn organizational purpose informs discussions and decisions about policy in all circles, in which the power of argument prevails over the power of rank or vote, due to the decision rule of informed consent.

Moreover, organizational purpose also informs the differentiation of the organization's hierarchy into different levels of abstraction and accountability; for example, any organizational purpose implying a broad portfolio of products and services will require a longer sequence of accountability levels than a single product offering. Similarly, any organizational purpose defined in value created for clients, users, or customers might also motivate a search for a legal ownership arrangement in which the organization "owns itself" and any exclusive claims (e.g. of shareholders) are avoided.

The "capacity for distributed management and learning" is at the heart of the model in Figure 6.1. This capacity arises from self-organizing circles as well as the creation of double linkages between these circles. In turn, these processes are driven and informed by the practice of making decisions on policy—including the election of delegates and functional leaders—by informed consent.

In addition, the praxis of distributed management and learning in circles is enhanced when all participants make (new) sense of hierarchy as a sequence of levels of accountability. The analysis earlier in this chapter also suggests the hypothesis that organizations that own themselves are more likely to sustain their capacity for distributed management over a long period of time, compared to organizations for which a (group of) legal owner(s) at some point in time can decide to have its own interest prevail over the interests and purposes of the organization at large.

Finally, the model in Figure 6.1 entails the hypothesis that a higher capacity for distributed management and learning will positively affect the performance and long-term viability of the organization, and vice versa.

Has Circular Organizing Been Sufficiently Validated?

The framework for a professional body of knowledge developed in Chapter 3 suggests that validation can be conducted regarding at least five "outputs": values, constructs, models, principles, and instantiations. Most scholarly work pertaining to circular organizing has been in the area of principles and instantiations, drawing on case studies (Romme and Reijmer 1997; Romme 1998, 1999; Romme and Endenburg 2006; Romme and Damen 2007). Other work has served to further develop and theorize key constructs such as circularity, ownership, authority, and hierarchy (Romme 1996, 1999), triple loop learning (Romme and Van Witteloostuijn 1999), and informed consent and decomposability (Romme 2004). A number of these studies and their findings were discussed earlier.

Notably, the population of organizations applying the circular approach is still too small and diverse to effectively allow survey-based research or other systematic comparative approaches. One of the few attempts in this area is the survey by Buck (2003), who finds that employees of Dutch organizations applying the circular approach express a statistically significant higher level of organizational commitment than their counterparts in other organizations. In general, however, it is almost impossible to disentangle the effect of any organizational method or intervention from the effect of many other conditions and interventions in relatively small samples of organizations. In this respect, circular principles are often applied in combination with other methods and principles, for example in the area of quality management or balanced scorecards. Thus, a systematic comparison between organizations applying circular organizing with those not applying it is only effective when both populations are large enough to be able to assume that all other (latent) variables affect both populations in a similar way.[13]

Few attempts have been undertaken to validate the dimension of values (as research output in Table 3.1) in circular organizing. Endenburg (1974, 1998) defined several key values such as equivalence and psychological safety, and his early exposure to these values has been critical to the development of circular organizing (Quarter 2000). However, as observed earlier, all key ideas and principles of circular organizing can also be derived from cybernetics and systems theory. Interestingly, the work of several political philosophers discussed in Chapter 2 suggests the (ideal) moral structure of organizations and their management systems is a matter of elevated utilitarian thinking, in which morality is equated with collective maximization. The circular organizing model represents such an ideal structure, inferred from a set of basic ideas about search, adaptation, and collaboration.

The limited number of managers and organizations that has been adopting the circular management approach suggests it can be further developed in many ways. This future growth and diffusion of circular management can take place at the level of values, constructs, models, principles, and/or instantiations. At the level of instantiations only, the initial model developed by Endenburg is not likely to be adopted widely, in view of the barriers it is facing in the area of vocabulary, ownership, and legal entities. In Chapter 5, I discussed ongoing work in applying and adapting circular principles in the area of public administration as well as the holacratic interpretation of these principles in a growing number of technology-driven firms. These examples suggest that future growth and diffusion of the circular model appears to be contingent on the further development and renewal of key values, constructs, and principles as well as the preliminary theoretical model outlined earlier.

Implications for the Professionalization Quest

The professionalization of disciplines such as law and civil engineering has resulted in establishing conditions and regulations for entry to the profession as well as sanctions and penalties regarding unprofessional conduct. This professionalization approach, says Barker (2010), only applies to professional activities such as those of lawyers who draw on well-defined expertise,

> whereas the manager is a jack-of-all-trades and master of none—the antithesis of the professional. . . . The lawyer writes a contract and charges for her time; her work is finite. Even when she has an ongoing relationship with a corporate client, her contribution is always a specialized input, measurable in terms of the amount billed. But the manager is responsible for the combined value generated by all inputs to the firm. Inputs are managed at varying stages in a product's life cycle, and at any given time products are at different stages in that life cycle—meaning the manager's job is never done. The manager's contribution is inherently difficult

to measure and has an indeterminable impact on a variety of outcomes. The difference between the lawyer's world and the manager's is rather like that between the value of a single revenue transaction and the value of a company as a whole. As a completed output with a monetary value, the revenue transaction is relatively objective. A company's share price is subjective—dependent on imprecise assumptions concerning a range of inputs, and ultimately a best guess about the future. (Barker 2010: 57)

Barker rightly points out that the current state of the management discipline is the antithesis of the professional. Indeed, it has not yet produced a robust and consistent body of knowledge. In this respect, the circular management approach suggests that any successful effort to professionalize management has to cover the entire territory of knowledge mapped in Chapter 3. For one, that means that both creative discovery and scientific validation are essential to the professionalization agenda. As also observed in Chapter 3, too few management scholars engage in the discovery side of their profession, which makes real progress in the quest for professionalism almost entirely dependent on pioneering practitioners such as Gerard Endenburg and Brian Robertson. Notably, empirical validation of theoretical constructs and models is critical to the evidence-based nature of the profession, but without discovery there is hardly anything to validate.

Representational, Dialogical, and Instrumental Knowledge

The available body of knowledge about power draws on description, explanation, interpretation, and critical evaluation in terms of key constructs, models, and values—that is, *episteme* and *phronesis* in the upper cells of Table 3.1 in Chapter 3. Most studies focus on discovering and validating constructs and models of how specific aspects of authority and power are used (Dahl 1989; Courpasson 2000; Ethiraj and Levinthal 2004; Lukes 2005). In addition, the literature on phronesis calls for uncovering and assessing values in relation to how power is distributed and rationalized (e.g. Clegg 1989; Flyvbjerg 1998).

The case of circular organizing suggests instrumental knowledge, Aristotle's *techne*, is also of critical importance. The engineering background of people like Endenburg and Robertson appears to provide a mindset aimed at developing and trying out principles and instantiations.[14] This mindset serves to develop synthetic action-oriented principles and engage in the instantation of these principles and their underlying constructs, models and values (i.e. the two lowest rows in Table 3.1). For the professionalization quest in management, instrumental knowledge is obviously as important as dialogical reflection and representational knowledge. The circular organizing case suggests that any professional engagement in the area of management and power will have to incorporate each of the three types of knowledge identified by Aristotle, as the argument in Chapter 3 also implies.

Pioneers in circular organizing have engaged with fundamental questions and challenges in the area of authority, hierarchy, ownership, and power. As such, the conventional wisdom about management appears to actually marginalize many opportunities for professionalizing management, especially in the area of management as technology. The highly ambiguous and complex configuration of ownership and decision authority in many publicly traded corporations, discussed earlier, is a case in point. Similarly, the vast majority of management scholars have also been marginalizing issues of power (as observed by Abegglen and Stalk 1989; Flyvbjerg 1998; Pfeffer 2013; Ridley-Duff and Bull 2014). In this regard, management studies has apparently not changed much since Van Maanen and Barley (1984: 347) observed that research in this area too often "represents a sort of effete innocence which speaks of attitudes, values, supervision, structure, goals, rules, ethos, culture, and communication, but not of conflict and power." The next chapter further explores these fundamental challenges.

Notably, my argument here does not boil down to some "conspiracy theory," a secret scheme of powerful agents seeking to prevent the further professionalization of management. Rather, the current intellectual and institutional stasis of the field of management appears to arise from the interaction and co-evolution of the purpose, knowledge, behavior, and expectation mechanisms in management practice and its scholarship, as argued in Chapter 1. There is no deliberate strategy that has created this stasis. However, the current stalemate will require a purposeful multi-level effort, sustained over several decades, to significantly grow the level of professionalism of management beyond its current adolescent state.

Concluding Remarks

This chapter kicked off with a quote from Bertrand Russell, who argued power is the most fundamental concept in management, similar to energy as the central notion in physics. The emergence of circular organizing is to some extent a "proof of concept" of Russell's idea, in the sense that it demonstrates power is a promising pivotal concept in the quest for professionalism in management.

In this respect, the circular organizing model provides an interesting response to calls for dialogical systems focusing on problem-solving and social experimentation to replace an unsatisfactory present with more satisfactory and hopeful futures (e.g. Habermas 1998; Rorty 1999). Interestingly, this response comes from a somewhat unexpected source: management professionals with engineering backgrounds. This suggests the need for management scholars to embrace the notion of management as technology, or Aristotle's techne. Instrumental knowledge appears to be as essential to the professionalization agenda as its representational and phronetic counterparts. Of course, the notion of instrumental knowledge is not a new one. In fact, the first generations of pioneers and thought leaders in management focused on this type of knowledge (Wren and Bedeian 2008), as management consultants and other reflective practitioners today still do. Therefore, a key challenge in the quest for professionalism is establishing an instrumental perspective on management as a technology, for example for distributing leadership and learning throughout the organization.

Notes

1. This chapter partly draws on ideas and arguments previously published in: A. G. L. Romme (1996), "A note on the hierarchy-team debate," *Strategic Management Journal* 17: 411–17; A. G. L. Romme (1999), "Domination, self-determination and circular organizing," *Organization Studies* 20: 801–32; and A. G. L. Romme and G. Endenburg (2006), "Construction principles and design rules in the case of circular design," *Organization Science* 17: 287–97.
2. This section is largely based on Romme (1996).
3. As such, I argued that teams and hierarchy are the two *primary* "human" information systems in any organization. Notably, there are many *secondary* systems and devices (e.g. rules, operating routines, IT systems) that merely manipulate and process data, rather than also attributing human meaning to these data. Teams and hierarchies thus constitute the key human systems that produce or use these secondary systems (Romme 1996).
4. A few decades earlier, Likert (1961) developed the so-called participative group organization, also known as *system 4* organization, which has been very influential in setting up new production plants in the US, particularly in the form of joint ventures with Japanese partners (Likert 1976). The participative group organization involves a multiple, overlapping team structure with every team making decisions by consensus. Likert argued that this kind of organization would promote upward feedback, while recognizing the importance of hierarchy (Likert 1961, 1976).
5. This section is largely based on Romme (1999).
6. The concept of self-determination is also inextricable from the idea of democracy, and, following Dahl, self-determination in its pure form would make domination impossible or at least illegitimate "since any group facing coercion on any matter could demand and through secession gain autonomy" (Dahl 1989: 196–7). The antagonism between domination and self-determination as concepts of power may therefore help to explain why many attempts to create higher participation levels by way of, for example, T-groups, quality of working life programs, work councils,

quality circles or labor representation at the shopfloor, have failed to produce substantial and sustained increases in participation (e.g. Burawoy 1979; Ledford et al. 1988; Rothstein 1995; Collins 1997; Romme 1997). In fact, non-participation tends to be the modal response of employees to participation programs (Leitko et al. 1985; McCarthy 1989).

7. For detailed descriptions and illustrations of the procedure for disconnecting someone from a circle (work unit), to either reconnect him/her to another circle or lay him/her off from the company all together, see Endenburg (1998) and Romme (1999). Generally speaking, this procedure for untying someone from the circle implies the incumbent employee can participate in the discussion to voice his concerns, but leaves the meeting room before the rest of the circle takes a decision by informed consent; if the circle then decides to untie this person, the next higher circle (if any) will explore whether this employee can be placed in another circle/unit; if that is not possible, the contract with this employee will be terminated. A similar procedure is used when the partners in a professional services firm intend to decide on the (forced) exit of one partner. Note that this synthesis between employment and partnership respects the key principle of "separation of interests" between the two parties in any contract.

8. These initial conditions also enabled Ricardo Semler, as the majority owner of Semco Partners, to implement a radical form of industrial democracy in this Brazilian company (Semler 1993). Semler appears to have maintained his ultimate authority as majority shareholder until today: www.semco.com.br/en/ (retrieved March 11, 2015).

9. This distribution of power and authority and the agency problems arising from it have been widely studied (e.g. Berle and Means 1932; Jensen and Meckling 1976), but never adequately solved. In fact, there is an ongoing debate on whether shareholders of publicly traded corporations should be re-empowered or not (e.g. Charkham and Simpson 1999; Deakin 2014; Kay 2014).

10. Shareholders of publicly traded corporations typically are only interested in the current and expected value of the equity position they have; as a result, the executives and directors (formally appointed by and accountable to the shareholders meeting) will use their discretion and authority to run and (possibly) change the company in ways that do not require any authorization of the shareholders. Any transformation to a circular organization evidently requires such active engagement and authorization of the shareholders.

11. This culture of silence and defensiveness regarding "undiscussable" issues in and around boardrooms has been extensively documented and analyzed by Argyris and his collaborators (e.g. Argyris and Schön 1978; Argyris et al. 1985; Argyris 2004). Other examples of initiatives toward empowerment and self-organization at local levels of the organization, which ultimately fail because managers are unable to effectively delegate decision rights, are described by Foss (2003) and Oetringer and De Monchy (2013).

12. There are many examples of people in publicly traded corporations who question the authority and power of those believed to be in charge, and then decide to leave or are forced to do so. An example is the narrative of Greg Smith, "Why I am leaving

Goldman Sachs," *The New York Times*, March 14, 2012—retrieved from: www.nytimes.com/2012/03/14/opinion/why-i-am-leaving-goldman-sachs.html?

13. Another interesting research question that might inform future work in this area involves the (potentially) ceremonial and ritual nature of instantiations of circular organizing principles (Trice and Beyer 1984; Nijholt and Benders 2007). In other words, what is the level of consistency between the espoused theory of circular organizing and how it actually works in practice (cf. Argyris et al. 1985). Chapter 5 provides some initial evidence regarding this consistency, but this evidence is obviously far from conclusive.

14. Brian Robertson was trained as a software engineer and Gerard Endenburg obtained an undergraduate degree in electrotechnical engineering. Interestingly, Russell Ackoff, who developed another interpretation of circular organizing, first obtained an undergraduate degree in architecture before switching to management studies.

7

Beyond Shareholders and Stakeholders

Introduction

In view of the changing nature of organizations and their management, Kets de Vries and Korotov (2010: 2) advocate a distributed view of leadership that shifts "the focus from the traditional single leader into an intricate and complex web of leaders who possess a range of abilities and experiences necessary to ensure that the leadership function is carried out to the benefit of the wider organization." This call concurs with the case of circular organizing, explored in the two preceding chapters. More broadly speaking, the circular approach to management raises several fundamental questions and dilemmas in the quest for professionalism, which I will address here.

First, I will explore the implications for the notion of leadership as it is widely understood. More specifically, the case of circular organizing suggests a more professional approach to management needs to go beyond established notions of leadership. The antagonism between the conventional wisdom on leadership and the notion of distributed leadership is discussed in the next section.

Subsequently, I return to shareholder value maximization and multi-stakeholder management, and compare these with circular organizing as an emerging management approach. This comparison also serves to demonstrate how both the shareholder value and the multi-stakeholder literatures have been avoiding and marginalizing fundamental issues and challenges in the area of ownership, authority, and power. The circular approach suggests we can only resolve these challenges and dilemmas by addressing and explicating key notions, models, and principles in the area of power and authority. By reviewing and comparing shareholder value maximization, multi-stakeholder management and circular organizing, this chapter also contributes toward the development of a preliminary (professional) body of knowledge on governance and management.

Beyond Leadership as We Know it

Established notions of management and entrepreneurship are implictly based on a general conception of the manager or entrepreneur as a "leader." The circular organizing case goes beyond established notions of leadership and might, in fact, turn the conventional notion of leadership upside down.

Leadership as We Know it

As a construct, *leadership* can be defined as the process of social influence in which a person can enlist the aid and support of others in accomplishing common tasks (Chemers 1997). This notion of leadership informs both popular wisdom on management and many theories in this area, especially those that attribute organizational success and failure largely to leadership (e.g. Anderson and Escher 2010; Covey 1989; Tichy and Bennis 2009; Vroom and Jago 1988). Therefore, narratives about heroic, charismatic, or "excellent" leadership—or lack thereof—continue to prevail in the popular press. In a similar way, the academic literature on management and leadership continues to emphasize the central role of leadership skills and leadership development (Day and Harrison 2007; McCallum and O'Connell 2009; Nahavandi 2015).

The conventional wisdom on leadership essentially says that organizational roles are adapted, or made to fit, to individual managers and their subordinates. This role then becomes an integral part of their identity in the organization. As a result, roles and people tend to become *tightly coupled*. The largely implicit praxis of people being tightly coupled to their role and position in the organization becomes manifest in cases of a perceived "mismatch," underperformance, or misconduct. For example, when superiors perceive one of their subordinates to severely underperform and are no longer willing to accept this, they almost automatically initiate a process of "voluntary" or forced exit. Obviously, prominent examples of such exits are CEOs or other high-level executives at multinational companies.[1]

Beyond Leadership as We Know it

Circular organizing suggests a novel perspective on leadership, one that reflects a culture of authority in which leaders acknowledge and appreciate their dependence on "followers" and the latter feel confident enough to challenge their leaders (Hirschhorn 1997). This type of perspective on leadership also resonates well with Senge's (2006) call for leaders championing a "learning organization" as facilitators, stewards, and designers.

In circular organizing, roles are clearly distinguished from the people appointed or elected to fulfill, or energize, these roles—with people often combining multiple roles. Moreover, informed by organizational purpose and objectives, a system of self-organizing circles is instrumental in appointing people to particular roles and tasks. People are thus linked to roles for an explicitly defined and limited period of time, and can also be decoupled from any of these roles, to appoint them to other roles and tasks, and so forth.

This clear distinction between roles and the people who energize them also applies to, for example, the CEO or general manager. The CEO role is preferably assigned to an internal candidate, for a pre-determined period (say two years). Consequently, at the end of this pre-determined period, she can be rather easily disconnected from that role again—if someone else is better qualified to fulfill that role and/or her competences can be better exploited in another capacity elsewhere in the organization. This organizational routine of allocating roles and tasks to people on a regular basis makes the organization more resilient and adaptive, and moreover, might prevent unnecessary exit bonus and severance payments.

Tacit and Explicit Knowledge

Tacit knowledge is pervasive in managerial work and performance, and the body of explicit knowledge on management is rather fragmented and therefore not very actionable, as observed in Chapter 3. As a result, management practices are largely informed by individual judgment and experience, in the absence of an advanced body of actionable knowledge grounded in evidence (Barker 2010). This nascent status of the field makes the pliable and malleable construct of leadership highly attractive. The pivotal role of the notion of leadership therefore also appears to arise from the adolescent state of the management discipline.

This is not to say that tacit knowledge on management is problematic in itself. Rather, the key point here is that the current balance between tacit and explicit knowledge in management (cf. Figure 3.1) tips too much toward the tacit side. As argued in Chapter 3, all professional work involves some tacit knowledge. The challenge in professionalizing management as a nascent profession is to build an explicit body of knowledge that makes the balance between tacit and explicit knowledge tip more toward the latter (professional) side. In particular, a robust body of knowledge on how to distribute management and leadership throughout any organization will make management as a professional activity less dependent on leadership embodied in a few people at the top.

Distributed Leadership

Research in the area of leadership therefore needs to pay more attention to the semi-permanent structures that leaders can help design, develop, adapt, and sustain over time, also in terms of the interaction between structure and agency (e.g. Giddens 1984; Elias and Scotson 1994). The emergence of circular organizing, pioneered by "leaders" with engineering backgrounds, demonstrates that these new structures can be effectively created and sustained. These instantiations of the circular approach are obviously not the only answer to the leadership challenge. But they demonstrate that the leadership construct can be expanded toward systems of *distributed leadership*, in which leadership is not confined to a few people at the top of the organization, but is distributed throughout (e.g. Kets de Vries 1999; Axelrod and Cohen 2000; Thorpe et al. 2011; Wheatley 2005).

In this respect, advocates of distributed leadership and distributed organizing have been highly antagonistic to traditional notions of hierarchy and authority (Kets de Vries 1999; Wheatley 2005; Hlupic 2014). The case of circular organizing illustrates what it takes to develop and sustain a distributed system of self-organizing agents and units in which power is released and activated throughout the organization. Rather than completely abandoning established notions of hierarchy and authority (cf. Kets de Vries 1999), the circular perspective suggests ways to redefine these constructs and their instantiations.

Overall, the experiences with circular organizing go beyond the received wisdom on leadership as an individual process of influencing and motivating other people. Accordingly, leadership is re-conceptualized as a distributed organizational system. More generally, the emergence of these distributed leadership systems may give us hope (cf. Hlupic 2014). It also suggests truly professional approaches to leadership and management only arise from a deliberate engagement with issues of power, authority, and ownership.

Beyond Shareholders and Stakeholders

The shareholder–stakeholder dilemma was introduced in Chapter 1, to illustrate that management is currently, at best, a nascent profession. This section returns to the shareholder value and multi-stakeholder perspectives. I first discuss shareholder value maximization and multi-stakeholder management in terms of core values, constructs, models, principles, and instantiations, and then compare both perspectives with circular organizing.

Shareholder Value Maximization

Shareholder value proponents argue that corporations and their managers should focus on maximizing shareholder value (SV) as the ultimate measure of the corporation's success (Rappaport 1998; Aretz and Bartram 2010). A key assumption here is that all other stakeholders are best served if the corporation is steered toward the highest possible value for shareholders as residual claimants. These residual claimants get paid only after customers have effectively been served and all other claimants such as suppliers, employees, and managers have been paid (Fama and Jensen 1983). By focusing the corporation on the interests of shareholders, the argument goes, everyone else also benefits.

Table 7.1 outlines the key values, constructs, and principles of SV maximization. Most theoretical models in the literature focus on how SV depends on revenue, operating margin, cost of capital, and other financial parameters (e.g. Rappaport 1986; Bender 2014). Drawing on agency theory (Jensen and Meckling 1976; Blair 1995), the broader managerial model essentially proposes that maximization of SV occurs when the interests of executives and shareholders are aligned. In turn, executive compensation based on stock options as well as disclosure of information between executives and directors serve to create this alignment of interests. Full disclosure of information is also assumed to arise from the need to comply with prevailing corporate governance codes. Overall, the model of SV maximization says that the focus on SV involves a virtuous feedback cycle. This cycle starts from stock-based executive compensation and full disclosure of information, via alignment of interests between shareholders and executives, to maximizing SV, which in turn helps to reinforce the (legitimacy of the) compensation arrangement as well as the full disclosure process. Figure 7.1 summarizes this managerial model of SV maximization.

Until about a hundred years ago, the standard model of SV maximization outlined in Figure 7.1 was valid. In those days many equity investors acted like, what we would now call, informal investors. These investors personally knew the (other) owners and managers and got involved in managing and supervising the affairs of the corporation. Moreover, these investors

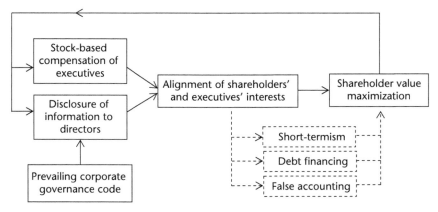

Figure 7.1. Model of shareholder value maximization (solid boxes and lines refer to standard model)

committed their money to the company, not for short-term gains, but for the long run. Indeed, any attempt to increase SV for these committed owner-investors would have implied that other stakeholders were also better off.

But the world has changed (Mizruchi and Kimeldorf 2005). In the early twentieth century, several national governments passed securities laws, attempting to create efficient equity markets that would be safe for distant and transient providers of capital. In the United States, for example, these securities laws were passed in 1933–4. These laws require companies to provide audited financial statements, disclose information about top executives and board members, and prohibit insider trading and other forms of market manipulation (Bhide 1994). These attempts to create efficient equity markets have, however, also created highly deficient corporate governance practices (discussed later). In this respect, equity appears to be a highly ambiguous asset that cannot be effectively traded on an arm's length basis (Bhide 1994).[2]

Even very large institutional investors have therefore developed a strong preference for short-term liquidity over long-term commitment to any of their equity positions (Gillan and Starks 1998). For these investors, any sustained attempt to exercise influence on and control over the management of a corporation in their equity portfolio would raise an unacceptable cost (Coffee 1991). Investors operating on equity markets are therefore more concerned about the liquidity of their investments than building up a concentrated ownership position that would provide the opportunity to truly influence decision-making in the incumbent corporation (cf. Bender 2014).[3]

Notably, advocates of SV maximization acknowledge the lack of interest and commitment of the vast majority of investors-shareholders (Rappaport 1986; Keasey et al. 1997). SV advocates seek to fill this power vacuum by aligning the interests of executives with those of the shareholders, by incorporating stock options in the compensation schemes for executives. However, managers whose sole objective is to maximize SV—also motivated by the stock options they have—are very likely to end up achieving the opposite, that is, destroying SV (as observed in Chapter 1). Examples are Enron, ICI, Worldcom, Global Crossing, and Xerox. By contrast, companies like Apple and Microsoft have deliberately avoided a commitment to SV, and instead have successfully focused on creating customer value (Martin 2011).

The main reason why Enron and other corporations have failed, where Apple and other firms have survived and thrived, is the invalidity of the standard SV model outlined in Figure 7.1. This model is invalid because shareholders appear to be primarily interested in the liquidity and short-term financial value of their investments; by aligning the interests of executives with those of the shareholders, executives become highly motivated to maximize SV in the short run—at the cost of strategies and investments that would increase it in the long run. This *short-termism* effect of aligning the interests of shareholders and executives explains why SV is often not maximized, or is even ultimately destroyed. Figure 7.1 includes this negative effect as an extension of the standard model of SV maximization.

The dashed part of Figure 7.1 also includes two related reasons for the failure of SV maximization: *debt financing* and *false accounting* (discussed more extensively in Chapter 1). Extreme forms of debt financing as well as false accounting also appear to arise from the perverse alignment of executive interests with shareholders primarily interested in the liquidity of their investments. While debt financing and false accounting may increase the SV in the next quarterly reports, in the longer run they severely undermine the company's viability and SV.

Common attempts to reduce these risks and problems include (adapting) corporate governance codes, changes in the composition of the board of directors, extending and codifying the legal duties of directors, adapting executive pay arrangements, changing the accounting treatment of stock options, and creating conditions that would help to re-engage institutional investors (e.g. Charkham and Simpson 1999; MacNeil and Xiao 2006; Marnet 2007; Patterson 2009; Hayes et al. 2012; Williamson et al. 2014). However, all these measures tend to fail, because they do not question the conditions and causal mechanisms widely believed to produce and maximize shareholder value.

Fixing the Shareholder Value Game

A prominent critic of SV maximization is Martin (2011) who, next to changing the rules and regulations of the equity markets and limiting the power of hedge funds, advocates two ways to "fix the game." He argues the authenticity of the lives of executives should be restored, and also recommends fundamentally redesigning the role and structure of the board of directors.

First, Martin argues that the *authenticity* of the lives of executives needs to be restored. He defines authenticity as "the degree to which one stays true to one's own character and morals while dealing with external forces" (Martin 2011: ch. 3). To restore authenticity, executives need to focus on customers rather than shareholders, and the use of stock-based compensation must be eliminated as an incentive.[4] Stock options create a powerful incentive to try to keep expectations rising continuously, which in the longer run is undoable. As a result, executives are pushed toward managing expectations, rather than real performance, and end up "doing work devoid of deeper meaning" (Martin 2011: ch.1). Instead, useful monetary incentives can be grounded entirely in the real markets the company operates in, says Martin. Such incentives can draw on measurements regarding return on invested capital, market share, staff turnover and retention, project management, or any other measurement of customer value. Monetary rewards based on such measurements can be structured as a royalty, to capture long-term value creation and demotivate short-termism (Martin 2011).

Another way to fix the SV game, Martin argues, is addressing *board govern-ance*. He believes it is time to fundamentally rethink the role and structure of boards. Particularly in the case of a publicly traded corporation, the board has a tricky task at the intersection between the expectation-driven equity market and the real markets the corporation is serving. Board members have to act on behalf of outside shareholders, but also interact closely with executives who work for the real market yet are exposed to incentives arising from stock-based compensation. These executives have "deep insider knowledge" (Martin 2011: ch. 4), and are thus always a few steps ahead of both directors and shareholders. This makes the job of the directors—ensuring that executives do not use their preferential access to information at the expense of SV—a very difficult, if not impossible one. These difficulties arise from the (lack of) capabilities of directors as well as how they are selected and compensated (Martin 2011).

For example, Martin observes that companies like P&G, who put customers first and focus on the long term, have nothing to hide and therefore tend to have great, thoughtful directors and full disclosure of information between executives and directors. By contrast, he observes that executives who have something to hide, at corporations such as Enron and Qwest, will look for weaker directors. In these corporations, executives prefer not to disclose the truth to their directors, and will keep them as ignorant as possible regarding the company's activities. Thus, Martin believes it is ironic to observe that in those corporations where the best directors are most needed, they are least likely to be found; and where highly capable and motivated directors are least needed, they are most likely to be found. To address these board governance issues, board membership needs to be redefined as a highly valued public service that is instrumental not only in protecting shareholders, but also in the functioning of the entire economy (Martin 2011).

Martin's analysis is thought-provoking and hard to disagree with. However, it does not question established notions of ownership, hierarchy, and author-ity in the corporate governance discourse (cf. Charkham and Simpson 1999; Hayes et al. 2012; Williamson et al. 2014). In turn, this raises fundamental questions as to whether the changes he recommends are likely to be con-sidered and adopted in publicly traded corporations, especially those whose directors and executives are committed to SV.[5] Attempts to introduce circular organizing in publicly traded companies, described and analyzed in Chapter 5 and 6, suggest the odds are not good. Publicly traded companies have developed highly ambiguous and complex configurations of ownership and decision authority, which in turn tend to inhibit fundamental transformations of any kind.

This is not to convict the executives, directors, or shareholders of these companies. Rather, immensely complex arrangements of ownership and decision authority have been co-evolving from numerous changes and adaptations in securities laws and regulations, corporate constitutions and their by-laws, governance codes, non-disclosure agreements, employment contracts, and many other arrangements and documents. The resulting, highly ambiguous stalemate appears to demotivate any attempt to accomplish a transformation that, to be successful, would indeed require a collective effort to clean up the mess (cf. Martin 2011). As argued earlier, an entirely different type of management system might be required to effectively change the rules of the game.

Multi-stakeholder Management

An important alternative to SV maximization is the *multi-stakeholder* perspective. Advocates of multi-stakeholder management consider an organization as a social institution that promotes its operations, products, and services in the interests of a variety of stakeholders such as employees, investors, customers, and the broader community (e.g. Freeman 1984; Freeman et al. 2007). The central idea is that any organization creates or destroys value through interactions with its stakeholders. Effective stakeholder management therefore involves developing and utilizing relationships with these stakeholders for mutual benefit (Post et al. 2002).

Accordingly, managers are expected to balance the interests of all interest groups, actors, claimants, or institutions that exert a hold on the incumbent organization (Mitroff 1983; Freeman 1984; Kay 2014). These stakeholders typically include customers, suppliers, employees, union representatives, investors, banks and other financial intermediaries, (local) government, and trade associations. Key stakeholders of publicly traded corporations are also shareholders, especially those with substantial equity positions; particular (e.g. environmental) interest groups; investment analysts; and the public and social media.

As such, the multi-stakeholder perspective has a strong ethical foundation, in which values, purpose, and societal interests play a key role (Phillips 2003; Freeman et al. 2007; Miles 2012). Key constructs thus include ethical leadership, stakeholder power, stakeholder interest, legitimacy, urgency, and salience (Mitchell et al. 1997; Freeman et al. 2007). Freeman's (1984) pioneering work on the stakeholder perspective draws on a variety of theoretical sources, including systems theory, organization theory, corporate social responsibility, and corporate planning. This broad intellectual base may also account for the various descriptive, instrumental, as well as normative models that have been developed (Donaldson and Preston 1995; Friedman and Miles 2006; Freeman et al. 2007).

For example, a key typology with descriptive as well as normative properties has been derived by Mitchell et al. (1997: 872), who assume "first, that managers who want to achieve certain ends pay particular kinds of attention to various classes of stakeholders; second, that managers' perceptions dictate stakeholder salience; and third, that the various classes of stakeholders might be identified based upon the possession, or the attributed possession, of one, two, or all three of the attributes: power, legitimacy, and urgency." In this respect, power is the extent to which the stakeholder has the means to impose its will in the relationship with the organization. Legitimacy refers to a general perception or assumption that the actions of the incumbent stakeholder "are desirable, proper, or appropriate" (Mitchell et al. 1997: 869). And urgency is about the degree to which claims of the stakeholder are so time sensitive and critical that they require immediate attention. By examining the combination of these attributes in a binary manner, eight types of stakeholders are identified. Figure 7.2 provides an overview of the resulting typology. Mitchell et al. (1997) spelled out the implications of each type of stakeholder, in terms of its salience and other conditions under which managers (do not) attend to this stakeholder.

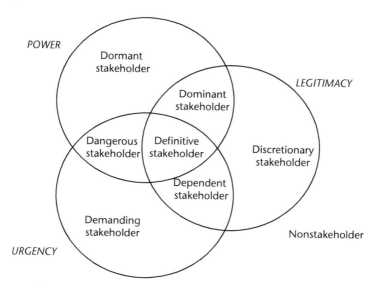

Figure 7.2. Stakeholder typology based on three attributes
Source: Mitchell et al. (1997: 874).

Despite the broad scope of this type of multi-stakeholder model, most practical solutions for embracing stakeholder interests focus on only a single type of stakeholder, such as customers or employees (e.g. Cheney 2000; Nayar 2010; O'Grady 2014). Obviously, the key challenge in practicing the multi-stakeholder approach is how to actually balance the interests of the stakeholders involved (Jones 1995; Mitchell et al. 1997). This tends to involve very laborious negotiations (Blattberg 2004), informed by tools developed for mapping stakeholder interests, understanding the needs and strategies of stakeholders, developing strategies for stakeholders, and creating modes of interaction with them (Freeman et al. 2007; Mitchell et al. 1997).

While multi-stakeholder advocates criticize the key values informing the shareholder value perspective, they do not question the conventional wisdom about authority and ownership, and, more generally, power and empowerment. The multi-stakeholder perspective serves to define power, legitimacy, and related constructs as attributes of the interaction between the incumbent organization and each of its stakeholders, as illustrated earlier. As such, it implicitly accepts any given distribution of authority and power in the organization.[6] Overall, multi-stakeholder management offers a very interesting antithesis to SV maximization, but does not appear to provide any systemic answers to questions of power, authority, and ownership, raised earlier in The Quest for Professionalism.

Circular Organizing Reconsidered

Admittedly, these assessments of the shareholder value and multi-stakeholder perspectives are somewhat biased by the circular organizing approach explored earlier. Table 7.1 summarizes the key values, constructs, principles, model, and instantiations of circular organizing. This overview draws on the detailed description and interpretation of the circular approach in preceding chapters.[7]

The research evidence on circular organizing is still limited, as observed in Chapter 6. The model proposed in that chapter may therefore inform and guide future research in this area. Overall, the circular approach offers an interesting response to some of the challenges arising from SV maximization and multi-stakeholder management. Created by practitioners and embraced by a growing number of organizations, the circular approach offers a professional model and technology for managing any type of company or organization. By distributing the capacity for leadership and management in a transparent manner throughout the organization, circular organizing may thus offer a systemic alternative in the quest for professionalizing management and entrepreneurship.

As illustrated in Chapter 5 and discussed in Chapter 6, the circular approach involves a pragmatist synthesis of hierarchical and heterarchical modes of managing and organizing. Shkliarevsky (2015) argues that the current political unrest, observed around the globe, reflects ongoing tensions between hierarchical and non-hierarchical interactions (see also Mintzberg 2015). Moreover, he believes the opposition between hierarchical and non-hierarchical mechanisms is socially constructed, and therefore subject to our control. In this respect, circular organizing provides an exemplar of how hierarchy and heterarchy can be synthesized—for managers and entrepreneurs as well as political leaders and public administrators.

Comparing Three Management Approaches

Each of the management approaches explored earlier in this section offers a philosophy, model as well as technology of "management"—defined earlier as the activity of connecting and coordinating people and resources to create value that no single individual can create alone. Table 7.1 provides an overview. As a philosophy of management, each approach draws on values that guides the behavior and attention of professionals in particular directions. These values also inform which constructs and models are created, adopted, and validated. Each approach also offers a management technology, codified in instrumental principles and instantiated in management practices.[8] Table 7.1 serves to compare the values, constructs, models, principles, and instantiations of shareholder value, multi-stakeholder, and circular organizing.

Notably, the three approaches are not entirely incompatible. For example, the top management of Royal Dutch Shell has adopted the multi-stakeholder approach in many ways (Post et al. 2002), while Shell's position as a publicly traded corporation on the capital market also implies some level of compliance with the shareholder value perspective. Similarly, some organizations using the circular approach also draw on stakeholder management principles and tools (Romme and Endenburg 2006). Especially at the level of instantiation, elements from different approaches can therefore be combined.

However, the management philosophies of the three approaches are far from compatible. This mutual exclusiveness is especially evident in how values are translated into a conception of what the firm/organization is, in terms of its constituencies and ownership. The SV perspective assumes that shareholders are the exclusive (legal) owners of the corporation, while multi-stakeholder advocates tend to remain silent regarding ownership, thereby implicitly accepting the status quo. The circular approach, by contrast, advocates a legal setting in which the organization owns itself.

The overview in Table 7.1 can perhaps also be interpreted in terms of differences in "stakeholder focus." Accordingly, the multi-stakeholder approach

Table 7.1. An overview of shareholder value maximization, multi-stakeholder management, and circular organizing

	Shareholder value maximization	Multi-stakeholder management	Circular organizing
Values	Shareholders legally own the company; shareholder value (SV) as ultimate measure of the company's performance and viability; focus on SV, as residual claim, also serves the interests of all other stakeholders.	Any organization creates value and wealth through interactions with its stakeholders; society is therefore best served by pursuing the shared interests of all stakeholders of the organization.	Infused by organizational purpose, every member of the organization should be able to (a) influence decisions that directly affect him/her, and (b) make and implement decisions that affect no one other than the decision makers.
Constructs	Shareholder value (SV) as residual claim; separation of ownership and control; corporate governance code; stock-based compensation; disclosure of information.	Organizational purpose and values; ethical leadership; stakeholder interest; stakeholder power, legitimacy, urgency and salience; balancing multiple interests; modes of interaction with stakeholders; etc.	Weaving between boundaries; organizational purpose; hierarchy; informed consent; psychological safety; circular process (leading–operating–measuring); circle as unit of people with shared objectives; double linking between circles; requisite organization; etc.
Model	Most models of SV focus on how it depends on revenue, operating margin, cost of capital and other financial parameters; Figure 7.1 outlines the key management model of SV maximization.	A variety of descriptive, normative, and instrumental models have been developed for mapping stakeholder interests, understanding their needs and strategies, and so forth; Figure 7.2 reproduces the typology developed by Mitchell et al. (1997).	Several normative and instrumental models (e.g. of double linking) have been developed; Figure 6.1 in Chapter 6 depicts the key theoretical model.
Principles	Most principles guiding SV maximization are in the area of corporate finance, focusing on how SV is derived from revenue growth, margin improvement and asset efficiency; key management principles include: • align the interests of executives with those of the shareholders, by offering the former stock options as key component of their compensation; • systematically connect strategic	Several authors have listed principles for managing stakeholder relationships; for example, the set of principles provided by Freeman et al. (2007) includes e.g.: • stakeholder interests go together over time; • find solutions for issues that satisfy multiple stakeholders; • everything we do serves stakeholders; we never trade off the interests of one versus the other	Distribute leadership, authority and power (and thus capacity to learn) throughout the organization by: • shaping administrative hierarchy as sequence of accountability levels; • distinguish roles and people, to be able to systemically assign roles to people; • set up circles for policy decisions (made by informed consent);

	plans and decisions to SV analysis, e.g. by mapping strategic initiatives to their contribution to shareholder value (Lukac and Frazier 2012).	continuously over time; • actively engage stakeholders and manage these relationships ourselves, rather than leaving it to government; • constantly monitor and redesign processes to better serve our stakeholders.	• create double links between these circles; • adapt the ownership structure of the organization, so that it owns itself.
Instantia-tions	Many publicly traded corporations (especially in English-speaking countries such as the US, UK, Canada, and Australia) that focus on their accountability to financial markets.	Publicly and privately traded corporations and other organizations, especially those that are (increasingly) held accountable by non-financial actors and pressure groups.	Privately traded companies and other organizations, mainly in Europe and North America; especially technology-driven start-ups and firms are adopting the holacratic version of circular organizing.

can be said to embrace all stakeholders, SV maximization focuses on shareholders as the primary stakeholder, and the circular approach seems to focus on employees as the key stakeholder. However, this high-level interpretation is incorrect. Advocates of SV maximization essentially say that, by maximizing the value for shareholders as the residual claimants, the company also effectively serves the interests of other stakeholders. In a similar way, the redistribution of power and authority in circular organizing is instrumental in enhancing organizational resilience and performance, which evidently is also in the interest of customers, suppliers, and others with a stake in the organization. Moreover, the top circle (i.e. board of directors) in organizations applying the circular approach typically involves at least three external directors representing stakeholders other than employees. Thus, the stakeholder lens is not helpful in comparing the management approaches outlined in Table 7.1.

Each of the three management approaches also starts from the idea that value creation for customers or clients is what drives and enables the organization. For publicly traded corporations that seek to maximize SV, producing value for customers is instrumental in generating value for shareholders. Within these corporations, customer value tends to become exclusively defined in financial terms, that is, the premium or margin that customers (are willing to) pay on top of the cost price of the product or service offered.

Multi-stakeholder management as well as circular organizing draw on an understanding of customers and customer value that is more broadly applicable. As a result, the multi-stakeholder approach has been applied in both publicly and privately traded companies (e.g. Freeman et al. 2007; Post et al. 2002) and circular organizing has been applied in a variety of privately traded companies and nonprofit organizations, and is currently being tested and applied in public governance settings.

SV maximization therefore does not offer a management approach that can be applied outside publicly traded corporations. Instead, multi-stakeholder management and circular organizing are more broadly applicable in terms of their philosophical, theoretical, as well as instrumental dimensions. However, the multi-stakeholder approach does not question the prevailing distribution of authority, power, and leadership. Whereas SV maximization tends to make management scholars the "hired hands" of shareholders, the multi-stakeholder idea is likely to make them the hired hands of executives and other managers (cf. Khurana 2007). Here, circular organizing might offer a management approach that fundamentally redistributes power and authority throughout the organization. Circular organizing thus reduces the isolation and pressure that many top managers suffer from (cf. Kets de Vries 1989; De Janasz and Peipert 2015) by avoiding the assumption that management is equated with a few leaders at the top of the organization.

In many ways, circular organizing invites managers and entrepreneurs to start operating like professional surgeons or aircraft pilots. As an advanced system for distributed management, it is the analogy of a state-of-the-art operating room for surgeons or a modern aircraft for pilots. Without this kind of advanced management technology, the growing expectations of management as a professional discipline might be difficult to meet.

Concluding Remarks

This chapter assessed the learning that arises from circular organizing as a rather unconventional approach to management. Some of this learning pertains to the shift from established notions of leadership toward systems of distributed leadership. Here, a professional body of knowledge on distributing management and leadership throughout the organization will make professionalism in management less dependent on a few leaders at the top.

Drawing on the perspective of circular organizing, I also argued that the shareholder value and multi-stakeholder perspectives have been avoiding and marginalizing fundamental professional challenges in the area of ownership, authority, and power. The exemplar of circular organizing suggests that key values, constructs, models, and principles in the area of power and authority have to be explicated and addressed in any effort to further professionalize management. Moreover, the overview of shareholder value maximization, multi-stakeholder management, and circular organizing in this chapter might provide a first step toward a professional body of knowledge on management.

Notes

1. Two examples, taken from an almost infinite list of executives who either chose to leave their position (and therefore the company) or were "asked" to leave, are the exit of Linda Cook from Royal Dutch Shell in 2009 and the exit of William Johnson from Heinz in 2013. Sources: "Linda Cook quits Shell after missing out on top job," *The Guardian*, May 26, 2009, retrieved via www.theguardian.com/business/2009/may/26/linda-cook-quits-shell; J. Jargon and S. Thurm, "Heinz CEO's golden exit deal," *The Wall Street Journal*, March 4, 2013, retrieved via http://www.wsj.com/articles/SB10001424127887324539404578340843926547954 March 15, 2015.

2. This is one example, among many others, that demonstrates how the model of shareholder value maximization exclusively draws on economics language and assumptions. More generally speaking, Ferraro et al. (2005) argue and illustrate that the language and assumptions of economics largely shape today's management practices. That is, economic vocabulary and assumptions have become taken for granted and normatively valued, in ways that make them self-fulfilling, entirely independent of their empirical validity.

3. Martin (2011) argues that the equity market is an expectation-oriented market that focuses on trading value around rather than building it. In contrast to real markets in which, for example, materials, products, or services are traded that create some individual and societal good, an expectation-oriented market creates a downward spiral that threatens both individual well-being and the health of the overall economy. Martin here proposes to change the rules of the equity market, in a similar way as the National Football League (NFL) manages and regulates their market. The rules set by the NFL focus on the fans (customers), putting a product on the field that is maximally enjoyable for them. As such, the NFL appears to operate on a deep understanding that its rules must be tweaked continuously to keep ahead of those who would seek to game and abuse these rules (Martin 2011). The challenge of changing the institutions and regulations of the equity markets is beyond the scope of this book. As in previous chapters, I will focus here on professional management and entrepreneurship at the organizational level.

4. For Martin (2011) this does not mean that executives should not buy equity in their company. Executives would be free to buy stock, but according to Martin should be prevented from selling any stock while serving at the company in an executive capacity, as well as for several years after leaving their posts.

5. The agency-structure discourse can offer some guidance regarding the feasibility of changes at the behavioral level that are not complemented by systemic changes in the broader institutions, such as those that structure and regulate the global equity markets (Giddens 1984; Barley and Tolbert 1997).

6. In this respect, the multi-stakeholder idea implicitly draws on the idea of the corporation as "social contract," which might undermine key principles on which any market economy is based (Mansell 2013). This also makes the "stakeholder" construct itself highly contested (Miles 2012). Anyway, the focus of the multi-stakeholder literature on relationships and interactions with *external* stakeholders may explain why it largely neglects the relationships and interactions *within* the organization.

7. In creating the high-level overview of circular organizing in Table 7.1, I have, for example, filtered away some of Gerard Endenburg's personal values that historically motivated the development of circular organizing, but which are not critical to understanding it as a management philosophy, model, and technology.

8. The term "management technology" here refers to instrumental (i.e. means–end) knowledge about bringing together and coordinating people and resources in order to create value that no single individual can create alone. This definition is consistent with how "management" and "technology" (cf. Aristotle's techne) were defined earlier. It is also consistent with how the "management technology" construct is used elsewhere (e.g. Bloom et al. 2015).

8

Implications and Conclusions

Introduction

Developing the management discipline into a profession is one of the grand challenges of our time. The Quest for Professionalism therefore draws on a multi-level understanding of this quest. Moreover, rather than developing a single response, I have sought to create multiple paths out of the current intellectual stasis of the field. This chapter synthesizes the main findings and conclusions arising from The Quest for Professionalism.

The first part of the chapter outlines several paths for professionalizing management practice and scholarship, arising from the combined findings and conclusions of the previous seven chapters. At this very early stage of the professionalization quest, the most important path involves creating a shared sense of professional purpose and responsibility, embedded in a culture of dialogical encounter. Another path may lead toward a professional body of knowledge informed by both discovery and validation, which also enables dialogical encounters between management professionals. Third, management as a nascent profession needs more trading zones that offer opportunities for (professionals with) different voices and interests to meet. Effective trading zones provide attractive platforms for participants with highly different backgrounds and interests to meet and collaborate. The fourth path outlined in this chapter implies that the expectations of professionalism in management can be raised in several ways, for example by creating conditions that enable employees and other internal stakeholders to speak up freely.

Finally, I will explore the implications of these professionalization paths for management education. These implications include the need to initiate discussions on the purpose of management as early as possible in the curriculum; engaging and immersing students in different management approaches and systems; and improving the alignment between espoused and actual behavior.

Pathways for Revitalizing the Quest

The level of professionalism of the management discipline is rather low, due to the absence of a shared sense of purpose and responsibility toward society, a highly fragmented body of academic knowledge on management which is loosely connected to practice and practical knowledge, actual behavior by managers that is often not in line with what they say they do, and public opinion leaders and other observers accepting the widespread lack of professionalism among managers as normal and unavoidable. This initial analysis in Chapter 1 suggests that the professionalization quest needs to aim at each of the P-K-B-E levels: the generative mechanisms of purpose, knowledge, behavior, and expectation. Chapters 2 to 4 analyzed and explored these levels in more detail, and Chapters 5 to 7 assessed whether and how circular organizing can offer a novel perspective on the professionalization challenge in management.

A key objective of The Quest for Professionalism is to uncover and create paths that may enable progress in this quest. In the remainder of this section, I outline four complementary pathways for revitalizing the quest. While each path starts at a single level, the argument on each path goes beyond this initial level, by using and integrating relevant findings and conclusions with regard to other generative mechanisms as well as the case of circular organizing. The following paths are explored and discussed:

- developing a shared sense of purpose and responsibility;
- moving toward a professional body of knowledge;
- creating trading zones where different voices and interests meet;
- raising expectations of management as a professional discipline.

Developing a Shared Sense of Purpose and Responsibility

At the heart of each (emerging) profession is a shared sense of purpose and responsibility toward society. For example, civil engineers share a sense of purpose regarding the reliability, robustness, and user convenience of the roads, bridges, tunnels, docks, and other artifacts they design and create (Muller and Gewirtzman 2004). The respect for human life and the commitment to heal people, expressed in the Hippocratic oath, reflects a shared sense of purpose and responsibility among medical professionals (Miles 2004).

These and many other professions also demonstrate that a shared purpose serves to cultivate diversity and pluralism. This may, at first sight, seem somewhat paradoxical. Here, the need for some common ground is similar to a basic agreement on the rules of any game—for example, in design competitions or in competitive sports such as tennis, soccer, or basketball—in which individuals or teams compete against another (Lampel et al. 2012).

Without any common ground, the game is not likely to come about. Diversity and dissent can therefore only be truly cultivated if all participants share some common ground.

Such common ground is, however, currently not available in the management discipline. Therefore, in Chapter 2 a proposal for a shared purpose and responsibility of management and its scholarship was developed. In sum, this proposal says management professionals would need to share the following purpose and responsibility:

- *Management should be(come) a profession* that serves the greater good by connecting and coordinating people and resources to create value that no single individual can create alone.

- *Practicing and knowing co-constitute each other.* Practicing and knowing are co-constitutive dialogic processes.

- *Shared interest in outcomes and implications.* A shared interest in outcomes and implications serves to facilitate productive exchange and dialogue across maps based on distinctions such as qualitative–quantitative, positivism–constructivism, and description–prescription.

- *Learning to see from different perspectives.* Practitioners and scholars learn to see themselves, their personal background, their organizational settings, and their own presuppositions from a range of different perspectives.

- *Pluralism is essential.* Pluralism in philosophical, theoretical, and methodical positions is a great asset to the profession, which implies "real doubt" is central in management and management scholarship.

- *Dialogical encounter.* In dialogical encounters, researchers and other professionals regularly expose themselves to fundamentally different views, as an opportunity to reconsider their central presuppositions.

This proposal for a shared purpose and responsibility is likely to raise fundamental questions, especially from scholars with a strong interest in critical management studies—as signalled in Chapter 2. These questions pertain to, for example, whether management can be conceived as a nascent profession, and the retorical and possibly self-serving nature of phrases like the "greater good." These are valid concerns. However, professionalism is at the heart of what management practitioners and scholars do and (say they) believe in, and the societal costs and risks arising from mismanagement and other forms of unprofessional management are too high. So we cannot simply walk away and abandon the professionalization quest.

If anything, the emergence of circular organizing might give us hope. Circular organizing provides a management perspective and technology that serves to connect "people and resources to create value that no single individual can create alone" (as proposed earlier). It distributes management and leadership throughout the organization, rather than equating management and leadership with a select group of people that exclusively operates the chain of command. Moreover, the circular approach appears to cultivate pluralism and dissent, by giving each organizational member a voice in decisions that directly affect him or her. As an organizational system in which power, authority, and information flow circularly, circular organizing may therefore provide an exemplar of an organizational culture of dialogical encounter.

This exemplar suggests the management discipline will benefit from a culture of dialogical encounter in which management practitioners and scholars draw on different management perspectives and philosophical assumptions, while also regularly exposing themselves to fundamentally different views. In dialogical encounters with each other, management professionals learn to see themselves, their personal background, their organizational settings, and their own presuppositions from a range of different perspectives, thus enabling them to engage more reflexively with their work and profession.

The pragmatist interest in outcomes and implications, already shared by many management scholars and practitioners, can inform the dialogue on a (potentially shared) sense of professional purpose and responsibility. The common interest in outcomes and implications might initiate conversations between highly different voices in the profession, by raising straightforward questions about what participants consider to be "firm performance," "organizational resilience," "dynamic capability," or any other outcome utility.

Overall, a shared sense of purpose and responsibility enhances the identity of management as an emerging profession. Given the embryonic stage of the discourse on the purpose and responsibility of our discipline, any attempt toward closure of this discourse will not be successful at this stage. In this respect, the prototype of professional purpose and responsibility, proposed earlier, is deliberately created to revitalize and re-open the debate. Future conversations on this prototype, or any alternative proposals, are best shaped in the form of dialogical encounters in public settings.

Moving Toward a Professional Body of Knowledge

The first business schools were established to train professional managers. However, efforts to avoid "wastelands of vocationalism" (Simon 1991a: 139) and instead build academic respectability have led most management scholars and business schools to retreat from that goal. Central to any attempt to revitalize the transformation to science-based professionalism is a specialized body of knowledge, in which discovery and validation activities inform a productive discourse on instantiated practices—in terms of their underlying values, constructs, models and principles. Interestingly, many elements of this body of knowledge are already present in the literature, albeit in a scattered and fragmented manner. In Chapter 3, I therefore presented a map of a future professional body of knowledge that facilitates dialogical encounters in this fragmented landscape (see Table 3.1). This map connects creative discovery to scholarly validation.

Chapter 3 also served to develop an agenda for future work on a professional body of knowledge. While many elements of this body of knowledge already appear to be present, many opportunities to better connect them remain untapped. Also in view of the findings arising from the circular approach to management, key points on this agenda are as follows:

- Developing and growing the awareness of the *role of values* in management and its scholarship. The comparison of shareholder value maximization, multi-stakeholder management and circular organizing in Chapter 7 illustrates the pervasive influence of values on what kind of constructs, models, principles, and instantiations are created. A broad discourse on professional values such as rigor and relevance is also critical. Rather than merely comparing and discussing these key values, the framework outlined in Chapter 3 suggests we would be better off by addressing academic rigor (including validity and reliability) and practical relevance on its own terms, that is, in the context of validation or discovery as professional activities.

- Management scholars need to invest more time and resources in discovering and validating constructs and models that help practitioners respond to *challenges* such as those in the area of empowerment and organizational resilience. Discovery-oriented work serves to identify empirical problems and anomalies, and mobilizes our creativity and ingenuity. As such, it thrives on the generative role of doubt. At the same time, the case of circular organizing illustrates that key theoretical constructs in mainstream management studies, such as Simon's bounded rationality and Hayek's dispersed knowledge, can be essential in professionalizing the management discipline. More generally speaking, we need a professional discourse that systematically connects the discovery and validation of theoretical constructs and models.

- *Principles* are critical in translating generic constructs and models to contextualized instantiated practices. While principles as a separate category of research in/output have only been recently introduced in the management literature, several proven methods can be used to develop them (see Chapter 3 as well as Appendix 2). A key implication is that the materials for training new generations of managers and scholars have to be revised, to equip them with tools and skills that connect the neat and tidy (analytical) world of scholarship to the fuzzy and embedded (synthetical) world of practice. The ability to distill, infer, or extract principles from a variety of sources may also offer opportunities for new forms of inter-action between practitioners and researchers—for example, by comparing principles extracted from practical experiences in the field with those distilled from validated research findings.

- In the early days of management scholarship, direct engagements in experimentation and prototyping were central to all scholarly work, but today the act of *instantiation* is typically left to management practitioners. Clearly, the quest for professionalism implies that work on creating and evaluating instantiations needs to become as academically respectable as other forms of research informing a professional body of knowledge. Discovering new management practices and transforming extant ones are core activities in both management practice and scholarship. Without creative discovery by management pioneers, the management profession would lose its vitality and adaptability to new challenges.

- The professional body of knowledge mapped in Table 3.1 suggests we should not only study how management approaches, tools, and other instantiations are actually used in practice, but also distill constructs and principles that can proactively inform the design of new instantiations or the adaptation of existing ones. This also invites longitudinal studies of whether and how these principles are actually used, and how evidence-based instantiation processes and outcomes compare to those not informed by evidence. Any research program covering the *entire map* of a professional body of knowledge will generate substantial theoretical progress as well as practical relevance and application. A promising research program, arising from the previous chapter, would be one that assesses shareholder value maximization, multi-stakeholder management and circular organizing in more detail, both empirically and theoretically. This type of research pro-gram is likely to have a major impact on the management profession.

Creating Trading Zones Where Different Voices and Interests Meet

A key barrier to professionalizing management arises from the tribal nature of the behavior of management practitioners and scholars alike. The level of engagement of management scholars with practice is generally poor, and most scholars only talk to and write for their own tribes. The notion of trading zones was therefore adopted in Chapter 4 to explore how dialogical encoun-ters can be practically facilitated and sustained. The same chapter also depicted several examples of existing "trading zones"—such as new business incubators, management labs, and professional degree programs—that already appear to enable more meaningful dialogues between highly different voices and interests. The trading zone perspective is a highly pragmatist one, because it avoids the need for major institutional changes that would be rather difficult to realize.

As one of the grand challenges of our time, the quest for professionalism in management is still at a very early stage. At this stage, the best shot at making progress is to experiment in many different trading zones. Nonetheless, some trading zones appear to be more promising than others, in terms of the criteria for successful trading zones proposed in Chapter 4 (e.g. durability and psychological safety). For example, professional degree programs offered by business schools might offer favorable conditions for dialogical encounters between management practitioners and scholars—particularly in professionalizing management in established companies and organizations. Such favorable conditions arise especially when those in charge of a *professional degree* (DBA) program can motivate their school's best scholars to actively work with students enrolled in the program, and these individual DBA projects are part of a long-term collaborative program between the business school and the companies employing the DBA students.

The *incubators* for new business creation that many universities and their business schools have established also offer very promising trading zones. Some of these incubators are founded as relatively autonomous units or companies, others have been embedded in so-called Technology Transfer Offices. Collaborative work between practitioners and scholars in these incubation environments has already led to a coherent and actionable body of knowledge on, for example, technology entrepreneurship, technology transfer, and university spinoff creation. Incubators are also very interesting as trading zones because they enable and promote collaboration between scholars and (nascent) entrepreneurs and their stakeholders. The case of circular organizing demonstrates that entrepreneurs have more discretion to experiment with new management perspectives than managers in established organizational settings. Indeed, major management innovations are more likely to arise in settings where a single entrepreneur, or a small group of entrepreneurial partners, has the ultimate authority to initiate such an innovation—even when this innovation itself implies a fundamental redistribution of power and authority throughout the organization.[1]

Theoretically, this suggests trading zones are best developed in areas with a minimum of regulatory and institutional constraints. Management practices in highly regulated organizational settings, such as in publicly traded corporations and government agencies, will evidently also benefit from the quest for professionalism. However, these highly constrained settings are not likely to generate, and experiment with, profound management innovations. Entrepreneurship is therefore not only relevant to the management profession because all organizations (to be managed) first have to be created, but also because entrepreneurial settings offer more degrees of freedom to discover and try out new values, constructs, and models for managing any organization (cf. Dorado and Ventresca 2013). The future of management scholarship might therefore, to some extent, depend on trading zones where scholars and entrepreneurs can pioneer, experiment, and engage with new ways of managing.

Raising Expectations of Management as Professional Discipline

If investors, employees, journalists, and many others raise their expectations of management professionals, the latter will tend to internalize these expectations, which in turn will inspire and guide them to perform and deliver their best. This raises the question of how we can trigger such a virtuous circle. Established professions such as medicine and law are often equated with conditions and regulations for entry to the profession as well as sanctions and penalties regarding unprofessional conduct. However, these regulations and sanctions tend to have counterproductive effects on professional conduct—especially by transforming the (initially) intrinsic commitment to professional standards into an extrinsic one.

There are several ways to initiate the self-reinforcing effect of higher expectations. First, the transformation of silenced employees into assertive ones is fundamental to raising the expectations of those (internal stakeholders) that managers work with on a daily basis.[2] By creating organizational conditions that enable employees and other internal stakeholders to *speak up freely and signal problems*, the expectations of professionalism at all management levels are raised almost immediately. Key conditions are psychological safety in informal and formal meetings (also attended by superiors), so that employees and others will speak up freely and address sensitive issues; and informed consent in decision making, which assures that each employee can contribute to decisions that affect him or her directly. Circular organizing appears to create at least some of these conditions, which Habermas, Rorty, and other philosophers have explored in terms of the socio-political requirements for free and authentic dialogue. The case of circular organizing also suggests that these socio-political conditions go far beyond conventional approaches to participative management and organizational democracy.

Second, the circular organizing case suggests that internal and external accountability can be broadened to include a variety of *non-financial performance measures*. This serves to redirect the attention of many managers, who otherwise would continue to focus on financial performance, supported by accounting and control systems that report costs, expenditure, and financial results. The example of circular organizing implies that non-financial objectives need to be defined precisely and consistently, so performance can be measured accordingly. Regarding the "non-financial" dimension, directors and external auditors are too easily satisfied with general statements about employee turnover and absence rates, mandatory meetings with work councils, and so forth. When the non-financial dimension is specified in measurable constructs—such as circles, double linking between circles, and decision making by informed consent—then directors and auditors as well as anyone else can effectively monitor whether the instantiations of these constructs meet the expectations and standards set for these non-financial aspects. More generally, measuring and assessing the quality level of non-financial processes serves to distinguish between *capability* and *performance*. This distinction is important because capabilities first have to be built and sustained, to then be able to perform—similar to how the technical state and capabilities of an aircraft can be assessed, tested, and maintained while on the ground, between flights during which it actually performs. In the current state of the management discipline, the capability to accomplish something is too easily equated with performance and results. As a result, management scholars as well as practitioners tend to misunderstand and underestimate the generative role and long-term impact of (investing in and maintaining) management capabilities and technologies.

Third, the ultimate test of professionalism is whether our actual behavior is consistent with what we say we are doing. By covering up our actual behavior, or that of others, for example by narratives about how much we appreciate and endorse "transparency" and "employee voice," we tend to sustain the low level of expectations others have of our professionalism. Most employees and managers have become so accustomed to malfunctioning managerial practices that they accept it as normal and unavoidable. Here, the level of expectations can be significantly raised by paying much more attention to the tensions and gaps between actual and espoused behavior, be it our own behavior or that of others. The next section explores this professionalization strategy in more detail.

Implications for Management Education

At the heart of management as a nascent profession is the aspirational and vocational alignment between purpose, knowledge, behavior, and expectation. Attempts to professionalize management by regulating and certifying management education have largely failed (Khurana 2007; Spender 2007; Somers et al. 2014). This "outside-in" strategy to professionalize management has primarily been shaped by national and international bodies that accredit business schools and their educational programs. In contrast, I have adopted an "inside-out" strategy in *The Quest for Professionalism*, by returning to fundamental issues at the level of professional purpose, knowledge, behavior, and expectation. This strategy served to develop a vision of management as a collaborative profession that thrives on a productive discourse about newly discovered as well as established ways to engage in management.

While the overall focus of *The Quest for Professionalism* here is on management practice and scholarship, the findings arising from this quest have major implications for management education. Management education has, to a large extent, got a life of its own. The regulatory mechanisms developed by national accreditation bodies and international ones such as AACSB, AMBA, and EQUIS appear to have successfully "professionalized" management education, by defining and implementing a specialized body of knowledge as well as accreditation procedures, even as management itself has yet to become a profession (Spender 2007). Notably, all three accreditation bodies advocate standards that reflect the "science-based professionalism" vision for management arising from the Ford and Carnegie reports in the 1950s, discussed in Chapter 1. For example, EQUIS espouses that it

> looks for a balance between high academic quality and the professional relevance provided by close interaction with the corporate world. A strong interface with the world of business is, therefore, as much a requirement as a strong research potential. EQUIS attaches particular importance to the creation of an effective learning environment that favours the development of students' managerial and entrepreneurial skills, and fosters their sense of global responsibility.[3]

Despite the image created by accreditation bodies such as EQUIS and AACSB, management education as actually practiced in most business schools has been widely criticized. Seeking academic respectability, almost all management professors treat students as consumers of course content rather than apprentices in management and entrepreneurship as professional activity (Mintzberg 2004; Khurana 2007; Rousseau 2012b). Moreover, the content of these courses tend to overemphasize the role of analysis and science, at the cost of critical reflection, entrepreneurial imagination and professional development (e.g. Chia 1996; Mintzberg and Gosling 2002; Grey 2004; Gray 2007; Learmonth 2007; Roglio and Light 2009; Khurana and Spender 2012). As a result, business schools tend to produce many graduates with underdeveloped skills in reflection, imagination, and self-criticism (Mintzberg and Gosling 2002; Learmonth 2007; Roglio and Light 2009).

In terms of the initial "science-based professionalism" mission of the management discipline, academic quality now prevails over professional relevance in how management education is actually practiced. Some management educators have been pioneering with course content and formats that enhance the professional development of students (e.g. Currie and Knights 2003; Romme 2003b; Gray 2007; Randolph 2011), to shift the emphasis from educating *about* to educating *for* management and entrepreneurship (Kirby 2004). Relatively speaking, however, these attempts have had a small impact, if any at all, because the vast majority of management students never gets exposed to such educational innovations (Learmonth 2007).

In the remainder of this section, I therefore recommend several changes in the course content and format of programs offered by business and management schools. Each of these changes does not require systemic changes in the entire curriculum, but involves targeted changes that enable and motivate dialogical encounters on the purpose, nature, and praxis of management among students and professors.

Initiate Discussion on the Purpose of Management as Early as Possible

The findings from *The Quest for Professionalism*, outlined previously, suggest one very obvious way to create awareness of the professionalization idea. The moral core of any profession arises from its "social contract" with society (Khurana and Nohria 2008), but the management discipline does not yet have such a social contract with the broader public. A good place to start conceiving this (emerging) social contract is to discuss the notions of purpose and responsibility that management students and their educators bring to the table.

Notably, a single "business ethics" course tends to be the only place in the curriculum where professors address moral issues. However, the discourse about professional purpose and responsibility is better initiated in introductory courses in the first semester, possibly later expanded in core courses on, for example, strategic management, accounting, and organizational behavior.

For any introductory course, excellent reading materials are Khurana and Nohria's (2008) call for a professional code, Anderson and Escher's (2010) MBA Oath, and key chapters from Mintzberg's (2004) criticism of management education. These readings will generate lively discussions between professors and students. In addition, fundamentally different perspectives such as shareholder value maximization, multi-stakeholder management, and distributed management (e.g. circular organizing) can inform and extend the discussion on professional purpose in relation to strategy, organization design, human resources, accounting, and finance.

Engage and Immerse Students in Management Practices and Technologies

New management practices and technologies are required to effectively redirect and revitalize the professionalization of management. As an alternative to shareholder value maximization and multi-stakeholder management, the emergence of circular organizing was explored in earlier chapters. This circular approach to distributing management throughout the organization can be effectively used in teaching management and entrepreneurship, especially by creating opportunities for students to practice new approaches to management and entrepreneurship.

In a variety of teaching roles, I observed that students learn a lot from getting directly engaged in exploring how circular organizing as well as other management technologies are actually practiced—both at the undergraduate and graduate levels (Romme 2003b; Romme and Putzel 2003). Whereas, for example, Mintzberg (2004) believes it makes no sense to teach management to undergraduates without any managerial experience, my own experiences as well as those of others suggest undergraduate students can be directly immersed in organizational and managerial settings, which generates the direct experiences they can reflect on (e.g. Romme and Putzel 2003; Jones and Iredale 2010; Neck and Greene 2011). At both the undergraduate and graduate level, this type of management and entrepreneurship education enables students to self-manage their learning process and also serves to develop skills in critical reflection (Romme 2003b; Jones and Iredale 2010; Van Seggelen-Damen and Romme 2014).

Many educational formats for engaging students in management and entrepreneurship can be implemented in a single course, without much interference with the rest of the curriculum (Neck and Greene 2011). Professors and program managers that are more adventurous can decide to adopt the management or entrepreneurship method (they prefer) in managing the entire curriculum or program. For example, we have used circular organizing to manage an undergraduate program with up to 700 students and 40 faculty members (e.g. Romme and Eltink 2002). Similarly, others have been drawing on different approaches to design and manage graduate programs for students with management experience. For example, the Major Projects Leadership Academy, initiated by Bent Flyvbjerg and funded by the UK government, draws on multi-stakeholder management to train senior managers of UK government departments in the skills and knowledge required to deliver major (e.g. big infrastructure) projects on time and on budget.[4] Another prominent example is the International Masters in Practicing Management (IMPM), that has been arising from Mintzberg's (2004) vision of management development as a reflective, practical, and hands-on process.[5]

Reduce the Gap between Actual and Espoused Behavior

The final implication involves the gap between actual and espoused behavior, that is, the lack of consistency between what we do and what we say we do. This is perhaps the most self-evident dimension of the quest for professionalism in management. While I have previously suggested several ways to engage and immerse students in management practice, they are not likely to exploit these opportunities when their skills in critically reflecting on their own experiences as well as those of others are absent or underdeveloped. Moreover, the conventional wisdom about management often tends to marginalize many opportunities for professionalizing management (cf. Ferraro et al. 2005), for example the opportunity to fundamentally redistribute power, leadership, and authority.

Therefore, any program in management education should include professional skills in questioning inconsistencies between what we do and what we say we do, to better align the two. Argyris, Schön, and others have done pioneering work in this area. They have codified and validated the core values (e.g. "suppress negative feelings") that sustain and mask inconsistencies between actual and espoused behavior, as well as the values (e.g. "free and informed choice") that support an open discussion about such inconsistencies. Moreover, constructs such as dispositional and causal attributions have been developed, to inform models of "limited" versus "effective" learning systems that explain whether and how learning about these inconsistencies occurs. In addition, a portfolio of tools (e.g. ladder of inference), intervention strategies (e.g. puzzle intervention and left-hand/right-hand column writing) and other instantiations have been created, evaluated, and validated in detailed case studies (e.g. Argyris and Schön 1978; Argyris et al. 1985; Argyris 1993).

Whereas some of these training tools and strategies are widely used in management and organizational development, the vast majority of business and management schools does not offer any (e.g. MBA) courses that explicitly draw on these tools and strategies.[6] Leading business schools as well as accreditation bodies such as AACSB and EQUIS may want to take action in this area, because learning to "walk your talk" is pivotal to any future progress in the quest for professionalism.

Concluding Remarks

In the Introduction to *The Quest for Professionalism* I kicked off with the example of professional pilots flying aircrafts, to illustrate that our expectations of management and entrepreneurship are often highly ambiguous and undefined. This was one of the observations motivating the search for ways to revitalize the professionalization quest in management and entrepreneurship. While this quest is contested and has a highly uncertain outcome, management and entrepreneurship scholars have a moral responsibility to revitalize it.

While many people pay lip-service to the idea of professionalizing management, the argument in *The Quest for Professionalism* demonstrates that it truly is a grand societal challenge for which there are no quick fixes. I therefore explored several paths that may help get us out of the current deadlock, to renew the momentum toward an intrinsic notion of science-based professionalism. Together, these paths might create a growing number of opportunities to engage in a viable and productive discourse on professionalizing the work of managers and entrepreneurs and those studying them. In this vein, I conclude here with a quote from a poem written by Margaret Wheatley (2014: 1), inspired by Parker Palmer's *The Active Life*:

> The true professional is one
> who does not obscure grace
> with illusions of technical prowess,
> the true professional is one
> who strips away all illusions to reveal
> a reliable truth
> a reliable truth in which
> the human heart can rest.

Notes

1. The observation that entrepreneurial organizations have more discretion has been theorized in the literature on the initial logics of organizing. In this respect, founder-entrepreneurs bring initial logics of organizing and managing to their organizations in the first few years. These so-called "founder blueprints" tend to become imprinted on the organization and subsequently mold its development—long after the founders have left (Stinchcombe 1965; Baron et al. 1996; Baron et al. 1999; Hannan et al. 2006; Romme et al. 2012). An example of the long-term effect of founder blueprints is when directors of an increasingly innovation-driven corporation continue to appoint executives with outspoken "command-and-control" leadership styles (e.g. Carlson 2015), even though the evidence is mounting that the key challenge for innovation-driven companies is to orchestrate and manage innovation activities distributed across numerous self-governing enterprises and corporate ventures (e.g. Baldwin 2012).
2. Given the prevailing assumption that subordinates are hardly able to affect how their bosses treat them, field studies are not likely to provide any evidence in this area. Oc et al. (2015) therefore draw on an experimental research design to demonstrate that candid (rather than compliant) feedback from subordinates to powerholders leads to a less self-interested allocation of resources by these powerholders, and thus enhances the likelihood that they allocate resources in ways that contribute to the "greater good."
3. "EQUIS–EFMD Quality Improvement System," retrieved from: https://www.efmd. org/accreditation-main/equis April 12, 2015.
4. Source: "Major Projects Leadership Academy," retrieved April 16, 2015 from: www.sbs.ox.ac.uk/programmes/execed/custom/our-clients/major-projects-leadership-academy.

5. The website of the IMPM program is: http://www.impm.org/.

6. The IMPM program mentioned earlier is one of these exceptions. A key condition for truly open discussions about the (in)consistency between actual and espoused behavior appears to be a high level of psychological safety (e.g. James 1996; Kolb and Kolb 2005). The power asymmetry between professor and student, prevailing in many undergraduate classrooms, may be the key barrier to creating and sustaining settings for dialogical encounters that are psychologically safe (Romme and Putzel 2003).

APPENDIX 1

Example of Symposium

This appendix provides an example of the kind of dialogical encounters advocated in Chapter 2, in the form of an All-Academy Symposium conducted at the Academy of Management conference (August 2015). This symposium draws on a process that was deliberately designed to continue and extend the dialogue on professional purpose and responsibility.

Title of Symposium

Professionalism in a Pluralistic World: The Quest for Common Ground in Governance and Management.

Organizers and Panelists

Organizers: Georges Romme (Eindhoven University of Technology) and David Denyer (Cranfield University). *Panelists:* Jean Bartunek (Boston College), Timothy Devinney (University of Leeds), Mark Learmonth (Durham University), Denise Rousseau (Carnegie Mellon University), Andrew van de Ven (University of Minnesota).

Abstract

The purpose and nature of corporate governance practices are contested, as is the professional nature of scholarship in the area of governance and management. As a result, the highly fragmented landscape of management research constitutes a major barrier for scholars to contribute to the professionalization of governance and management practice. In this symposium we explore opportunities for establishing some minimum amount of common ground that would provide a basic notion of purpose, responsibility, and mutual respect—to be shared by management scholars and practitioners alike. We will debate the possibility and desirability of developing a shared sense of (professional) purpose and responsibility, and also whether and how it could inform the professionalization of management and governance practices. The symposium draws on an unconventional format, informed by design science.

Background and Overview of Symposium

Mary Parker Follett (1927: 117) argued that management would need to become a profession based on "a foundation of science and a motive of service." Now, almost 90 years later, the nature of professionalism in management is by no means settled, and most business schools and management scholars appear to have abandoned the quest for professionalization (Khurana 2007). In this respect, there is a broad consensus that the field of management currently is *not* a profession (e.g. Learmonth and Harding 2006; Khurana and Nohria 2008; Barker 2010; Rousseau 2012b), while some strongly believe that it *might and should* become one (Khurana and Nohria 2008; Augier and March 2011; Pfeffer 2012; Rousseau 2012b).

The lack of a shared professional purpose is reflected in the ongoing debate between advocates of shareholder value maximization and those advocating a multi-stakeholder perspective; the former argue that corporations and their managers should focus on maximizing shareholder value (Rappaport 1986; Aretz and Bartram 2010), whereas advocates of the stakeholder approach believe managers should balance the interests of all stakeholders, including customers, employees, suppliers, investors, and society at large (Freeman 1984; Devinney et al. 2013a). As such, the deep and abiding commitment of executives, directors, and investors to the idea that the purpose of the firm is to maximize shareholder value has been giving rise to a string of accounting scandals, options-backdating schemes, investment debacles, and other ethics breaches (e.g. Martin 2011). Evidently, the unresolved nature of the shareholder–stakeholder debate in academia has not been helpful in addressing, in whatever way, these corporate governance practices (cf. Ghoshal 2005; Devinney et al. 2013b; Tihanyi et al. 2014).

More broadly speaking, the purpose and nature of management scholarship is contested, as evidenced by debates on the quest for professionalism (Khurana and Nohria 2008; Barker 2010), evidence-based management (Learmonth 2006; Learmonth and Harding 2006; Rousseau 2006a), the rigor–relevance gap (Hodgkinson and Rousseau 2009; Kieser and Leiner 2009; Hughes et al. 2011; Learmonth et al. 2012), and mode 2 research and design science (Mohrman 2007; Pandza and Thorpe 2010; Bartunek 2011). While the *Academy of Management* has a long history of initiating debates on the purpose and nature of management scholarship, through its annual conferences as well as journals (e.g. Huff 2000; Rynes et al. 2001; Bartunek 2003; Van de Ven and Johnson 2006; Rousseau et al. 2008; Rousseau 2012a), more recently this debate appears to have been subdued.

An example is the discourse on Mode 2 and 3 research and ways to connect rigor and relevance (Huff 2000; Huff and Huff 2001). Both Tranfield and Starkey's (1998) and Huff's (2000) initial advocacy of mode 2 and other work in this area (e.g. Starkey and Madan 2001) expressed optimism for a future for management scholarship based on teamwork and trans-disciplinarity. About a decade later, Bartunek observed that the Mode 2 discourse on ways to link rigor and relevance had not progressed substantially (Bartunek 2011). As such, disputes on the purpose and nature of management research appear to have taken on some characteristics of language games, rather than of a discourse that would evoke productive movement (Starkey et al. 2009; Bartunek 2011).

In this symposium we aim to reignite this debate. One key idea discussed is that the highly fragmented landscape of management (practice as well as scholarship) lacks a capability for dialogue across this landscape, and that this capability can only develop if there is a *shared sense of responsibility* (Rolin 2010). The conventional view here is that a culture of dialogue has not come alive in the management discipline due to the philosophical barriers that appear to inhibit such a culture (e.g. Jackson and Carter 1991; Tadajewski 2009), that is, the fragmented nature of the landscape of management studies (Tranfield and Starkey 1998; Gulati 2007). However, others have argued that it is not so much the pluralistic and fragmented nature of management scholarship and practice that is inhibiting genuine dialogue between otherwise highly different voices, but rather, the lack of a shared sense of responsibility. For example, Rolin's (2010) analysis implies the field of organization and management studies would only be able to truly cultivate diversity and dissent if it subscribed to, and acted upon, some shared norm of intellectual responsibility (also known as epistemic responsibility)—a norm that is currently missing. Similarly, Khurana and Nohria (2008) observe that a shared sense of professional responsibility, or what they call a code, is at the heart of any profession. This shared responsibility provides the profession with a collective identity. For example, the codes of the legal and medical professions define a shared purpose and responsibility that is embraced by practitioners as well as scholars in those professions (e.g. Miles 2004). Yet, such codes have also been subjected to heavy criticism and may, for example, merely serve as a cover for unethical practices (cf. Learmonth and Harding 2006; Barker 2010).

Developing Common Ground

In preparing and shaping this symposium, we apply a design approach (Romme 2003a; Van Aken 2004; Hodgkinson and Starkey 2011) to the challenge of developing common ground in the management discipline. The design cycle adopted is as follows.

Develop a set of requirements of the (shared) norm needed. Here, we formulated three requirements. This norm should (a) constitute a coherent set of the most basic ingredients of management scholarship, that is, a "minimum viable" set of heuristics (cf. Adner 2012) to which every management scholar can add more specific philosophical ideas, methodological perspectives, or theoretical lenses; (b) provide sufficient common ground at the epistemic level to facilitate dialogue across otherwise highly different voices (cf. Bakhtin 1981; Rolin 2010); and (c) accommodate the notion of shareholder value as well as the notion of accountability toward a broad set of stakeholders (Khurana and Nohria 2008), without the need to fully subscribe to either of these notions.

Assemble a group of scholars representing a plurality of voices. We assembled a highly diverse group of six scholars and a practitioner, with micro interests (i.e. individual and group behavior) as well as macro interests (e.g. strategy, culture, operations, design) and with epistemic backgrounds as varied as constructivism, critical realism, and positivism. The size of the group was sufficiently large to include highly different perspectives, while small enough to work as a team on the next step. The group included: Marie-José Avenier (Grenoble University), David Denyer (Cranfield University), Gerard Hodgkinson (University of Warwick), Krsto Pandza (University of Leeds), Georges Romme (Eindhoven University of Technology), Ken Starkey (University of Nottingham), and Nicolay Worren (Deloitte Consulting, Norway).

Develop an initial norm (alpha-testing). The group met at a European conference in 2013 to explore the territory and develop a first version of the norm. After this meeting, the group continued work on this norm, and over a period of more than 12 months converged on a first prototype (that we can thus consider to be alpha-tested). The next section describes the result.

Discuss and test the initial version of the norm in a public forum (beta-testing)—the symposium proposed here. In this symposium, a diverse group of scholars and practitioners is invited to scrutinize the proposed norm. The panel composed for the symposium share a concern about practice but is diverse in terms of micro–macro, quantitative–qualitative, as well as the realism–constructivism spectrum. In view of the potential bias arising from the European composition of the group that developed the first version of the norm, most panelists contributing to the symposium are based in Northern America. There will also be some time for questions and comments from the audience. In the wrap-up of the symposium, the chairman will also invite everyone to contribute to the last stage of the process. (The next section provides more information on the symposium.) After the conference, a report of the symposium will be drafted and checked by all panel members. Based on this report, the proposed norm will be adapted.

Test the adapted norm in online community settings (gamma testing). We will then use an online community setting, such as AoM Connect, to invite a large population of management scholars to evaluate the norm. Other online community forums, such as the EBMgt Google Group, will be used to involve practitioners in evaluating the norm. This will serve to explore whether the proposed norm is indeed instrumental in facilitating a discourse on the purpose and nature of management (scholarship) across different "tribes" (Gulati 2007). Finally, we will draw up a report of the entire design cycle and its key findings and outcomes.

Preparing and Chairing the Symposium

The previous section has served to outline the purpose and set-up of the symposium. Notably, we intend to stimulate debate rather than attempt merely to reach some form of consensus. Given the contested nature of management and governance as professional work, the panel is likely to disagree on some of the key issues raised.

The symposium will start with an introduction on the why and how of the symposium, which includes an overview of the current version of the proposed norm of professional purpose and responsibility. Mainly informed by the literature on professionalism (e.g. Khurana 2007; Van de Ven 2007; Khurana and Nohria 2008; Rousseau 2012b) and pragmatism (e.g. Bernstein 1991; Baert 2005; Locke et al. 2008; Zundel and Kokkalis 2010), the *proposed norm* of professional purpose and responsibility is as follows:

- *Management should be(come) a profession* that serves the greater good by bringing people and resources together to create value that no single individual can create alone.

- *Practicing and knowing co-constitute each other.* Practicing and knowing are co-constitutive dialogic processes and management scholars and practitioners alike engage in practicing as well as knowing (possibly in different proportions).

- *Shared interest in outcomes and implications.* Conceptual distinctions such as qualitative–quantitative, positivism–constructivism, and description–prescription provide maps that help scholars and practitioners find their way in the world.

A shared interest in outcomes and implications serves to facilitate productive exchange and dialogue across these maps.

- *Learning to see from different perspectives.* Practitioners and scholars learn to see themselves, their personal background, their organizational settings, and their own presuppositions from a range of different perspectives, thus enabling them to engage reflexively with their profession.

- *Pluralism is essential.* Pluralism in philosophical, theoretical, and methodical positions is a great asset to the profession. This also implies skepticism toward searching for a single logic of research—be it positivism, constructivism, realism (critical or otherwise), or any other ontology or epistemology. Rather than a single logic of research, what Peirce called "real doubt" is central to management and management scholarship.

- *Dialogical encounter.* In a culture of "dialogical encounter," researchers and other professionals engage in knowledge development by drawing on distinct philosophical assumptions but also regularly expose themselves to fundamentally different views, as an opportunity to reconsider their central presuppositions.

Subsequently, each panel member will have five minutes to pitch his/her comments and feedback. The chairman will deliberately guide the panelists' contributions and subsequent discussion toward a search for any common ground, that is, the minimum overlap between otherwise highly different worldviews and perspectives. Each panelist will thus be invited to prepare a pitch, based on the following *three questions*:

- ○ What do you believe is the common ground (if any) that ties together academics and practitioners in the field of management?

- ○ Do you object to (any of the statements in) the proposed norm, and if so, how would it have to be adapted to make it acceptable to you?

- ○ Will any shared norm, such as the one proposed earlier (possibly adapted), facilitate and promote dialogue between scholars/practitioners with highly different worldviews?

Each panelist can also comment on the proposed norm, drawing on his/her specific background and experiences. Subsequently, the audience will be invited to raise ideas, comments and questions regarding the "common ground" theme of the symposium. Given that only one practitioner was involved in developing the first version of the norm, the chairman will particularly seek the views of practitioners in the audience. Notably, the design challenge central to this symposium requires a discourse directed toward "informed consent," that is somewhat antagonistic to the culture of dissent and diversity prevailing in the academy (Gulati 2007; Walsh et al. 2006).

Program

Total length: 90 minutes.

- *David Denyer* (chair): introduction of the symposium *(2 minutes)*
- *Georges Romme*: Why and how of the quest for common ground, including a description of the set of norms described earlier *(≤ 8 minutes)*

- *Jean Bartunek* (panelist) will approach the three questions in the previous section by reflecting on the development of the discourse on mode 2 research ("What happened to mode 2?") as well as her broad experience in academic–practitioner collaborative research *(≤ 10 min.)*

- *Timothy Devinney* (panelist) will assess the proposed set of norms from the perspective of research in strategic management, social responsibility and corporate governance: can this set of norms, if truly agreed upon, somehow contribute to resolving the debate on the position of shareholders and other stakeholders in corporate governance? *(≤ 10 min.)*

- *Mark Learmonth* (panelist) will approach the three questions by drawing on a Critical Theory perspective, arguing that the idea of management as a (would-be) profession is deeply contested regarding, for example, the "evidence" it draws on; he will also draw on his extensive experience as a practicing manager in the health care industry to assess the proposed common ground *(≤ 10 min.)*

- *Denise Rousseau* (panelist) will respond to the three questions informed by her interest in revitalizing a Simonian perspective on our discipline; she will also draw on the experience of initiating and leading the Evidence-Based Management (EBMgt) collaborative, in which a highly diverse group of scholars and practitioners was brought together *(≤ 10 min.)*

- *Andrew van de Ven* (panelist) will assess the common ground proposed in the previous section by examining how it might be implemented and what factors might prevent their implementation, informed by his experience in conducting longitudinal field studies of the processes of organizational change as well as his more recent work on engaged scholarship *(≤ 10 min.)*

- Q&A and discussion with audience, including closure by the chairman *(≥ 30 min.)*

APPENDIX 2

Overview of Methods

This appendix provides an overview of research methods (broadly defined), categorized in terms of the dimensions used in Table 3.1. As argued in Chapter 3, "methods" could also be positioned as a separate, third axis of the framework outlined in Table 3.1, rather than integrating it in the horizontal "research activities" axis. To avoid the visual complexity of such a framework, Table 3.1 was formatted in two dimensions. However, as Spender (2015) observes, management scholars' key stock in trade is perhaps not so much "knowledge" but "method." This appendix therefore gives an idea of the various methods that can be used in any (combination of) cells in Table 3.1.

Notably, the overview in this appendix is far from complete; it merely serves to direct the reader to some prevailing research tools, procedures, heuristics, and frameworks employed in a particular combination of cells of this table. The list contains methods already widely used by management scholars and practitioners, but also includes several outside their normal scope. Obviously, the methods listed here are very diverse in terms of values and vocabulary, also a result of the fragmentation of the management discipline. In turn, this illustrates the complementarity of different methods in the context of a broad discourse on management as professional work informed by management scholarship. The codes (e.g. V1) in Table A.1 serve to link each of the methods listed below to particular cells in this table.

$$V_{1-2-3-4} \quad C_{1-2-3-4} \leftrightarrow I_{1-2}$$

Discovering and validating values and constructs that drive (the creation and evaluation of) espoused versus realized management/organizational practices: Argyris (2004), Argyris et al. (1985), Argyris and Schön (1978), Barrett (2006), Flyvbjerg (2001), Flyvbjerg et al. (2012), Grundstein (1983), and Schön (1987).

Table A.1. Overview of codes

	DISCOVERY		VALIDATION	
	Creating	Evaluating	Theorizing	Justifying
Values	V_1	V_2	V_3	V_4
Constructs	C_1	C_2	C_3	C_4
Models	M_1	M_2	M_3	M_4
Principles	P_1	P_2	P_3	P_4
Instantiations	I_1	I_2	I_3	I_4

$$V_{3-4} \quad C_{3-4} \quad M_{3-4} \quad P_{3-4}$$

Validating existing values in organizations from a variety of perspectives; including models and principles for managing a plurality of values: Gauthier (1986), McEwan (2001), and Pearson (1995).

$$C_1 \leftrightarrow C_2$$

Creating and evaluating constructs, by collecting and analyzing qualitative (e.g. language and text) data: Corbin and Strauss (2015), Denzin and Lincoln (2011), Riffe et al. (2013), and Silverman (2013).

$$C_{1-2} \leftrightarrow C_{3-4} \leftrightarrow M_{3-4}$$

Discovering and validating constructs, by drawing on content analysis of qualitative (e.g. language or text) data: Krippendorff (1980), Laver et al. (2003), and Tetlock et al. (2008).

$$C_{3-4} \quad M_{3-4}$$

Theorizing and justifying (testing) constructs and models, by collecting and analyzing qualitative and quantitative data: for example, textbooks on management research methods (e.g. Blumberg et al. 2011; Easterby-Smith et al. 2015), entrepreneurship research methods (e.g. Davidsson 2008), regression modeling and testing (e.g. Aiken and West 1991; Hair et al. 2010; Martin and Bridgmon 2012), and experimental studies (e.g. Aguinis and Bradley 2014).

$$C_{1-2-3-4} \quad M_{1-2-3-4} \leftrightarrow I_{1-2-3-4}$$

Iteratively discovering and validating constructs and models (to solve problems and address major challenges, such as continuous innovation): Kopec et al. (2012), Le Masson et al. (2010), Van Aken et al. (2007), and Wieringa (2014).

$$C_{3-4} \quad M_{3-4} \quad P_{3-4} \rightarrow I_{1-2}$$

Creating/discovering various organizational instantiations, drawing on a set of constructs, models and principles (mostly validated elsewhere in the literature): Galbraith et al. (2002), Jaques (1996), and Worren (2012).

$$C_{3-4} \quad M_{3-4} \rightarrow P_{1-2-3-4}$$

Systemically reviewing the literature and synthesizing the findings in (e.g. action or design) principles: Briner and Denyer (2012), Denyer et al. (2008), Tranfield et al. (2003), and Van Burg and Romme (2014).

$$C_{1-2-3-4} \quad M_{1-2-3-4}$$

Discovering and validating new theory (i.e. constructs and models): Alvesson and Karreman (2007), Locke et al. (2008), and Weick (1989) explore theorizing strategies that stretch the entire C and M rows. Examples of domain-specific theorizing are Czarniawska (2014) and Shane (2003).

$$C_{2-3-4} \quad M_{2-3-4} \quad (I_{2-3-4})$$

Process research methods for assessing, theorizing, and justifying instantiations in the form of processes of change and development at individual, group, organizational, or other levels: Langley (1999, 2007) and Van de Ven (2007).

$$C_{3-4} \ M_{3-4} \ I_{3-4} \rightarrow I_{1-2}$$

Creating and evaluating (e.g. value propositions, business models, and strategies of) ventures and enterprises by analyzing and exploiting opportunities, and drawing on academic research findings as well as practitioner insights: Byers et al. (2014), Clarysse and Kiefer (2011), MacIntosh and MacLean (2014), Osterwalder and Pigneur (2010), and Sarasvathy (2008).

$$M_1 \leftrightarrow M_2 \leftrightarrow M_3 \leftrightarrow M_4 \rightarrow P_1$$

Creating, assessing, theorizing, and justifying (dynamic) models that enable simulations of complex systems to design management policies/principles: Sterman (2000) and Davis et al. (2007).

$$P_{1-2} \leftrightarrow I_{1-2}$$

Idealized design (or "ideation") of instantiations and their guiding principles, including for example experience mapping, prototyping, and storytelling: Ackoff et al. (2006), Ackoff (1999), Brown (2009), Cooperrider and Whitney (1999), Kumar (2013), and Martin (2009).

$$I_{3-4} \ \leftrightarrow C_{3-4} \ M_{3-4}$$

Theorizing and justifying by collecting and analyzing case study data: Eisenhardt (1989, 1991), Eisenhardt and Graebner (2007), Miles et al. (2014), Van de Ven (2007), and Yin (2014).

$$I_1 \rightarrow I_{2-3} \ (P_{1-2-3})$$

Practitioners (self)reflecting on instantiations they created, including biographical accounts of prominent CEOs and entrepreneurs, and similar reflections published in social media (e.g. blogs): direct theorizing of these instantiations (possibly in terms of principles), but typically without any systematic development of constructs and/or models (e.g. Brandt 2011; Nayar 2010; Peters and Waterman 1982; Ries 2011): methods here include historical analysis in terms of "reasoned practice" (e.g. Collingwood 1999), for example using reflective journals, concept mapping, critical incident analysis, and other tools (Gray 2007; Uy et al. 2010).

$$I_2 \rightarrow P_{1-2}$$

Practitioner–academic collaborative teams creating and evaluating principles from given instantiations, based on, for example brainstorming, written documentation, narratives/stories, expert panels, and hypothetical scenarios: Krippendorff (2006) and Plsek et al. (2007).

$$I_{1-2} \rightarrow I_{3-4} \leftrightarrow C_{3-4} \ M_{3-4}$$

Reflexively discovering and validating instantiations of management processes/practices, drawing on ethnographic methods, action research, clinical methods, discourse analysis, and similar approaches: Bartunek and Louis (1996), Coughlan and Coghlan

(2002), Fairclough (2003), Hammersley and Atkinson (1995), Phillips and Hardy (2002), Reason and Bradbury (2001), and Schein (1987).

$$I_{3-4} \leftrightarrow C_{3-4} \; M_{3-4}$$

Practice-based methods for theorizing and justifying instantiated practices to interpret them from inside and outside as well as assess their social effects: Feldman and Orlikowski (2011), Gherardi (2012), and Jarzabkowksi and Kaplan (2015).

$$I_1 \leftrightarrow I_2 \leftrightarrow I_3 \leftrightarrow I_4 \quad (P_3)$$

Experimenting and prototyping (including co-creation and user innovation) to develop new ventures, products, services, management systems, or other instantiations; based on principles inferred from best practices and case studies in the area of experimentation, entrepreneurship, and so forth: Ries (2011), Thomke (2003), Thomke and Manzi (2014), and Von Hippel (2005).

Glossary of Terms

Abduction: the mental process that generates explanations, conjectures, theories, and hypotheses in situations where the outcome has not yet been established (as a belief) by induction and/or deduction.

Accountability: answerability and the expectation of account-giving.

Amateurism: a non-professional level of activity, typically arising when actors have little or no formal training (cf. knowledge) and low levels of expectation of their activity.

Authority: the right and/or justification to exercise power; this right or justification may originate from governmental rules and laws (e.g. in the case of police officers), established customs and habits (e.g. monarchs), academic knowledge and status (e.g. professors), corporate constitution (e.g. shareholders or boards of directors), or other sources.

Belief: any extreme position in favor of a particular idea or issue.

Bounded rationality: the idea that, when individuals act and/or decide, their rationality is limited by the information they have, the cognitive limitations of their minds, and the time available to decide.

CEO: Chief Executive Officer.

Circle: a functional work unit, involving a group of people with a common work objective who draw on circular processes to realize this objective; in circular organizing, the circle notion applies to all functional levels of the organization: from the board of directors to operational teams and units.

Circle process: see "Circular process."

Circular organizing: management approach that fundamentally redistributes leadership, authority and power throughout the organization, by setting up circles that are (double) linked.

Circular process: iterative management cycle involving leading, operating, and measuring activity; for this cycle to work effectively, the three activities need to be connected and interacting with each other (i.e. the cycle must be unbroken).

Circular system: network of (double linked) circles.

Circularity of power: the extent to which power flows upward as easily as downward in the organization, arising from the capacity to continually switch between domination and self-determination as organizational/human concerns.

Co-dependency: relationship between two entities, in which each entity is structurally dependent on the other one.

Consensus: agreement on an idea, topic, or proposed decision; in the case of taking decisions, such an agreement requires each participant to say "yes" to the proposed course of action.

Consent: see "Informed consent."

Construct: an ideal object conceived in the mind of a human subject (e.g. management scholar or practitioner); synomymously used with "notion" or "term" throughout this book. Constructs constitute the "vocabulary" for describing problems and challenges within a professional domain; most constructs in management research and practice involve concepts or variables that cannot be directly observed, and therefore are operationalized, estimated, or approximated.

Creating/Create: the initial act of conceiving a value, construct, model, principle, or instantiation that is (perceived as) new in the domain of the profession. As such, the act of creating might also involve introducing such an entity (e.g. construct) from other professional domains.

Creative discovery: see "Discovery."

Debt financing: taking on debt to increase shareholder value; the debt serves to leverage a (relatively) low baseline of equity in more shareholder value.

Decision: a course of action chosen/determined by an individual or a group of people.

Deduction: the mental process that starts from a given set of assumptions (not necessarily validated), such as axioms and postulates, and then uses formal reasoning to produce a conclusion with regard to an articulated statement (e.g. an initial hypothesis or conjecture).

Denotative: see "Denotation."

Denotation: the direct or explicit meaning of a word/phrase.

Design (as verb): any purposeful activity that involves devising courses of action to change an existing situation into a preferred one.

Design science: design-oriented research that develops knowledge that can be used by professionals (in the incumbent discipline) in creating, evaluating, theorizing, and justifying strategies and solutions in response to, or anticipation of, challenges and problems in their work.

Dialogical encounter: any form of encounter in which participants expose themselves to fundamentally different views, as an opportunity to reconsider their central presuppositions.

Disbelief: any extreme position against a particular idea or issue.

Discovery/Discover: research activities that serve to create new knowledge (e.g. in terms of values, constructs, models, principles, instantiations) with regard to management practices and processes that already exist or are currently emerging, or those that "might be" or "should be" created.

Distributed leadership: patterns and systems of leadership in which leadership is not confined to a few people at the top of the organization, but is distributed throughout.

Domination: the capacity of an agent to carry out its own will, despite resistance of other people involved.

Double linking: management principle in circular organizing which implies that two levels for policy decision making (i.e. circles) are linked by way of a representative chosen at the lower level (i.e. upward link) and a functional leader chosen at the higher level (i.e. top-down link).

Doubt: a tendency toward disbelief regarding a particular idea or issue, arising from the experience of not-knowing; as such, doubt promotes engaging in (some form of) inquiry.

Empirical phenomenon: an instantiation and/or its setting expressed in denotative statements. The term "empirical phenomenon" typically draws on a representational view of knowledge. (In the framework of Table 3.1, one can only talk about empirical phenomena in the context of the Validation of Constructs-Models-Instantiations.)

Entrepreneurship: identifying and exploiting opportunities to create value, by bringing people and/or resources together.

Episteme: Aristotle's notion of universal, invariable, and context-independent knowledge. (Aristotle defined episteme as one of three so-called "intellectual virtues," also including "techne" and "phronesis.")

Evaluating/Evaluate: the act of assessing (new) research in/output (i.e. values, constructs, models, principles, and instantiations) against criteria such as usefulness, novelty, and relevance.

Expectation: the act or state of looking forward to something (e.g. to happen or to be delivered).

Expertise: the core beliefs, insights, and tools required to perform professional work (general definition). The framework in Chapter 3 implies that expertise in the area of management (ideally) involves a coherent set of well-validated constructs, models, principles, and instantiations. Infused with values, expertise constitutes a professional body of knowledge on management.

Explicit knowledge: knowledge that has been articulated, codified, and/or stored in certain media.

False accounting: destroying, defacing, hiding, manipulating, or falsifying any record, registry, statement, or document that is required for accounting and/or annual reporting purposes.

Foundational fallacy: taking a (set of) construct(s) for granted, without the awareness that any construct is merely a nominal concept, created by human beings to help understand and solve specific problems.

Fractionated trading zone: a trading zone where disparate constituencies collaborate without (the need for) creating any shared meaning.

Grand (societal) challenge: a fundamental societal problem that is characterized by many interactions and nonlinear dynamics, has highly uncertain dimensions and consequences, and cuts across many jurisdictional boundaries.

Heterarchy: any collaborative ("horizontal") way to organize and coordinate work, in which agents have the same amount of power.

Hierarchy: vertical sequence of layers of accountability involving different degrees of abstraction.

Holacracy: see "Holacratic circular organizing."

Holacratic circular organizing: approach to circular organizing that draws on a system of self-organizing circles that decide on their own policies and allocate roles to people.

Inclination (toward belief): a tendency toward belief in a particular idea or issue.

Induction: the mental process that serves to draw conclusions from observations, experiments, or other data concerning an articulated hypothesis, conjecture, or other statement.

Information: data to which a human agent attributes meaning in a particular context.

Informed consent: decision rule implying that a decision is taken when there are no remaining "paramount" arguments against the proposal. Giving consent thus implies: "based on my understanding and appreciation of the relevant facts, implications, and consequences, I do not object to it."

Instantiation: the realization of an artifact (e.g. in a managerial context).

Instrumental knowledge: knowledge about means (e.g. conditions, methods, processes, techniques) that are, or can be, used to accomplish certain ends (e.g. objectives).

Justifying/Justify: enhancing the legitimacy of research in/output (i.e. values, constructs, models, principles and instantiations); for example, reviewing the available evidence in the literature, collecting and interpreting data, and/or statistically testing key causal mechanisms.

Knowledge: a familiarity, awareness, or understanding of someone or something.

Leadership: the process of social influence in which one enlists the aid and support of others in accomplishing common tasks.

Management: connecting and coordinating people and resources, to create value that no single individual can create alone.

Management technology: instrumental (i.e. means–end) knowledge about bringing together and coordinating people and resources in order to create value that no single individual can create alone. (Chapter 3 presents a framework implying that this type of instrumental knowledge can be best captured in terms of principles and instantiations.)

Model: a set of propositions or statements expressing relationships among constructs; this definition includes (what elsewhere may be called) theory, theoretical framework, conceptual framework, or mathematical model.

Near decomposability: property of all multi-celled organisms and organizations that consist of "a hierarchy of components, such that, at any level of the hierarchy, the rates of interaction within components at that level are much higher than the rates of interaction between different components" (Simon 2002: 587).

Nearly complete decomposability: see "Near decomposability."

Option (in corporate finance): a contract that gives the buyer-owner the right, but not the obligation, to buy or sell a particular asset at a specified price on or before a specified date.

Ownership: the state/fact of legally possessing something.

Perceptual judgement: the most basic form of inferencing, involving the (almost) instant mental transformation that takes place whenever sensory perception is at work. (Other forms of inferencing are abduction, induction, and deduction.)

Philosophical fallacy: see "Foundational fallacy."

Phronesis: Aristotle's notion of prudence, the reflective questioning and deliberating about how values and power work in current (e.g. management) practices. (Aristotle defined phronesis as one of three so-called intellectual virtues, also including "episteme" and "techne.")

Phronetic knowledge: reflective and deliberative knowledge about how values and power work in organizational and management practices.

Policy: the boundaries (limits) set for a certain operational or other process (to be) implemented or followed.

Power: the ability to influence somebody to do something that he/she otherwise would or might not do.

Pragmatism: philosophical perspective that avoids the search for a single foundation of knowledge; understands both theorizing and practicing as human activities; assumes doubt is essential in making us engage in inquiry; draws on a conception of knowledge as action that serves human purposes; and promotes dialogue between a plurality of voices.

Principles: solution concepts for a certain professional problem/challenge. In the area of management and entrepreneurship, principles tend to be heuristic in nature, incorporating ambiguity operators in predicate logic format. (Other labels often used are: design principles, design rules, design propositions, and technological rules.)

Profession: vocation founded upon specialized knowledge and training.

Professional (adjective): characterized by a high level of professionalism.

Professional (noun): member of a profession.

Professional body of knowledge (on management): the systematic collection of management activities and outcomes in terms of their values, constructs, models, principles, and instantiations, which (a) arises from continuous discovery and validation work by practitioners and scholars and (b) enables self-reflective growth and reproduction of management as professional activity.

Professionalism: the alignment between the incumbent profession's (a) shared purpose, (b) body of knowledge, (c) actual behavior in terms of actions and decisions, and (d) expectations held by various internal and external stakeholders.

Professional expertise: see "Expertise."

Professional purpose: see "Purpose."

Professional responsibility: a sense of obligation that professionals feel to themselves, to others, and to situations in which they act and perform.

Professional values: see "Value."

Professionalization: the (long-term) process toward more professionalism.

Proof of concept: an instantiation of a certain (set of) value(s), construct(s), model(s), and/or principle(s) that demonstrates its feasibility and potential of being used.

Psychological safety: a setting that participants perceive to be safe for interpersonal risk taking (e.g. they feel free to speak up about any issue).

Purpose: commitment to a "good" broader than self-interest.

Rationality (of action or decision): the level of conformity and consistency between one's action/decision and the facts and/or reasoning used to justify this action/decision.

Rationalization: the replacement of tradition, intuition, emotion, opportunism, or any other motivator perceived as largely "non-rational" with thoughts and actions that appear to be more rational and calculated.

Representational knowledge: knowledge about empirical matters that is universal, invariable and context-independent; the key idea/assumption here is that knowledge represents reality and can therefore be expressed in denotative statements regarding this reality as-it-is.

Research input/output: findings and outcomes arising from research activity, which can also serve as inputs for new research activity. Chapter 3 defines five categories of research input/output: values, constructs, models, principles, and instantiations.

Research method: a set of steps, for example in the form of a procedure or heuristic, which serves to perform a research activity.

Residual claim: the sole remaining claim on the company's net cash flows, after all other claimants have been paid.

Residual claimant: the economic agent who has the sole remaining (i.e. residual) claim on the company's net cash flows, after all other claimants have been paid.

Responsibility: a sense of obligation to oneself, to others, and to particular situations and challenges.

Requisite organization: the idea that any organization has an ideal or optimal (i.e. requisite) structure that "wants" to emerge, implying that a key task of managers is to uncover this structure.

Science-based professional body of knowledge: see "Professional body of knowledge."

Science-based professionalism: see "Professionalism." Throughout this book "professionalism" is equated with "science-based professionalism." Chapter 1 serves to distinguish science-based professionalism from other forms of professionalism.

Scientific validation: see "Validation."

Self-determination: the capacity to act autonomously (e.g. as individual or group).

Self-management: any form of management that implies work is (largely) self-determined and self-directed, typically by a group of individuals with a shared objective.

Self-organization: any process where some form of overall coordination or structure arises from the local interactions between components of an initially disordered system.

Shareholder: any individual person or legal entity that owns a share of stock in a (publicly or privately traded) company.

Shareholder value: for a publicly traded company, shareholder value (SV) is the market value of the company's equity (i.e. current shareprice × number of outstanding shares); SV of a privately held company is determined by using other valuation methods, in the absence of a market-based shareprice.

Shareholder value (maximization) perspective: the idea that a company and its managers should focus on maximizing shareholder value, as the ultimate measure of the company's success.

Short-termism: managerial focus on increasing the short-term value of their company rather than its long-term performance and viability.

Sociocracy: see "Sociocratic circular organizing."

Sociocratic circular organizing: approach to circular organizing that draws on a system of double linked circles, in which policy decisions are made by informed consent.

Stakeholder: an interest group, actor, claimant, or institution that exerts a hold on the incumbent organization; for a publicly traded company, stakeholders typically include suppliers, customers, employees, shareholders, investors, banks, and other financial intermediaries, (local) government, and the public media (including investment analysts).

Stakeholder management perspective: the idea that managers should balance the interests of all stakeholders of the organization.

Stock: the equity stake of the owners of a company.

Stockholder: see "Shareholder."

Stock option: an option to buy equity in a particular company, at a fixed price at a certain date in the future.

Tacit knowledge: knowledge that is not explicated.

Techne: Aristotle's notion of instrumental knowledge, based on a means–ends rationality. (Aristotle defined techne as one of three intellectual virtues, also including "episteme" and "phronesis.")

Technology: instrumental knowledge that is instantiated in some form (e.g. machines, products, processes, practices).

Theorizing/Theorize: producing propositions or statements that are generalizable as well as applicable to, or testable on, individual cases. Theorizing may thus serve to, for example, codify a particular value, use constructs and models to explain how or why something has happened (or instantiated), or use principles to brainstorm and speculate about whether an envisioned instantiation is likely to work.

Trading zone: space where communities with disparate meanings and logics collaborate despite their differences.

Tribal behavior: human behavior in societal settings organized largely on the basis of face-to-face communities, each bound together by kinship relations and reciprocal exchange. In Chapter 4, it serves to denote the behavioral patterns arising when scholars or practitioners operate in an exclusive group/community (e.g. focused on "rigorous research" or "shareholder value maximization") that primarily talks to itself and dismisses work done elsewhere.

Validation/Validate: research activities that serve to theorize and justify knowledge. The conventional objects of validation efforts in management research are theoretical constructs and models, but Chapter 3 serves to demonstrate that values, principles, and instantiations can also be theorized and justified.

Value: notions or imperatives that guide an individual in establishing the degree of importance a certain action has for her/him and what kind of action is best to do (cf. "right" conduct); professional values serve as a key mechanism in guiding professional work.

Vocation: occupational activity to which a person is specially drawn.

References

AACSB (2015). Academic and professional engagement. Retrieved December 18, 2014 from http://www.aacsb.edu/accreditation/standards/2013-business/academic-and-professional-engagement-standards/

Abbott, A. (1988). *The System of Professions. An Essay on the Division of Expert Labor.* Chicago, IL: University of Chicago Press.

Abegglen, J., and G. Stalk (1989). Whose company is it? In: M. L. Tushman, C. O'Reilly, and D. A. Nadler (eds.), *The Management of Organizations*, pp. 317–36. New York: Harper & Row.

Academy of Management (2015). Vision, mission, objectives & values. Retrieved January 15, 2015 via http://aom.org/

Ackoff, R. L. (1981). *Creating the Corporate Future.* New York: Wiley.

Ackoff, R. L. (1989). The circular organization: An update. *Academy of Management Executive* 3(1): 11–16.

Ackoff, R. L. (1994). *The Democratic Corporation.* New York: Oxford University Press.

Ackoff, R. L. (1999). *Re-Creating the Corporation: A Design of Organizations For the 21st Century.* New York: Oxford University Press.

Ackoff, R., and F. E. Emery (1973). *On Purposeful Systems.* Chicago, IL: Aldine-Atherton.

Ackoff, R. L., J. Magidson, and H. J. Addison (2006). *Idealized Design: Creating an Organization's Future.* Upper Saddle River, NJ: Prentice Hall.

Adamo, J. (2013). A great stock option scam. *Forbes*, August 12, 2013. Retrieved via www.forbes.com December 20, 2014.

Adler, P. S., S. Kwon, and C. Heckscher (2008). Professional work: The emergence of collaborative community. *Organization Science* 19: 359–76.

Adner, R. (2012). *The Wide Lens: A New Strategy for Innovation.* New York: Portfolio/Penguin.

Aguinis, H., and K. J. Bradley (2014). Best practice recommendations for designing and implementing experimental vignette methodology studies. *Organizational Research Methods* 17: 351–71.

Aguinis, H., D. L. Shapiro, E. P. Antonacopoulou, and T. G. Cummings (2014). Scholarly impact: A pluralist conceptualization. *Academy of Management Learning & Education* 13: 623–39.

Aiken, L. S., and S. G. West (1991). *Multiple Regression: Testing and Interpreting Interactions.* Thousand Oaks, CA: Sage.

Alvesson, M., and D. Karreman (2007). Constructing mystery: Empirical matters in theory development. *Academy of Management Review* 32: 1265–81.

References

Alvesson, M., and H. Willmott (eds.) (2003). *Studying Management Critically*. London: Sage.

Amabile, T. M., C. Patterson, J. Mueller, T. Wojcik, P. W. Odomirok, M. Marsh, and S. J. Kramer (2001). Academic–practitioner collaboration in management research: A case of cross-profession collaboration. *Academy of Management Journal* 44: 418–31.

Anderson, M., and P. Escher (2010). *The MBA Oath: Setting a Higher Standard for Business Leaders*. New York: Portfolio.

Ansell, C. K. (2011). *Pragmatist Democracy: Evolutionary Learning as Public Philosophy*. Oxford: Oxford University Press.

Aretz, K., and Bartram, S. M. (2010). Corporate hedging and shareholder value. *Journal of Financial Research* 33: 317–71.

Argyris, C. (1993). *Knowledge for Action*. San Francisco, CA: Jossey-Bass.

Argyris, C. (2004). *Reasons and Rationalizations: The Limits to Organizational Knowledge*. Oxford: Oxford University Press.

Argyris, C., and D. Schön (1978). *Organization Learning: A Theory of Action Approach*. Reading, MA: Addison Wesley.

Argyris, C., R. Putnam, and D. McLain Smith (1985). *Action Science: Concepts, Methods, and Skills for Research and Intervention*. San Francisco, CA: Jossey-Bass.

Armstrong, C. S., and R. Vashishtha (2012). Executive stock options, differential risk-taking incentives, and firm value. *Journal of Financial Economics* 104: 70–88.

Arthur, W. B. (2009). *The Nature of Technology: What It Is and How It Evolves*. London: Penguin.

Atchison, T. J. (1991). The employment relationship: untied or retied? *Academy of Management Executive* 5(4): 52–62.

Augier, M., and J. G. March (2011). *The Roots, Rituals, and Rhetorics of Change. North American Business Schools after the Second World War*. Stanford, CA: Stanford Business Books.

Augier, M., J. G. March, and B. N. Sullivan (2005). Notes on the evolution of a research community: Organization studies in Anglophone North America 1945–2000. *Organization Science* 16: 85–95.

Avenier, M. (2010). Shaping a constructivist view of organizational design science. *Organization Studies* 31: 1229–55.

Avenier, M. J., and A. Parmentier Cajaiba (2012). The dialogical model: Developing academic knowledge for and from practice. *European Management Review* 9: 199–212.

Axelrod, R. A., and M. D. Cohen (2000). *Harnessing Complexity: Organizational Implications of a Scientific Frontier*. New York: Free Press.

Backover, A. (2002). Another guilty plea in WorldCom fraud case. *USA Today*, October 7, 2002. Retrieved via http://www.usatoday.com/ December 27, 2014.

Baert, P. (2005). *Philosophy of the Social Sciences: Towards Pragmatism*. Cambridge, UK: Polity.

Bakhtin, M. M. (1981). *The Dialogic Imagination: Four Essays* (edited by M. Holquist). Austin: University of Texas Press.

Baldwin, C. Y. (2012). Organization design for distributed innovation. Harvard Business School Finance Working Paper No. 12-100. Available at SSRN: http://dx.doi.org/10.2139/ssrn.2055814

Barends, E., S. Ten Have, and F. Huisman (2012). Learning from other evidence-based practices: The case of medicine. In: D. M. Rousseau (ed.), *The Oxford Handbook of Evidence-Based Management*, pp. 25–42. New York: Oxford University Press.

Barker, R. (2010). No, management is *not* a profession. *Harvard Business Review* 88 (July–August): 52–60.

Barley, S. R., and P. S. Tolbert (1997). Institutionalization and structuration: Studying the links between action and institution. *Organization Studies* 18: 93–118.

Baron, J. N., M. D. Burton, and M. T. Hannan (1996). The road taken: Origins and evolution of employment systems in emerging companies. *Industrial and Corporate Change* 5: 239–75.

Baron, J. N., M. T. Hannan, and M. D. Burton (1999). Building the iron cage: Determinants of managerial intensity in the early years of organizations. *American Sociological Review* 64: 527–47.

Barr, S. H., T. Baker, S. K. Markham, and A. I. Kingon (2009). Bridging the valley of death: Lessons learned from 14 years of commercialization of technology education. *Academy of Management Learning & Education* 8: 370–88.

Barrett, F. J., and R. E. Fry (2005). *Appreciative Inquiry: A Positive Approach to Building Cooperative Capacity*. Chagrin Falls, OH: Taos Institute Publications.

Barrett, R. (2006). *Building a Values-Driven Organization: A Whole System Approach to Cultural Transformation*. New York: Routledge.

Bartlett, D. (2011). The neglect of the political: An alternative evidence-based practice for I-O psychology. *Industrial and Organizational Psychology: Perspectives on Science and Practice* 4: 27–31.

Bartunek, J. M. (2003). A dream for the Academy. *Academy of Management Review* 28: 198–203.

Bartunek, J. M. (2007). Academic–practitioner collaboration need not require joint or relevant research: Towards a relational scholarship of integration. *Academy of Management Journal* 50: 1323–33.

Bartunek, J. M. (2011). What has happened to Mode 2? *British Journal of Management* 22: 555–8.

Bartunek, J. M., and M. R. Louis (1996). *Insider/Outsider Team Research*. Newbury Park, CA: Sage.

Bartunek, J., and S. L. Rynes (2010). The construction and contributions of "implications for practice": What's in them and what might they offer? *Academy of Management Learning and Education* 9: 100–17.

Bartunek, J. M., and S. L. Rynes (2014). Academics and practitioners are alike and unlike: The paradoxes of academic–practitioner relationships. *Journal of Management* 40: 1181–201.

Bartunek, J. M., J. Balogun, and B. Do (2011). Considering planned change anew: Stretching large group interventions strategically, emotionally, and meaningfully. *The Academy of Management Annals* 5(1): 1–52.

Baskerville, R., and J. Pries-Heje (2010). Design logic and the ambiguity operator. In: R. Winter, J. L. Zhao, and S. Aier (eds.), *Global Perspectives on Design Science Research—Lecture Notes in Computer Science*, vol. 6105, pp. 180–93. Berlin/Heidelberg: Springer.

Bate, P. (2007). Bringing the design sciences to organization development and change management (introduction to special issue). *Journal of Applied Behavioral Science* 43: 8–11.

Bauer, P. C., M. Freitag, and P. Sciarini (2013). Political trust in Switzerland: Again a special case? Retrieved November 20, 2014 via SSRN: http://ssrn.com/abstract= 2471152

Bedeian, A. G. (1989). Totems and taboos: Undercurrents in the management discipline. *Academy of Management News* 19(4): 1–6.

Beer, M. (2009). *High Commitment High Performance: How to Build A Resilient Organization for Sustained Advantage*. San Francisco, CA: Jossey-Bass.

Beer, S. (1959). *Cybernetics and Management*. London: English Universities Press.

Bell, D. (1973). *The Coming of Post-Industrial Society: A Venture in Social Forecasting*. New York: Basic Books.

Bender, R. (2014). *Corporate Financial Strategy* (4th edn). New York: Routledge.

Benton, J. F. (1985). Trotula, women's problems, and the professionalization of medicine in the Middle Ages. *Bulletin of Historical Medicine* 59(1): 30–53.

Berle, A., and G. Means (1932). *The Modern Corporation and Private Property*. New York: Commerce Clearing House.

Bernstein, J. M. (1994). *Recovering Ethical Life: Jürgen Habermas and the Future of Critical Theory*. New York: Routledge.

Bernstein, R. J. (1991). *The New Constellation: The Ethical-Political Horizons of Modernity/Postmodernity*. Cambridge, UK: Polity.

Berson, Y., S. Oreg, and T. Dvir (2008). CEO values, organizational culture and firm outcomes. *Journal of Organizational Behavior* 29: 615–33.

Bhide, A. (1994). Efficient markets, deficient governance. *Harvard Business Review* 72(6): 128–39.

Billsberry, J., and A. Birnik (2010). Management as a contextual practice: The need to blend science, skills and practical wisdom. *Organization Management Journal* 7: 171–78.

Blair, M. (1995). *Ownership and Control: Rethinking Corporate Governance for the Twenty-First Century*. Washington, DC: Brookings Institution.

Blattberg, C. (2004). *From Pluralist to Patriotic Politics: Putting Practice First*. New York: Oxford University Press.

Bloom, N., C. Genakos, R. Sadun, and J. van Reenen (2012). Management practices across firms and countries. *The Academy of Management Perspectives* 26: 12–33.

Bloom, N., R. Sadun, and J. van Reenen (2015). Management as a technology? Working paper: http://web.stanford.edu/~nbloom/MAT.pdf (retrieved August 21, 2015).

Bloom, N., R. Lemos, R. Sadun, D. Scur, and J. van Reenen (2014). The new empirical economics of management. *Journal of the European Economic Association* 12: 835–76.

Blumberg, B., D. R. Cooper, and P. S. Schindler (2011). *Business Research Methods* (3rd edn). London: McGraw-Hill.

Bogers, M., and W. Horst (2014). Collaborative prototyping: Cross-fertilization of knowledge in prototype-driven problem solving. *Journal of Product Innovation Management* 31: 744–64.

Boggan, S. (2001). Nike admits to mistakes over child labour. *The Independent*, 20 October 2001.

Böhm, S., A. C. Dinerstein, and A. Spicer (2010). (Im)possibilities of autonomy: Social movements in and beyond capital, the state and development. *Social Movement Studies: Journal of Social, Cultural and Political Protest* 9: 17–32.

Boisot, M., M. Nordberg, S. Yami, and B. Nicquevert (eds.) (2011). *Collisions and Collaboration: The Organization of Learning in the ATLAS Experiment at the LHC.* Oxford: Oxford University Press.

Boisvert, R. D. (1998). *John Dewey: Rethinking Our Time.* Albany, NY: State University of New York Press.

Boland, R. J., and F. Collopy (2004). Toward a design vocabulary for management. In: R. J. Boland and F. Collopy (eds.), *Managing as Designing*, pp. 265–76. Stanford, CA: Stanford University Press.

Bouchikhi, H., and J. Kimberly (2001). It's difficult to innovate: The death of the tenured professor and the birth of the knowledge entrepreneur. *Human Relations* 54: 77–84.

Bovens, M., and A. Wille (2008). Deciphering the Dutch drop: Ten explanations for decreasing political trust in The Netherlands. *International Review of Administrative Sciences* 74: 283–305.

Bowman, J. S., and J. P. West (2011). Public administration as a profession: Promises, problems, and prospects. In: D. C. Menzel and H. L. White (eds.), *The State of Public Administration: Issues, Challenges, and Opportunities.* New York: M.E. Sharpe.

Boxenbaum, E., and L. Rouleau (2011). New knowledge products as bricolage: Metaphors and scripts in organizational theory. *Academy of Management Review* 36: 272–96.

Boyer, E. L. (1990). *Scholarship Reconsidered: Priorities of the Professorate.* Princeton, NJ: Carnegie Foundation.

Bradbury Huang, H. (2010). What is good action research? *Action Research* 8: 93–109.

Brandt, R. L. (2011). *The Google Guys: Inside the Brilliant Minds of Google Founders Larry Page and Sergey Brin.* New York: Portfolio/Penguin.

Bratton, W. W., and M. L. Wachter (2010). The case against shareholder empowerment. *University of Pennsylvania Law Review* 158: 653–728.

Briner, R. B., and D. Denyer (2012). Systematic review and evidence synthesis as a practice and scholarship tool. In: D. M. Rousseau (ed.), *The Oxford Handbook of Evidence-Based Management*, pp. 112–29. New York: Oxford University Press.

Brown, J. (2005). *The World Café: Shaping Our Futures Through Conversations That Matter.* San Francisco, CA: Berrett-Koehler.

Brown, S. L., and K. M. Eisenhardt (1998). *Competing on the Edge: Strategy as Structured Chaos.* Boston, MA: Harvard Business School Press.

Brown, T. (2009). *Change by Design.* New York: HarperCollins.

Buchanan, J. M., and G. Tullock (1962). *The Calculus of Consent.* Ann Arbor: University of Michigan Press.

Buck, J. (2003). *Employee Commitment in Sociocratic versus Conventional Organizations* (Master thesis). Washington, DC: George Washington University.

Buck, J., and S. Villines (2007). *We the People: Consenting to a Deeper Democracy.* Washington, DC: Sociocracy.Info.

Bunge, M. (1967). *Scientific Research II: The Search For Truth.* Berlin: Springer.

Burawoy, M. (1979). *Manufacturing Consent*. Chicago/London: University of Chicago Press.

Burgoyne, J., and K. Turnbull James (2006). Towards best or better practice in corporate leadership development: Operational issues in mode 2 and design science research. *British Journal of Management* 17: 303–16.

Burrell, G. (1994). Modernism, postmodernism and organizational analysis 4: The contribution of Jürgen Habermas. *Organization Studies* 15: 1–19.

Burton, R. M., and B. Obel (2004). *Strategic Organizational Diagnosis and Design: Developing Theory for Application*. Dordrecht, Netherlands: Kluwer.

Burton, R. M., and B. Obel (2011). Computational modeling for what-is, what-might-be, and what-should-be studies—and triangulation. *Organization Science* 22: 1195–202.

Bushe, G. R. (2011). Appreciative inquiry: Theory and critique. In: D. Boje, B. Burnes, and J. Hassard (eds.), *The Routledge Companion to Organizational Change*, pp. 87–103. Oxford: Routledge.

Bushe, G. R., and A. F. Kassam (2005). When is appreciative inquiry transformational? *Journal of Applied Behavioral Science* 41: 161–81.

Bushe, G. R., and R. J. Marshak (2009). Revisioning organization development: Diagnostic and dialogic premises and patterns of practice. *Journal of Applied Behavioral Science* 45: 348–68.

Byers, T. H., R. C. Dorf, and A. J. Nelson (2014). *Technology Ventures: From Idea to Enterprise* (4th edn). New York: McGraw-Hill.

Cameron, K. S., and R. E. Quinn (2011). *Diagnosing and Changing Organizational Culture: Based on the Competing Values Framework* (3rd edn). San Francisco, CA: Jossey-Bass.

Cameron, K. S., and D. A. Whetten (1983). A model for teaching management skills. *Journal of Management Education* 8(2): 21–7.

Carley, K. (1992). Organizational learning and personnel turnover. *Organization Science* 3: 20–46.

Carlile, P. R. (2002). A pragmatic view of knowledge and boundaries: Boundary objects in new product development. *Organization Science* 13: 442–55.

Carlson, N. (2015). *Marissa Mayer and the Fight to Save Yahoo*. New York: Hachette.

Cha, S. E., and A. C. Edmondson (2006). When values backfire: Leadership, attribution, and disenchantment in a values-driven organization. *The Leadership Quarterly* 17: 57–78.

Charkham, J., and A. Simpson (1999). *Fair Shares: The Future of Shareholder Power and Responsibility*. Oxford: Oxford University Press.

Chemers, M. M. (1997). *An Integrative Theory of Leadership*. New York: Lawrence Erlbaum Associates.

Cheney, G. (2000). *Values at Work: Employee Participation Meets Market Pressure at Mondragón*. Ithaca, NY: Cornell University Press.

Chesbrough, H. (2003). *Open Innovation: The New Imperative for Creating and Profiting from Technology*. Boston, MA: Harvard Business School Press.

Chia, R. (1996). Teaching paradigm shifting in management education: University business schools and the entrepreneurial imagination. *Journal of Management Studies* 33: 409–28.

Chichilnisky, G., and G. M. Heal (1983). Necessary and sufficient conditions for a resolution of the social choice paradox. *Journal of Economic Theory* 31: 68–87.

Citrin, J., M. Levy, and M. Wright (2014). Multicultural policy and political support in European democracies. *Comparative Political Studies* 47: 1531–57.

Clark, S. C., R. Callister, and R. Wallace (2003). Undergraduate management skills courses and students' emotional intelligence. *Journal of Management Education* 27(1): 3–23.

Clarysse, B., and S. Kiefer (2011). *The Smart Entrepreneur: How to Build for a Successful Business*. London: Elliott & Thompson.

Clarysse, B., M. Wright, A. Lockett, E. Van de Velde, and A. Vohora (2005). Spinning out new ventures: A typology of incubation strategies from European research institutions. *Journal of Business Venturing* 20: 183–216.

Clegg, S. R. (1989). *Frameworks of Power*. London: Sage.

Clegg, S. R., and T. S. Pitsis (2012). Phronesis and power research. In: B. Flyvbjerg, T. Landman and S. Schram (eds.), *Real Social Science: Applied Phronesis*, pp. 66–91. Cambridge: Cambridge University Press.

CMI (2015). Presidential team and trustees of Chartered Management Institute. http://www.managers.org.uk/about-us/governance/presidential-team-and-trustees retrieved January 23, 2015.

Coffee, J. (1991). Liquidity versus control: The institutional investor as corporate monitor. *Columbia Law Review* 91: 1277–368.

Coghlan, D., and A. B. Shani (2013). Organizational-development research interventions: Perspectives from action research and collaborative management research. In: H. S. Leonard, R. Lewis, A. M. Freedman, and J. Passmore (eds.), *The Wiley-Blackwell Handbook of the Psychology of Leadership, Change and Organizational Development*, pp. 443–60. Chichester, UK: Wiley.

Collingwood, R. G. (1999). *The Principles of History and Other Writings in Philosophy of History* (edited with an introduction by W. H. Dray and W. J. van der Dussen). Oxford: Oxford University Press.

Collins, D. (1997). The ethical superiority and inevitability of participatory management as an organizational system. *Organization Science* 8: 489–507.

Collins, H. M. (2001). Tacit knowledge, trust and the Q of sapphire. *Social Studies of Science* 31: 71–85.

Collins, H. M. (2010). *Tacit and Explicit Knowledge*. Chicago: University of Chicago Press.

Collins, H. M., and R. Evans (2007). *Rethinking Expertise*. Chicago: University of Chicago Press.

Collins, H., R. Evans, and M. Gorman (2007). Trading zones and interactional expertise. *Studies in History and Philosophy of Science Part A*, 38: 657–66.

Colquitt, J. A., and G. George (2011). From the editors: Publishing in AMJ—Part 1: Topic choice. *Academy of Management Journal* 54: 432–5.

Cooper, C. (2008). *Extraordinary Circumstances: The Journey of a Corporate Whistleblower*. Hoboken, NJ: Wiley.

Cooperrider, D. L., and D. Whitney (1999). *Appreciative Inquiry*. San Francisco, CA: Berrett-Koehler.

Cooperrider, D. L., F. Barrett, and S. Srivastva (1995). Social construction and appreciative inquiry: A journey in organizational theory. In: D. Hosking, H. P. Dachler, and K. J. Gergen (eds.), *Management and Organization: Relational Alternatives to Individualism*, pp. 157–200. Brookfield, VT: Avebury/Ashgate Publishing.

Copeland, C., and D. N. Laband (2002). Expressiveness and voting. *Public Choice* 110: 351–63.

Corbin, J., and A. Strauss (2015). *Basics of Qualitative Research: Techniques and Procedures for Developing Grounded Theory* (4th edn). Thousand Oaks, CA: Sage.

Corner, P. D., and K. Pavlovich (2014). Shared value through inner knowledge creation. *Journal of Business Ethics*, online pre-publication, December 2014. DOI: 10.1007/s10551-014-2488-x

Coughlan, P., and D. Coghlan (2002). Action research for operations management. *International Journal of Operations & Production Management* 22: 220–40.

Coughlan, P., and C. F. Ponto (2014). Leverage points and prototypes: Integrating systems thinking and design thinking to help organizations evolve. In: M. Grace and G. Graen (eds.), *Millennial Spring: Designing the Future of Organizations*, pp. 107–22. Charlotte, NC: Information Age.

Courpasson, D. (2000). Managerial strategies of domination. Power in soft bureaucracies. *Organization Studies* 21: 141–61.

Covey, S. R. (1989). *The 7 Habits of Highly Effective People*. New York: Fireside.

Cowan, R., and D. Foray (1997). The economics of codification and the diffusion of knowledge. *Industrial and Corporate Change* 6: 595–22.

Crowther-Heyck, H. (2005). *Herbert A. Simon: The Bounds of Reason in Modern America*. Baltimore: Johns Hopkins University Press.

Currie, G., and D. Knights (2003). Reflecting on a critical pedagogy in management education. *Management Learning* 34: 27–49.

Cyert, R. M., and J. G. March (1963). *A Behavioral Theory of the Firm*. Englewood Cliffs, NJ: Prentice-Hall.

Czarniawska, B. (1998). Who is afraid of incommensurability? *Organization* 5: 273–5.

Czarniawska, B. (2003). Social constructionism and organization studies. In: R. Westwood and S. Clegg (eds.), *Debating Organization: Point-Counterpoint in Organization Studies*, pp. 128–39. Malden, MA: Blackwell.

Czarniawska, B. (2014). *A Theory of Organizing*. Cheltenham, UK: Edward Elgar.

Daft, R. L. (2002). *The Leadership Experience*. Mason, OH: South-Western.

Daft, R. L., and N. B. Macintosh (1984). The nature and use of formal control systems for management control and strategy implementation. *Journal of Management* 10: 43–66.

Dahl, R. A. (1989). *Democracy and Its Critics*. New Haven: Yale University Press.

Dalton, R. (2004). *Democratic Challenges, Democratic Choices: The Erosion of Political Support in Advanced Industrial Democracies*. Oxford: Oxford University Press.

Dasgupta, S. (2003). Multidisciplinary creativity: the case of Herbert A. Simon. *Cognitive Science* 27: 683–707.

Davidsson, P. (2008). *The Entrepreneurship Research Challenge*. Cheltenham, UK: Edward Elgar.

Davis, J. P., K. M. Eisenhardt, and C. B. Bingham (2007). Developing theory through simulation methods. *Academy of Management Review* 32: 480–99.

Day, D. V., and M. M. Harrison (2007). A multilevel, identity-based approach to leadership development. *Human Resource Management Review* 17: 360–73.

Deakin, S. (2014). Against shareholder empowerment. In: J. Williamson, C. Driver, and P. Kenway (eds.), *Beyond Shareholder Value: The Reasons and Choices for Corporate Governance Reform*, pp. 36–40. London: TUC.

Deci, E. L. (1980). *The Psychology of Self-Determination*. Lexington, MA: Lexington Books.

Deetz, S. (1996). Describing differences in approaches to organization science: Rethinking Burrell and Morgan and their legacy. *Organization Science* 7: 191–207.

Deetz, S. (2003). Disciplinary power, conflict suppression and human resources management. In: M. Alvesson and H. Willmott (eds.), *Studying Management Critically*, pp. 23–45. London: Sage.

De Janasz, S., and M. Peipert (2015). Managing yourself: CEOs need mentors too. *Harvard Business Review* 93 (4): 100–3.

Deming, W. E. (1986). *Out of the Crisis*. Cambridge, MA: MIT Press.

De Munck, B., S. L. Kaplan, and H. Soly (2007). *Learning on the Shop Floor: Historical Perspectives on Apprenticeship*. New York/Oxford: Berghahn Books.

Denyer, D., D. Tranfield, and J. E. Van Aken (2008). Developing design propositions through research synthesis. *Organization Studies* 29: 393–413.

Denzin, N. K. (2011). The politics of evidence. In: N. K. Denzin and Y. S. Lincoln (eds.), *The Sage Handbook of Qualitative Research* (3rd edn), pp. 645–58. Thousand Oaks, CA: Sage.

Denzin, N. K., and Y. S. Lincoln (eds.) (2011). *The Sage Handbook of Qualitative Research*. Thousand Oaks, CA: Sage.

De Rond, M., and A. N. Miller (2005). Publish or perish: Bane or boon of academic life? *Journal of Management Inquiry* 14: 321–9.

Der Spiegel (2014). Korruptionsverdacht auf BER-Baustelle: Mehdorns Desaster ist perfekt [Suspicions of corruption at BER construction site: Mehdorn is a complete disaster]. *Der Spiegel*, 28 May 2014: www.spiegel.de/wirtschaft/unternehmen/hauptstadtflughafen-korruptionsverdacht-mehdorn-unter-druck-a-972277.html retrieved December 20, 2014.

Despotidou, L., and G. P. Prastacos (2012). Professionalism in business: Insights from ancient philosophy. In: G. P. Prastacos, F. Wang, and K. E. Soderquist (eds.), *Leadership through the Classics*, pp. 437–55. Berlin/Heidelberg: Springer.

Detert, J. R., and L. K. Trevino (2008). Speaking up to higher-ups: How supervisors and skip-level leaders influence employee voice. *Organization Science* 21: 249–70.

Devinney, T. M., A. M. Mcgahan, and M. Zollo (2013a). A research agenda for global stakeholder strategy. *Global Strategy Journal* 3: 325–37.

Devinney, T. M., J. Schwalbach, and C. A. Williams (2013b). Corporate social responsibility and corporate governance: Comparative perspectives. *Corporate Governance: An International Review* 21: 413–19.

Dewey, J. (1929). *The Quest for Certainty: A Study of the Relation of Knowledge and Action*. Minton, Balch & Company, New York. Reprinted in: J. Dewey (1984), *The Later Works: 1925–1953*, volume 4: 1929 (eds. J. A. Boydston and H. F. Simon), pp. 1–254. Carbondale and Edwardsville, IL: Southern Illinois University Press.

Dierdorff, E. C., D. J. Nayden, D. C. Jain, and S. C. Jain (2013). Ensuring and enhancing future value. In: GMAC (ed.), *Disrupt or Be Disrupted: A Blueprint for Change in Management Education*, pp. 21–56. San Francisco, CA: Jossey-Bass.

Donaldson, L. (2003). Position statement for positivism. In: R. Westwood and S. Clegg (eds.), *Debating Organization: Point-Counterpoint in Organization Studies*, pp. 116–27. Malden, MA: Blackwell.

Donaldson, T., and L. E. Preston (1995). The stakeholder theory of the corporation: Concepts, evidence, and implications. *Academy of Management Review* 20: 65–91.

Dorado, S., and M. J. Ventresca (2013). Crescive entrepreneurship in complex social problems: Institutional conditions for entrepreneurial engagement. *Journal of Business Venturing* 28: 69–82.

Dougherty, D. (2008). Bridging social constraint and social action to design organizations for innovation. *Organization Studies* 29: 415–34.

Drucker, P. F. (1974). *Management: Tasks, Responsibilities, Practices*. New York: HarperCollins.

Drucker, P. F. (1985). *Innovation and Entrepreneurship*. New York: Harper & Row.

Dubin, R. (1978). *Theory Development*. New York: Free Press.

Dunning, T. (2012). *Natural Experiments in the Social Sciences: A Design-Based Approach*. Cambridge: Cambridge University Press.

Easterby-Smith, M., R. Thorpe, and P. R. Jackson (2015). *Management and Business Research* (5th edn). London: Sage.

Edmondson, A. (1999). Psychological safety and learning behavior in work teams. *Administrative Science Quarterly* 44: 350–83.

Eisenhardt, K. M. (1989). Building theories from case study research. *Academy of Management Review* 14: 532–50.

Eisenhardt, K. M. (1991). Better stories and better constructs: The case for rigor and comparative logic. *Academy of Management Review* 16: 620–7.

Eisenhardt, K. M., and M. E. Graebner (2007). Theory building from cases: Opportunities and challenges. *Academy of Management Journal* 50: 25–32.

Elias, N., and J. L. Scotson (1994). *The Established and the Outsiders: A Sociological Enquiry into Community Problems* (2nd edn). Thousand Oaks, CA: Sage.

Emery, F. E. (1980). Designing socio-technical systems for "greenfield" sites. *Journal of Occupational Behaviour* 1: 19–27.

Emery, F. E., and E. Thorsrud (1976). *Democracy at Work*. Leiden (Netherlands): Nijhoff.

Emmerling, R. J., and D. Goleman (2005). Leading with emotion. *Leadership Excellence* 22(7): 9–10.

Endenburg, G. (1974). *Sociocratie: Een Redelijk Ideaal*. Zaandijk, Netherlands: Klaas Woudt.

Endenburg, G. (1988). *Sociocracy: The Organization of Decision-Making*. Rotterdam, Netherlands: Sociocratic Center.

Endenburg, G. (1998). *Sociocracy as Social Design*. Delft, Netherlands: Eburon.

Erickson, M. N. (2014). The art of conducting dynamic emergence. In: M. Grace and G. Graen (eds.), *Millennial Spring: Designing the Future of Organizations*, pp. 253–78. Charlotte, NC: Information Age.

Ethiraj, S. K., and D. A. Levinthal (2004). Bounded rationality and the search for organizational architecture: An evolutionary perspective on the design of organizations and their evolvability. *Administrative Science Quarterly* 49: 404–37.

Evetts, J. (2011). A new professionalism? Challenges and opportunities. *Current Sociology* 59: 406–22.

Fairclough, N. (2003). *Analysing Discourse: Textual Analysis for Social Research*. London: Routledge.

Fama, E. F., and M. C. Jensen (1983). Separation of ownership and control. *Journal of Law and Economics* 26: 301–26.

Fayol, H. (1949). *General and Industrial Management* (translated by Constance Storrs). London: Pitman & Sons.

Feldman, M. S., and W. J. Orlikowski (2011). Theorizing practice and practicing theory. *Organization Science* 22: 1240–53.

Fendt, J. (2013). Lost in translation? On mind and matter in management research. *SAGE Open* 3(2): 1–13.

Fendt, J., and R. Kaminska-Labbé (2011). Relevance and creativity through design-driven action research: Introducing *pragmatic adequacy*. *European Management Journal* 29: 217–33.

Ferraro, F., J. Pfeffer, and R. I. Sutton (2005). Economics language and assumptions: How theories can become self-fulfilling. *Academy of Management Review* 30: 8–24.

Ferraro, F., D. Etzion, and J. Gehman (2015). Tackling grand challenges pragmatically: Robust action revisited. *Organization Studies* 36: 363–90.

Flood, J. (2011). From ethics to regulation: The re-organization and re-professionalization of large law firms in the 21st Century. *Current Sociology* 59: 507–29.

Flood, P. C., M. J. Gannon, and J. Paauwe (1996). *Managing Without Traditional Methods*. Wokingham: Addison-Wesley.

Flyvbjerg, B. (1998). *Rationality and Power: Democracy in Practice*. Chicago: University of Chicago Press.

Flyvbjerg, B. (2001). *Making Social Science Matter: Why Social Inquiry Fails and How It Can Succeed Again*. Cambridge, UK: Cambridge University Press.

Flyvbjerg, B. (2006). From Nobel Prize to project management: Getting risks right. *Project Management Journal* 37(3): 5–15.

Flyvbjerg, B. (2008). Phronetic organizational research. In: R. Thorpe and R. Holt (eds.), *The Sage Dictionary of Qualitative Management Research*, pp. 153–5. Los Angeles: Sage.

Flyvbjerg, B. (2013). Mega delusional: The curse of the megaproject. *New Scientist*, December 2013, pp. 28–9.

Flyvbjerg, B., N. Bruzelius, and W. Rothengatter (2003). *Megaprojects and Risk: An Anatomy of Ambition*. Cambridge: Cambridge University Press.

Flyvbjerg, B., T. Landman, and S. Schram (eds.) (2012). *Real Social Science: Applied Phronesis*. Cambridge: Cambridge University Press.

Follett, M. P. (1927). Management as a profession. In: H. C. Metcalf (ed.), *Business Management as a Profession*, pp. 73–87. Reprinted in: J. T. Samaras (ed.), *Management Applications: Exercises, Cases, and Readings*, pp. 12–19. Englewood Cliffs, NJ: Prentice Hall.

Foray, D., and B.-Å. Lundvall (1996). The knowledge-based economy: From the economics of knowledge to the learning economy. In: D. Foray and B.-Å. Lundvall (eds.), *Employment and Growth in the Knowledge-Based Economy*, pp. 11–32. Paris: OECD.

Foss, N. J. (2003). Selective intervention and internal hybrids: Interpreting and learning from the rise and decline of the Oticon spaghetti organization. *Organization Science* 14: 331–49.

Foss, N. J., and P. G. Klein (2014). Hayek and Organization Studies. In: P. Adler, P. du Gay, G. Morgan, and M. Reed (eds.), *Oxford Handbook of Sociology, Social Theory and Organization Studies: Contemporary Currents*, pp. 467–86. Oxford: Oxford University Press.

Foucault, M. (1978). *Discipline and Punish: The Birth of the Prison.* New York: Pantheon Books.

Fox, L. (2003). *Enron: The Rise and Fall.* Hoboken, NJ: Wiley.

Frankel, M. S. (1989). Professional codes: Why, how, and with what impact? *Journal of Business Ethics* 8: 109–15.

Frankford, D. M., M. A. Patterson, and R. T. Konrad (2000). Transforming practice organizations to foster lifelong learning and commitment to medical professionalism. *Academic Medicine* 75: 708–17.

Frederickson, B. L. (2003). Positive emotions and upward spirals in organizations. In: K. S. Cameron, J. E. Dutton, and R. E. Quinn (eds.). *Positive Organizational Scholarship: Foundations of a New Discipline*, pp. 163–75. San Francisco, CA: Berrett-Koehler.

Freeman, R. E. (1984). *Strategic Management: A Stakeholder Approach.* Boston, MA: Pitman.

Freeman, R. E., J. S. Harrison, and A. C. Hicks (2007). *Managing for Stakeholders: Survival, Reputation, and Success.* New Haven & London: Yale University Press.

Friedman, A. L., and S. Miles (2006). *Stakeholders: Theory and Practice.* Oxford: Oxford University Press.

Fromm, E., and M. Maccoby (1970). *Social Character in a Mexican Village.* Englewood Cliffs, NJ: Prentice-Hall.

Gadamer, H.-G. (2004). *Truth and Method* (2nd edn). New York: Crossroad.

Galbraith, J., D. Downey, and A. Kates (2002). *Designing Dynamic Organizations: A Hands-On Guide for Leaders at All Levels.* New York: AMACOM.

Galison, P. (1997). *Image and Logic: A Material Culture of Microphysics.* Chicago: University of Chicago Press.

Garud, R., and P. Karnøe (2001). Path creation as a process of mindful deviation. In: R. Garud and P. Karnøe (eds.), *Path Dependence and Creation*, pp. 1–38. Mahwah, NJ: Lawrence Earlbaum Associates.

Garud, R., S. Jain, and P. Tuertscher (2008). Incomplete by design and designing for incompleteness. *Organization Studies* 29: 351–71.

Gauthier, D. (1986). *Morals by Agreement.* Oxford: Oxford University Press.

Gehman, J., L. K. Treviño, and R. Garud (2013). Values work: A process study of the emergence and performance of organizational values practices. *Academy of Management Journal* 56: 84–112.

George, G. (2014). From the editors: Rethinking management scholarship. *Academy of Management Journal* 57: 1–6.

Gherardi, S. (2012). *How to Conduct a Practice-Based Study: Problems and Methods.* Cheltenham, UK: Edward Elgar.

Ghoshal, S. (2005). Bad management theories are destroying good management practices. *Academy of Management Learning & Education* 4: 75–91.

Gibbons, M., C. Limoges, H. Nowotny, S. Schwartzman, P. Scott, and M. Trow (1994). *The New Production of Knowledge: The Dynamics of Science and Research in Contemporary Societies*. London: Sage.

Giddens, A. (1984). *The Constitution of Society*. Berkeley, CA: University of California Press.

Gigerenzer, G., R. Hertwig, and T. Pachur (eds.) (2011). *Heuristics: The Foundation of Adaptive Behavior*. Oxford: Oxford University Press.

Gillan, S. L., and L. T. Starks (1998). A survey of shareholder activism: Motivation and empirical evidence. *Contemporary Finance Digest* 2(3): 10–34.

Goold, M. and A. Campbell (2002). *Designing Effective Organizations: How to Create Structured Networks*. San Francisco, CA: Jossey-Bass.

Gordon, J. E. (1991). *The New Science of Strong Materials: Or Why You Don't Fall Through the Floor*. Hamondsworth, UK: Penguin.

Gorman, M. E. (2002). Levels of expertise and trading zones: A framework for multi-disciplinary collaboration. *Social Studies of Science* 32: 933–8.

Grant, R. M. (1996). Toward a knowledge-based theory of the firm. *Strategic Management Journal* 17: 109–22.

Gray, D., S. Brown, and J. Macanufo (2010). *Gamestorming—A Playbook for Innovators, Rulebreakers, and Changemakers*. Sebastopol, CA: O'Reilly Media.

Gray, D. E. (2007). Facilitating management learning: Developing critical reflection through reflective tools. *Management Learning* 38: 495–517.

Grey, C. (2004). Reinventing business schools: the contribution of critical management education. *Academy of Management Learning & Education* 3: 178–86.

Groth, A. (2015). Holacracy at Zappos: It's either the future of management or a social experiment gone awry. Retrieved from: http://qz.com/317918/holacracy-at-zappos-its-either-the-future-of-management-or-a-social-experiment-gone-awry/ March 5, 2015.

Grundstein, N. D. (1983). *The Futures of Prudence: Pure Strategy and Aristotelian and Hobbesian Strategists*. Hudson, OH: Zeus.

The Guardian (2012). Largest Dutch housing association faces mass sell-off of homes. *The Guardian*, February 29, 2012. http://www.theguardian.com/housing-network/2012/feb/29/dutch-housing-association-sell-homes retrieved September 10, 2014.

Gulati, R. (2007). Tent poles, tribalism, and boundary spanning: The rigor-relevance debate in management research. *Academy of Management Journal* 50: 775–82.

Habermas, J. (1984). *The Theory of Communicative Action: Volume 1*. Cambridge: Polity.

Habermas, J. (1998). *On the Pragmatics of Communication* (edited by M. Cooke). Cambridge, MA: MIT Press.

Hair, J. F., W. C. Black, B. J. Babin, and R. E. Anderson (2010). *Multivariate Data Analysis* (7th edn). Upper Saddle River, NJ: Prentice Hall.

Hambrick, D. C. (2007). The field of management's devotion to theory: Too much of a good thing? *Academy of Management Journal* 50: 1346–52.

Hamilton, W. D. (1975). Innate social aptitudes of man: An approach from evolutionary genetics. In: R. Fox (ed.), *Biosocial Anthropology*, pp. 115–32. New York: Wiley.

Hammersley, M., and P. Atkinson (1995). *Ethnography: Principles in Practice* (2nd edn). London: Routledge.

Haney, B., and J. Sirbasku (2011). *Leadership Charisma*. Waco, TX: S&H Publishing.

Hannan, M. T., J. N. Baron, G. Hsu, and Ö. Koçak (2006). Organizational identities and the hazard of change. *Industrial and Corporate Change* 15: 755–84.

Hansen, M. T., N. Nohria, and T. Tierney (1999). What's your strategy for managing knowledge? *Harvard Business Review* 77 (2): 106–16.

Hansmann, H. (1996). *The Ownership of Enterprise*. Cambridge, MA: Harvard University Press.

Hartley, J., D. Jacobsen, B. Klandermans, and T. van Vuuren (1991). *Job Insecurity*. Newbury Park: Sage.

Hartnett, T. (2011). *Consensus-Oriented Decision-Making: The CODM Model for Facilitating Groups to Widespread Agreement*. Gabriola Island, BC, Canada: New Society Publishers.

Hassard, J., and J. Wolfram Cox (2013). Can sociological paradigms still inform organizational analysis? A paradigm model for post-paradigm times. *Organization Studies* 34: 1701–28.

Hatchuel, A. (2001a). The two pillars of new management research. *British Journal of Management* 12 (special issue): S33–9.

Hatchuel, A. (2001b). Towards design theory and expandable rationality: The unfinished program of Herbert Simon. *Journal of Management and Governance* 5: 260–73.

Hatchuel, A., and B. Weil (2003). A new approach of innovative design: an introduction to CK theory. In: Proceedings of *International Conference on Engineering Design*, Stockholm, Sweden.

Hatchuel, A., and B. Weil (2009). CK design theory: An advanced formulation. *Research in Engineering Design* 19(4): 181–92.

Hatchuel, A., B. Weil, and P. Le Masson (2013). Towards an ontology of design: Lessons from C–K design theory and Forcing. *Research in Engineering Design* 24(2): 147–63.

Hawking, S., and L. Mlodinow (2010). *The Grand Design*. New York: Bantam Books.

Hayek, F. A. (1945). The use of knowledge in society. *American Economic Review* 35: 519–30.

Hayes, R. M., M. Lemmon, and M. Qiu (2012). Stock options and managerial incentives for risk taking: Evidence from FAS 123R. *Journal of Financial Economics* 105: 174–90.

Healey, M. P., G. P. Hodgkinson, R. Whittington, and G. Johnson (2014). Off to plan or out to lunch? Relationships between design characteristics and outcomes of strategy workshops. *British Journal of Management* 26(3): 507–28.

Hedberg, B. L. T., P. C. Nystrom, and W. H. Starbuck (1976). Camping on seesaws: Prescriptions for a self-designing organization. *Administrative Science Quarterly* 21: 41–65.

Hedlund, G. (1994). A model of knowledge management and the N-form corporation. *Strategic Management Journal* 15, Special issue on "Strategy: Search for New Paradigms": 73–90.

Hedström, P., and R. Swedberg (1996). Social mechanisms. *Acta Sociologica* 39: 281–308.

Hedström, P., and P. Ylikoski (2010). Causal mechanisms in the social sciences. *Annual Review of Sociology* 36: 49–67.

Helfat, C. E., S. Finkelstein, W. Mitchell, M. Peteraf, H. Singh, D. Teece, and S. G. Winter (2007). *Dynamic Capabilities: Understanding Strategic Change in Organizations*. Oxford: Blackwell.

Hendriks, F. (2009). Contextualizing the Dutch drop in political trust: Connecting underlying factors. *International Review of Administrative Sciences* 75: 473–91.

Heracleous, L. (2011). Introduction to the special issue on Bridging the Scholar–Practitioner Divide. *Journal of Applied Behavioral Science* 47: 5–7.

Heugens, P., and M. J. Mol (2005). So you call that research?: Mending methodological biases in strategy and organization departments of top business schools. *Strategic Organization* 3: 117–28.

Heusinkveld, S., and J. Benders (2002). Between professional dedication and corporate design: Exploring forms of new concept development in consultancies. *International Studies of Management and Organization* 32: 104–22.

Hildebrand, D. L. (2003). *Beyond Realism & Anti-Realism: John Dewey and the Neopragmatists*. Nashville, TN: Vanderbilt University Press.

Hirschhorn, L. (1997). *Reworking Authority: Leading and Following in the Post-Modern Organization*. Cambridge, MA: MIT Press.

Hlupic, V. (2014). *The Management Shift: How to Harness the Power of People and Transform Your Organization for Sustainable Success*. New York: Palgrave Macmillan.

Hodgkinson, G. P. (2012). The politics of evidence-based decision making. In: D. M. Rousseau (ed.), *The Oxford Handbook of Evidence Based Management*, pp. 404–19. Oxford: Oxford University Press.

Hodgkinson, G. P., and M. P. Healey (2008). Toward a (pragmatic) science of strategic intervention: design propositions for scenario planning. *Organization Studies* 29: 435–57.

Hodgkinson, G. P., and D. M. Rousseau (2009). Bridging the rigour–relevance gap in management research: It's already happening! *Journal of Management Studies* 46: 534–46.

Hodgkinson, G. P., and K. Starkey (2011). Not simply returning to the same answer over and over again: Reframing relevance. *British Journal of Management* 22: 355–69.

Hodgkinson, G., R. Whittington, G. Johnson, and M. Schwarz (2006). The role of strategy workshops in strategy development processes: Formality, communication, co-ordination and inclusion. *Long Range Planning* 39: 479–96.

Hofstede, G., and G. J. Hofstede (2005). *Cultures and Organizations: Software of the Mind* (2nd edn). New York: McGraw-Hill.

Honig, B., and A. Bedi (2012). The fox in the hen house: A critical examination of plagiarism among members of the Academy of Management. *Academy of Management Learning & Education*, 11: 101–23.

Huff, A. S. (2000). Presidential address: Changes in organizational knowledge production. *Academy of Management Review* 25: 288–93.

Huff, A. S., and J. O. Huff (2001). Re-focusing the business school agenda. *British Journal of Management* 12 (special issue): S49–S54.

Hughes, T., D. Bence, L. Grisoni, N. O'Regan, and D. Wornham (2011). Scholarship that matters: Academic–practitioner engagement in business and management. *Academy of Management Learning & Education* 10: 40–57.

Hurd, P. D. (1998). Scientific literacy: New minds for a changing world. *Science Education* 82: 407–16.

Iannello, K. P. (1992). *Decisions Without Hierarchy*. New York: Routledge.

IAOIP (2015). International Association of Innovation Professionals. Retrieved January 26, 2015 from: http://iaoip.org/

Jackall, R. (2010). *Moral Mazes: The World of Corporate Managers*. Oxford: Oxford University Press.

Jackson, J. A. (1970). Professions and professionalization—editorial introduction. In: J. A. Jackson (ed.), *Professions and Professionalization*, pp. 3–16. Cambridge: Cambridge University Press.

Jackson, N., and P. Carter (1991). In defence of paradigm incommensurability. *Organization Studies* 12: 109–27.

James, P. (1996). Learning to reflect: A story of empowerment. *Teaching and Teacher Education* 12: 81–97.

Jaques, E. (1990). In praise of hierarchy. *Harvard Business Review* 68 (1): 127–33.

Jaques, E. (1996). *Requisite Organization: A Total System for Effective Managerial Organization and Managerial Leadership for the 21st Century*. Arlington, VA: Cason Hall.

Jarzabkowksi, P., and S. Kaplan (2015). Strategy tools-in-use: A framework for understanding "technologies of rationality" in practice. *Strategic Management Journal* 36: 537–58.

Jarzabkowski, P., S. A. Mohrman, and A. G. Scherer (2010). The generation and use of academic knowledge about organizations: Introduction to the special issue. *Organization Studies* 31: 1189–207.

Jeannet, J.-P., and H. Schreuder (2015). *From Coal to Biotech: The Transformation of DSM with Business School Support*. Berlin/Heidelberg: Springer.

Jelinek, M., A. G. L. Romme, and R. J. Boland (2008). Organization studies as a science for design: Creating collaborative artifacts and research (introduction to special issue). *Organization Studies* 29: 317–29.

Jensen, M. C. (1989). Eclipse of the public corporation. *Harvard Business Review* 67 (5): 61–74.

Jensen, M. C., and W. Meckling (1976). The theory of the firm: Managerial behavior, agency costs and ownership structure. *Journal of Financial Economics* 3: 305–60.

Johns, T., and L. Gratton (2013). The third wave of virtual work. *Harvard Business Review* 91(1): 2–9.

Johnson, T. J. (1972). *Professions and Power*. London: Palgrave Macmillan.

Jones, B., and N. Iredale (2010). Enterprise education as pedagogy. *Education + Training* 52: 7–19.

Jones, T. M. (1995). Instrumental stakeholder theory: A synthesis of ethics and economics. *Academy of Management Review* 20: 404–37.

Joyner, B. E., and D. Payne (2002). Evolution and implementation: A study of values, business ethics and corporate social responsibility. *Journal of Business Ethics* 41: 297–311.

Kahle-Piasecki, L. (2011). Making a mentoring relationship work: What is required for organizational success. *Journal of Applied Business and Economics* 12: 46–56.

Kaplan, A. (2014). European management and European business schools: Insights from the history of business schools. *European Management Journal* 32: 529–34.

Kay, J. (2014). What became of the stakeholder society? In: J. Williamson, C. Driver, and P. Kenway (eds.), *Beyond Shareholder Value: The Reasons and Choices for Corporate Governance Reform*, pp. 56–9. London: TUC.

Keasey, K., S. Thompson, and M. Wright (1997). Introduction: the corporate governance problem—competing diagnoses and solutions. In: K. Keasey, S. Thompson, and M. Wright (eds.), *Corporate Governance: Economic, Management, and Financial Issues*, pp. 1–17. Oxford: Oxford University Press.

Kellogg, K. C., W. J. Orlikowski, and J. A. Yates (2006). Life in the trading zone: Structuring coordination across boundaries in postbureaucratic organizations. *Organization Science* 17: 22–44.

Kelly, K. J. (2009). Jack Welch ends Business Week column. *New York Post*, November 13, 2009. Retrieved September 12, 2013 from: http://nypost.com/2009/11/13/jack-welch-ends-businessweek-column/

Kenworthy, T., and W. E. McMullan (2013). Finding practical knowledge in entrepreneurship. *Entrepreneurship Theory and Practice* 37: 983–97.

Kessler, E. H., and J. Bartunek (2014). Designing management maps and apps: Insights for discovering and creating our management realities (book review). *Academy of Management Review* 39: 234–43.

Kets de Vries, M. F. R. (1989). *Prisoners of Leadership*. New York: Wiley.

Kets de Vries, M. F. R. (1999). High performance teams: Lessons from the Pygmies. *Organizational Dynamics* 27(3): 66–77.

Kets de Vries, M. F. R., and K. Korotov (2010). *Developing Leaders and Leadership Development*, INSEAD working paper. Available at SSRN via: http://ssrn.com/abstract=1684001

Khurana, R. (2007). *From Higher Aims to Hired Hands: The Social Transformation of American Business Schools and the Unfulfilled Promise of Management as a Profession*. Princeton, NJ: Princeton University Press.

Khurana, R., and N. Nohria (2008). It's time to make management a true profession. *Harvard Business Review* 86 (10): 70–7.

Khurana, R. and J. C. Spender (2012). Herbert A. Simon on what ails business schools: More than "A problem in organizational design." *Journal of Management Studies* 49: 619–39.

Kidder, T. (2003). *Mountains Beyond Mountains: The Quest of Dr. Paul Farmer, a Man Who Would Cure the World*. New York: Random House.

Kieser, A., and L. Leiner (2009). Why the rigour-relevance gap in management research is unbridgeable. *Journal of Management Studies* 46: 516–33.

Kirby, D. A. (2004). Entrepreneurship education: Can business schools meet the challenge? *Education + Training* 46: 510–19.

Knudsen, H. (1995). *Employee Participation in Europe*. London: Sage.

Koedinger, K. R. and A. Corbett (2006). Technology bringing learning sciences to the classroom. In: R. K. Sawyer (ed.), *The Cambridge Handbook of the Learning Sciences*, pp. 61–75. New York/Cambridge: Cambridge University Press.

Koestler, A. (1968). *The Ghost in the Machine*. New York: Macmillan.

Kolb, A. Y., and D. A. Kolb (2005). Learning styles and learning spaces: Enhancing experiential learning in higher education. *Academy of Management Learning & Education* 4: 193–212.

Kopec, D., E. Sinclair, and B. Matthes (2012). *Evidence-Based Design: A Process for Research and Writing*. Upper Sadlle River, NJ: Pearson Prentice Hall.

References

Krippendorff, K. (1980). *Content Analysis: An Introduction to its Methodology*. Newbury Park, CA: Sage.

Krippendorff, K. (2006). *The Semantic Turn: A New Foundation For Design*. Boca Raton, FL: CRC Press.

Kumar, V. (2013). *101 Design Methods: A Structured Approach for Driving Innovation in Your Organization*. Hoboken, NJ: Wiley.

Lackéus, M., and K. Williams Middleton (2011). Venture creation programs: Entrepreneurial education through real-life content. Paper presented at *BCERC 2011* conference. http://vcplist.com/wp-content/uploads/2013/08/Lack%C3%A9us-Williams-Middleton-Venture-Creation-Programs-BCERC11.pdf

Lai, E. R. (2011). *Motivation: A Literature Review*. Retrieved January 20, 2015 via: https://nibeer.s3.amazonaws.com/uploads/publication/pdf/7/Motivation_Review_final.pdf

Lalonde, C. (2004). In search of archetypes in crisis management. *Journal of Contingencies and Crisis Management* 12: 76–88.

Laloux, F. (2014). *Reinventing Organizations*. Brussels: Nelson Parker.

Lampel, J. (2011). Torn between admiration and distrust: European strategy research and the American challenge. *Organization Science* 22: 1655–62.

Lampel, J., and A. D. Meyer (2008). Field-configuring events as structuring mechanisms: How conferences, ceremonies, and trade shows constitute new technologies, industries, and markets. *Journal of Management Studies* 45: 1025–35.

Lampel, J., P. J. Pushkar, and A. Bhalla (2012). Test-driving the future: How design competitions are changing innovation. *Academy of Management Perspectives* 26: 71–85.

Langley, A. (1999). Strategies for theorizing from process data. *Academy of Management Review* 24: 691–711.

Langley, A. (2007). Process thinking in strategic organization. *Strategic Organization* 5: 271–82.

Latour, B. (1999). *Pandora's Hope: Essays on the Reality of Science Studies*. Cambridge, MA: Harvard University Press.

Laver, M., K. Benoit, and J. Garry (2003). Extracting policy positions from political texts using words as data. *American Political Science Review* 97: 311–31.

LawBrain (2014). Corporate fraud. http://lawbrain.com/wiki/Corporate_Fraud (retrieved January 5, 2015).

Lazonick, W., and M. O'Sullivan (2000). Maximizing shareholder value: A new ideology for corporate governance. *Economy and Society* 29: 13–35.

Learmonth, M. (2006). Dialogue. *Academy of Management Review* 31: 1089–91.

Learmonth, M. (2007). Critical management education in action: Personal tales of management unlearning. *Academy of Management Learning & Education* 6: 109–13.

Learmonth, M., and N. Harding (2006). Evidence-based management: The very idea. *Public Administration* 84: 245–66.

Learmonth, M., A. Lockett, and K. Dowd (2012). Promoting scholarship that matters: The uselessness of useful research and the usefulness of useless research. *British Journal of Management* 23: 35–44.

Ledford, G., E. Lawler, and S. Mohrman (1988). The quality circle and its variations. In: J. Campbell and R. Campbell (eds.), *Productivity in Organizations*. San Francisco, CA: Jossey-Bass.

Lee, F., A. C. Edmondson, S. Thomke, and M. Worline (2004). The mixed effects of inconsistency on experimentation in organizations. *Organization Science* 15: 310–26.

Lee, T. (1995). The professionalization of accountancy: A history of protecting the public interest in a self-interested way. *Accounting, Auditing & Accountability Journal* 8(4): 48–69.

Leitko, G., A. Greil, and S. A. Peterson (1985). Lessons at the bottom: Worker non-participation in labor management committees as situational adjustment. *Work and Occupations* 12: 285–306.

Le Masson, P., B. Weil, and A. Hatchuel (2010). *Strategic Management of Innovation and Design*. Cambridge: Cambridge University Press.

Leten, B., W. Vanhaverbeke, and N. Roijakkers (2013). IP models to orchestrate innovation ecosystems: IMEC, a public research institute in Nano-electronics. *California Management Review* 55(4): 51–64.

Levitt, B., and J. G. March (1988). Organizational learning. *Annual Review of Sociology* 14: 319–40.

Lewis, M. W., and M. L. Kelemen (2002). Multiparadigm inquiry: Exploring organizational pluralism and paradox. *Human Relations* 55: 251–75.

Leymann, H. (1996). The content and development of mobbing at work. *European Journal of Work and Organizational Psychology* 5: 165–84.

Likert, R. (1961). *New Patterns of Management*. New York: McGraw-Hill.

Likert, R. (1976). *The Human Organization*. New York: McGraw-Hill.

Locke, K., and K. Golden-Biddle (1997). Constructing opportunities for contribution: Structuring intertextual coherence and problematizing in organizational studies. *Academy of Management Journal* 40: 1023–63.

Locke, K., K. Golden-Biddle, and M. S. Feldman (2008). Making doubt generative: Rethinking the role of doubt in the research process. *Organization Science* 19: 907–18.

Loorbach, D. (2010). Transition management for sustainable development: A prescriptive, complexity-based governance framework. *Governance* 23: 161–83.

Louis, M. R. (1994). In the manner of friends: Learning from Quaker practice for organizational renewal. *Journal of Organizational Change Management* 7: 42–60.

Ludema, J. D., D. Whitney, B. J. Mohr, and T. J. Griffin (2003). *The Appreciative Inquiry Summit*. San Francisco, CA: Berrett-Koehler.

Luhmann, N. (1990). The autopoiesis of social systems. In: N. Luhmann (ed.), *Essays on Self-Reference*, pp. 1–20. New York: Columbia University Press.

Lukac, E. G., and D. Frazier (2012). Linking strategy to value. *Journal of Business Strategy* 33(4): 49–57.

Lukes, S. (2005). *Power: A Radical View* (2nd edn). New York: Palgrave Macmillan.

Lyotard, J.-F. (1984). *The Postmodern Condition: A Report on Knowledge*. Harmondsworth, UK: Penguin.

McCallum, S., and D. O'Connell (2009). Social capital and leadership development: Building stronger leadership through enhanced relational skills. *Leadership & Organization Development Journal* 30: 152–66.

McCarthy, S. (1989). The dilemma of non-participation. In: C. J. Lammers and G. Széll (eds.), *International Handbook of Participation in Organizations*, volume I, pp. 115–29. Oxford: Oxford University Press.

References

McEwan, T. (2001). *Managing Values and Beliefs in Organisations*. Harlow, UK: Pearson Education.

MacIntosh, R., and D. MacLean (2014). *Strategic Management: Strategists at Work*. New York: Palgrave Macmillan.

McKenna, C. D. (2006). *The World's Newest Profession: Management Consulting in the Twentieth Century*. Cambridge: Cambridge University Press.

MacNeil, I., and L. Xiao (2006). Comply or explain: Market discipline and non-compliance with the combined code. *Corporate Governance: An International Review* 14: 486–96.

Maister, D. H. (2000). *True Professionalism: The Courage to Care about Your People, Your Clients, and Your Career*. New York: Touchstone.

Mansell, S. (2013). *Capitalism, Corporations and the Social Contract: A Critique of Stakeholder Theory*. Cambridge: Cambridge University Press.

Manz, C. C., and H. P. Sims, Jr (1987). Leading workers to lead themselves: The external leadership of self-managing work teams. *Administrative Science Quarterly* 32: 106–28.

March, S. T., and G. F. Smith (1995). Design and natural science research on information technology. *Decision Support Systems* 15: 251–66.

Markides, C. (2011). Crossing the chasm: How to convert relevant research into managerially useful research. *Journal of Applied Behavioral Science* 47: 121–34.

Markus, L., A. Majchrzak, and L. Gasser (2002). A design theory for systems that support emergent knowledge processes. *MIS Quarterly* 26: 179–212.

Marnet, O. (2007). History repeats itself: The failure of rational choice models in corporate governance. *Critical Perspectives on Accounting* 18: 191–210.

Martela, F. (2015). Fallible inquiry with ethical ends-in-view: A pragmatist philosophy of science for organizational research. *Organization Studies* 36: 537–63.

Martin, R. (2009). *The Design of Business: Why Design Thinking is the Next Competitive Advantage*. Boston, MA: Harvard Business Press.

Martin, R. (2011). *Fixing the Game: How Runaway Expectations Broke the Economy, and How to Get Back to Reality* (ebook version). Boston, MA: Harvard Business Review Press.

Martin, W. E., and K. D. Bridgmon (2012). *Quantitative and Statistical Research Methods: From Hypothesis to Results*. San Francisco, CA: Jossey-Bass.

Massa, M., and A. Simonov (2009). Experimentation in financial markets. *Management Science* 55: 1377–90.

Matlack, C. (2013). Research fraud allegations trail a German B-School wunderkind. *Bloomberg Business Week* June 24, 2013. Retrieved via www.businessweek.com October 15, 2014.

Maurer, C. C., P. Bansal, and M. M. Crossan (2011). Creating economic value through social values: Introducing a culturally informed resource-based view. *Organization Science* 22: 432–48.

Mayr, O. (1970). *The Origins of Feedback Control*. Cambridge, MA: MIT Press.

Mays, K. (2013). Interview with the "CEO" of David Allen Company. Retrieved from: http://holacracy.org/blog/interview-with-the-ceo-of-david-allen-company accessed March 11, 2015.

MBA Oath (2015). *MBA Oath*. Retrieved via mbaoath.org/accessed 15 Janaury 15, 2015.

Merton, R. K. (1968). *Social Theory and Social Structure*. New York: Free Press.

Metcalf, H. C. (1926). *Scientific Foundations of Business Administration*. Baltimore, MD: Williams & Wilkins Company.

Metcalf, H. C. (ed.). (1927). *Business Management as a Profession*. Chicago, IL: A.W. Shaw Company.

Miceli, M. P., and J. P. Near (1989). The incidence of wrongdoing, whistle-blowing, and retaliation: Results of a naturally occurring field experiment. *Employee Responsibilities and Rights Journal* 2: 91–108.

Miles, M. B., A. M. Huberman, and J. Saldaña (2014). *Qualitative Data Analysis: A Methods Sourcebook* (3rd edn). Thousand Oaks, CA: Sage.

Miles, S. (2012). Stakeholders: Essentially contested or just confused? *Journal of Business Ethics* 108: 285–98.

Miles, S. H. (2004). *The Hippocratic Oath and the Ethics of Medicine*. Oxford: Oxford University Press.

Milliken, F. J., E. W. Morrison, and P. F. Hewlin (2003). An exploratory study of employee silence: Issues that employees don't communicate upward and why. *Journal of Management Studies* 40: 1453–76.

Mills, D. Q. (1991). *Rebirth of the Corporation*. New York: Wiley.

Mintzberg, H. (2004). *Managers, not MBAs: A Hard Look at the Soft Practice of Managing and Management Development*. San Francisco, CA: Berrett-Koehler.

Mintzberg, H. (2015). *Rebalancing Society: Radical Renewal Beyond Left, Right, and Center* (version January 5, 2015). Retrieved via www.mintzberg.org April 13, 2015.

Mintzberg, H., and J. Gosling (2002). Educating managers beyond borders. *Academy of Management Learning & Education* 1: 64–76.

Mitchell, R. K., B. R. Agle, and D. J. Wood (1997). Toward a stakeholder identification and salience: Defining the principle of who and what really counts. *Academy of Management Review* 22: 853–86.

Mitroff, I. I. (1983). *Stakeholders of the Organizational Mind: Toward a New View of Organizational Policy Making*. San Francisco, CA: Jossey-Bass.

Mizruchi, M. S., and H. Kimeldorf (2005). The historical context of shareholder value capitalism. *Political Power and Social Theory* 17: 213–21.

Mohrman, S. A. (2007). Having relevance and impact: The benefits of integrating the perspectives of design science and organizational development. *Journal of Applied Behavioral Science* 43: 12–22.

Mohrman, S. A., C. B. Gibson, and A. M. Mohrman (2001). Doing research that is useful to practice: A model and empirical exploration. *Academy of Management Journal* 44: 357–75.

Monarth, H. (2014). A company without job titles will still have hierarchies. *Harvard Business Review* January 28, 2014, retrieved from: https://hbr.org/2014/01/a-company-without-job-titles-will-still-have-hierarchies/

Mueller, F. (1994). Teams between hierarchy and commitment: Change strategies and the internal environment. *Journal of Management Studies* 31: 383–403.

Mulder, M. (1971). Power equalization through participation? *Administrative Science Quarterly* 16: 31–8.

Muller, F., and J. Gewirtzman (2004). Section 2: Design management. In: J. T. Ricketts, M. K. Loftin, and F. S. Merritt (eds.), *Standard Handbook for Civil Engineers* (5th edn). New York: McGraw-Hill.

Munzer, S. R. (1990). *A Theory of Property*. Cambridge: Cambridge University Press.

Muzio, D., and I. Kirkpatrick (2011). Introduction: Professions and organizations—a conceptual framework. *Current Sociology* 59: 389–405.

Myers, J. W., and F. Thompson (2006). Ethical reasoning, epistemology, and administrative inquiry. *Research in Public Policy Analysis and Management* 14: 261–87.

Nadler, G., and S. Hibino (1999). *Creative Solution Finding*. Rocklin, CA: Prima.

Nahavandi, A. (2015). *The Art and Science of Leadership* (7th edn). Upper Saddle, NJ: Pearson.

Nayar, V. (2010). *Employees First, Customers Second*. Boston, MA: Harvard Business Press.

Neck, H. M., and P. G. Greene (2011). Entrepreneurship education: Known worlds and new frontiers. *Journal of Small Business Management* 49: 55–70.

Nijholt, J. J., and J. Benders (2007). Coevolution in management fashions: The case of self-managing teams in The Netherlands. *Group and Organization Management* 32: 628–52.

Nonaka, I. (1994). A dynamic theory of organizational knowledge creation. *Organization Science* 5: 14–37.

Nonaka, I., and H. Takeuchi (1995). *The Knowledge Creating Company: How Japanese Companies Create The Dynamics of Innovation*. Oxford: Oxford University Press.

Nurmi, H. (1999). *Voting Paradoxes and How to Deal With Them*. Berlin: Springer.

Nutt, P. C. (1999). Suprising but true: Half the decisions in organizations fail. *Academy of Management Executive* 13(4): 75–90.

Nutt, P. C. (2011). Making decision-making research matter: Some issues and remedies. *Management Research Review* 34(1): 5–16.

Oc, B., M. R. Bashshur, and C. Moore (2015). Speaking truth to power: The effect of candid feedback on how individuals with power allocate resources. *Journal of Applied Psychology* 100: 450–63.

O'Connell Davidson, J. (1994). The sources and limits of resistance in a privatized utility. In: J. M. Jermier, D. Knights, and W. R. Nord (eds.), *Resistance and Power in Organizations*, pp. 69–101. London: Routledge.

Oetringer, E., and C. de Monchy (2013). *Bridging the Gap Between Central Organisations and the Field* (white paper). Netherlands: ComDyS Business Services. Retrieved April 15, 2015 via www.ipma-library.org/Player/eKnowledge/bridgingthegapv1.pdf

O'Grady, F. (2014). Workers' voice in corporate governance. In: J. Williamson, C. Driver, and P. Kenway (eds.), *Beyond Shareholder Value: The Reasons and Choices for Corporate Governance Reform*, pp. 69–73. London: TUC.

O'Mahony, S., and B. A. Bechky (2008). Boundary organizations: Enabling collaboration among unexpected allies. *Administrative Science Quarterly* 53: 422–59.

Orlikowski, W. J. (2000). Using technology and constituting structures: A practice lens for studying technology in organizations. *Organization Science* 11: 404–28.

Orlikowski, W. J. (2002). Knowing in practice: Enacting a collective capability in distributed organizing. *Organization Science* 13: 249–73.

Orlikowski, W. J. (2004). Managing and designing: Attending to reflexiveness and enactment'. In: R. J. Boland and F. Collopy (eds.), *Managing as Designing*, pp. 90–5. Stanford, CA: Stanford University Press.

Osterwalder, A. (2004). *The Business Model Ontology—A Proposition in a Design Science Approach* (Doctoral dissertation). Lausanne, Switzerland: University of Lausanne.

Osterwalder, A., and Y. Pigneur (2010). *Business Model Generation*. Hoboken, NJ: Wiley.

Osterwalder, A., and Y. Pigneur (2013). Designing business models and similar strategic objects: The contribution of IS. *Journal of the Association for Information Systems* 14: 237–44.

Ouchi, W. G. (1979). A conceptual framework for the design of organizational control mechanisms. *Management Science* 25: 833–48.

Ouchi, W. G. (1981). *Theory Z*. Reading: Addison-Wesley.

Owen, J. (1983). *Sleight of Hand: The $25 Million Nugan Hand Bank Scandal*. Sydney: Colporteur Press.

Palmer, D., B. Dick, and N. Freiburger (2009). Rigor and relevance in organization studies. *Journal of Management Inquiry* 18: 265–72.

Pandza, K., and R. Thorpe (2010). Management as design, but what kind of design? An appraisal of the design science analogy for management. *British Journal of Management* 21: 171–86.

Pascal, A., C. Thomas, and A. G. L. Romme (2013). Developing a human-centred and science-based approach to design: The knowledge management platform project. *British Journal of Management* 24: 264–80.

Patterson, D. A. (2009). Scientists and engineers on boards will keep focus on the long term. *Harvard Business Review*, October 23, 2009. Retrieved via https://hbr.org/ December 26, 2014.

Pawson, R. (2000). Middle-range realism. *Archives Européennes de Sociologie* 41: 283–325.

Pawson, R. (2006). *Evidence-Based Policy: A Realist Perspective*. London: Sage Publications.

Pearson, G. (1995). *Integrity in Organizations: An Alternative Business Ethic*. London: McGraw-Hill.

Peirce, C. S. (1934). *Collected Papers of Charles Sanders Peirce, vol. 5: Pragmatism and Pragmaticism* (C. Hartshorne and P. Weiss, eds.). Cambridge, MA: Harvard University Press.

Pentland, B. T. (1993). Getting comfortable with the numbers: Auditing and the micro-production of macro-order. *Accounting, Organizations and Society* 18: 605–20.

Perkmann, M., and A. Spicer (2014). How emerging organizations take form: The role of imprinting and values in organizational bricolage. *Organization Science* 25(6): 1785–806.

Perkmann, M., V. Tartari, M. McKelvey, E. Autio, A. Broström, P. D'Este, R. Fini, A. Geuna, R. Grimaldi, A. Hughes, S. Krabel, M. Kitson, P. Llerena, F. Lisson, A. Salter, and M. Sobrero (2013). Academic engagement and commercialisation: A review of the literature on university-industry relations. *Research Policy* 42: 423–42.

Perrow, C. (1986). *Complex Organizations: A Critical Essay* (3rd edn). New York: Random House.

Peters, T. (1987). *Thriving on Chaos*. London: Pan Books.

Peters, T. J., and R. H. Waterman (1982). *In Search of Excellence: Lessons from America's Best-Run Companies*. New York: Harper & Row.

Pfeffer, J. (1992). *Managing With Power: Politics and Influence in Organizations*. Boston, MA: Harvard Business School Press.

Pfeffer, J. (1993). Barriers to the development of organizational science: Paradigm development as a dependent variable. *Academy of Management Review* 4: 599–620.

Pfeffer, J. (2012). Foreword. In: D. M. Rousseau (ed.), *The Oxford Handbook of Evidence-Based Management*, pp. vii–x. New York: Oxford University Press.

Pfeffer, J. (2013). You're still the same: Why theories of power hold over time and across contexts. *Academy of Management Perspectives* 27: 269–80.

Pfeffer, J., and C. T. Fong (2002). The end of business schools? Less success than meets the eye. *Academy of Management Learning & Education* 1: 78–95.

Pfeffer, J., and R. I. Sutton (2000). *The Knowing-Doing Gap: How Smart Companies Turn Knowledge into Action*. Boston, MA: Harvard Business School Press.

Phillips, N., and C. Hardy (2002). *Discourse Analysis: Investigating Processes of Social Construction*. Newbury Park, CA: Sage.

Phillips, R. (2003). *Stakeholder Theory and Organizational Ethics*. San Francisco, CA: Berrett-Koehler.

Plsek, P., J. Bibby, and E. Whitby (2007). Practical methods for extracting explicit design rules grounded in the experience of organizational managers. *Journal of Applied Behavioral Science* 43: 153–70.

Poiesz, T. (2014). *Redesigning Psychology: In Search of the DNA of Behavior*. The Hague, Netherlands: Eleven.

Polanyi, M. (1958). *Personal Knowledge: Towards a Post-Critical Philosophy*. Chicago: University of Chicago Press.

Polanyi, M. (1966). *The Tacit Dimension*. London: Routledge & Kegan Paul.

Posner, B. Z., J. M. Kouzes, and W. H. Schmidt (1985). Shared values make a difference: An empirical test of corporate culture. *Human Resource Management* 24: 293–309.

Post, J. E., L. E. Preston, and S. Sachs (2002). *Redefining the Corporation: Stakeholder Management and Organizational Wealth*. Stanford, CA: Stanford University Press.

Prahalad, C. K., and G. Hamel (1990). The core competence of the corporation. *Harvard Business Review* 68(3): 79–91.

Proust, M. (1929). *The Captive* (translated by C. K. Scott Moncrieff). New York: Random House.

PwC (2013). *PwC's Next Gen: A Global Generational Study*. Retrieved via www.pwc.com March 11, 2015.

Quarter, J. (2000). *Beyond the Bottom Line: Socially Innovative Business Owners*. Westport, CT: Quorum Books.

Randolph, W. A. (2011). Developing global business capabilities in MBA students. *Journal of Management Inquiry* 20: 223–40.

Rappaport, A. (1986). *Creating Shareholder Value: The New Standard for Business Performance*. New York: Free Press.

Rappaport, A. (1998). *Creating Shareholder Value: A Guide for Managers and Investors*. New York: Free Press.

Rasche, A., and D. U. Gilbert (2015). Decoupling responsible management education: Why business schools may not walk their talk. *Journal of Management Inquiry* 24: 239–52.

Rawls, J. (1971). *A Theory of Justice*. Cambridge, MA: Harvard University Press.

Reason, P. and H. Bradbury (eds.) (2001). *The Handbook of Action Research*. London: Sage.

Reed, M. (1996). Organizational theorizing: A historically contested terrain. In: S. R. Clegg, C. Hardy, and W.R. Nord (eds.), *Handbook of Organization Studies*, pp. 31–56. London: Sage.

Research Councils UK (2015). Pathways to Impact. Retrieved January 16, 2015 via: http://www.rcuk.ac.uk/ke/impacts/

Ribeiro, R., and H. Collins (2007). The bread-making machine: Tacit knowledge and two types of action. *Organization Studies* 28: 1417–33.

Ridley-Duff, R., and M. Bull (2014). *Solidarity Co-operatives* (Keynote to 2014 Social Innovation and Entrepreneurship Research Colloquium), Melbourne. Retrieved from http://shura.shu.ac.uk Janaury 12, 2015.

Ries, E. (2011). *The Lean Startup: How Today's Entrepreneurs Use Continuous Innovation to Create Radically Successful Businesses*. New York: Crown Business.

Riffe, D., S. Lacy, and F. G. Fico (2013). *Analyzing Media Messages: Using Quantitative Content Analysis in Research* (3rd edn). New York: Routledge.

Robertson, B. J. (2007). *Organization at the Leading Edge: Introducing Holacracy*. Retrieved from http://integralesleben.org/fileadmin/user_upload/images/DIA/Flyer/Organization_at_the_Leading_Edge_2007-06_01.pdf (retrieved January 15, 2015).

Robertson, B. J. (2015). *Holacracy: The New Management System for a Rapidly Changing World*. New York: Henry Holt & Company.

Roglio, K. D., and G. Light (2009). Executive MBA programs: The development of the reflective executive. *Academy of Management Learning & Education* 8: 156–73.

Rolin, K. (2010). Diversity and dissent in the social sciences: The case of organization studies. *Philosophy of the Social Sciences* 41: 470–94.

Romme, A. G. L. (1996). A note on the hierarchy-team debate. *Strategic Management Journal* 17: 411–17.

Romme, A. G. L. (1997). Work, authority and participation: The scenario of circular organizing. *Journal of Organizational Change Management* 10: 156–66.

Romme, A. G. L. (1998). Toward the learning organization: The case of circular re-engineering. *Knowledge and Process Management* 5: 158–64.

Romme, A. G. L. (1999). Domination, self-determination and circular organizing. *Organization Studies* 20: 801–32.

Romme, A. G. L. (2003a). Making a difference: Organization as design. *Organization Science* 14: 558–73.

Romme, A. G. L. (2003b). Organizing education by drawing on organization studies. *Organization Studies* 24: 697–720.

Romme, A. G. L. (2004). Unanimity rule and organizational decision making: A simulation model. *Organization Science* 15: 704–18.

Romme, A. G. L., and I. Damen (2007). Toward science-based design in organization development: Codifying the process. *Journal of Applied Behavioral Science* 43: 108–21.

Romme, A. G. L., and S. Eltink (2002). Naar integraal onderwijs op basis van kringorganisatie. *Tijdschrift voor Arbeid en Participatie* 24: 193–204.

Romme, A. G. L., and G. Endenburg (2001). Naar een nieuwe vormgeving van het aandeel. *Tijdschrift voor Management & Organisatie* 55(3): 40–53.

Romme, A. G. L., and G. Endenburg (2002). Het hoe en waarom van consentaandelen. *Maandblad voor Accountancy en Bedrijfseconomie* 76: 243–7.

Romme, A. G. L., and G. Endenburg (2006). Construction principles and design rules in the case of circular design. *Organization Science* 17: 287–97.

Romme, A. G. L., and R. Putzel (2003). Designing management education: Practice what you teach. *Simulation & Gaming* 34: 512–30.

Romme, A. G. L., and A. Reijmer (1997). Kringorganiseren en het dilemma tussen centrale sturing en zelforganisatie. *M&O Tijdschrift voor Management en Organisatie* 51(6): 43–59.

Romme, A. G. L., and A. van Witteloostuijn (1999). Circular organizing and triple loop learning. *Journal of Organizational Change Management* 12: 439–53.

Romme, A. G. L., E. P. Antonacopoulou, D. E. M. Mulders, and M. S. Taylor (2012). The dynamism of organizational practices: The role of employment blueprints. *British Journal of Management* 23: 561–74.

Romme, A. G. L., M.-J. Avenier, D. Denyer, G. P. Hodgkinson, K. Pandza, K. Starkey, and N. Worren (2015). Towards common ground and trading zones in management research and practice. *British Journal of Management* 26(3): 544–59.

Rorty, R. (1979). *Philosophy and the Mirror of Nature*. Princeton, NJ: Princeton University Press.

Rorty, R. (1982). *Consequences of Pragmatism*. New York: University of Minnesota Press.

Rorty, R. (1989). *Contingency, Irony, and Solidarity*. Cambridge: Cambridge University Press.

Rorty, R. (1999). *Philosophy and Social Hope*. Hamondsworth: Penguin.

Rothschild, J., and T. D. Miethe (1994). Whistleblowing as resistance in modern work organizations: The politics of revealing organizational deception and abuse. In: J. M. Jermier, D. Knights, and W.R. Nord (eds.), *Resistance and Power in Organizations*, pp. 252–73. London: Routledge.

Rothstein, L. R. (1995). The empowerment effort that came undone. *Harvard Business Review* 73 (1): 20–6.

Rousseau, D. M. (2006a). Is there such a thing as evidence-based management? *Academy of Management Review* 31: 256–69.

Rousseau, D. M. (2006b). Keeping an open mind about evidence-based management: A reply to Learmonth's commentary. *Academy of Management Review* 31: 1091–3.

Rousseau, D. M. (ed.) (2012a). *The Oxford Handbook of Evidence-Based Management*. Oxford: Oxford University Press.

Rousseau, D. M. (2012b). Designing a better business school: Channelling Herbert Simon, addressing the critics, and developing actionable knowledge for professionalizing managers. *Journal of Management Studies* 49: 600–18.

Rousseau, D. M., J. Manning, and D. Denyer (2008). Evidence in management and organizational science: Assembling the field's full weight of scientific knowledge through reflective reviews. *Academy of Management Annals* 2: 475–515.

Rubinstein, A. (1998). *Modeling Bounded Rationality*. Cambridge, MA: MIT Press.

Russell, B. (1938). *Power: A New Social Analysis*. London: George Allen & Unwin.

Rynes, S. L. (2007). Editor's afterword. Let's create a tipping point: What academics and practitioners can do, alone and together. *Academy of Management Journal* 50: 1046–54.

Rynes, S. L., and K. G. Brown (2011). Where are we in the "long march to legitimacy?": Assessing scholarship in management learning and education. *Academy of Management Learning & Education* 10: 561–82.

Rynes, S. L., J. M. Bartunek, and R. L. Daft (2001). Across the great divide: Knowledge creation and transfer between practitioners and academics. *Academy of Management Journal* 44: 340–55.

Sandberg, J., and H. Tsoukas (2011). Grasping the logic of practice: Theorizing through practical rationality. *Academy of Management Review* 36: 338–60.

Sarasvathy, S. D. (2003). Entrepreneurship as a science of the artificial. *Journal of Economic Psychology* 24: 203–20.

Sarasvathy, S. D. (2008). *Effectuation: Elements of Entrepreneurial Expertise*. Cheltenham, UK: Edward Elgar.

Sarasvathy, S. D., and S. Venkataraman (2011). Entrepreneurship as method: Open questions for an entrepreneurial future. *Entrepreneurship Theory and Practice* 35: 113–35.

Sass, S. A. (1982). *The Pragmatic Imagination: A History of the Wharton School, 1881–1981*. Philadelphia, PA: University of Pennsylvania Press.

Schein, E. H. (1987). *The Clinical Perspective in Fieldwork*. London: Sage.

Schein, E. H. (1988). *Process Consultation, Volume I: Its Role in Organization Development* (2nd edn). Reading, MA: Addison-Wesley.

Schön, D. A. (1979). Generative metaphor: A perspective on problem solving in social policy. In: A. Orthony (ed.), *Metaphor and Thought*, pp. 254–83. Cambridge: Cambridge University Press.

Schön, D. A. (1983). *The Reflective Practitioner: How Professionals Think in Action*. London: Temple Smith.

Schön, D. A. (1987). *Educating the Reflective Practitioner*. San Francisco, CA: Jossey-Bass.

Schwarz, R. (2002). *The Skilled Facilitator: A Comprehensive Resource for Consultants, Facilitators, Managers, Trainers, and Coaches*. San Francisco, CA: Jossey-Bass.

Schultz, M., and M. J. Hatch (1996). Living within multiple paradigms: The case of paradigm interplay in organizational culture studies. *Academy of Management Review* 21: 529–57.

Scott, M. C. (1998). *The Intellect Industry: Profiting and Learning from Professional Services Firms*. Chichester, UK: Wiley.

Seidl, D. (2007). General strategy concepts and the ecology of strategy discourses: A systemic-discursive perspective. *Organization Studies* 28: 197–218.

Semler, R. (1993). *Maverick: The Success Story Behind the World's Most Unusual Workplace*. New York: Warner Books.

Sen, A. K. (1979). *Collective Choice and Social Welfare*. Amsterdam: Elsevier Science.

Sen, A. (1995). Rationality and social choice. *American Economic Review* 85: 1–24.

Senge, P. M. (2006). *The Fifth Discipline: The Art and Practice of the Learning Organization* (2nd edn). New York: Currency/Bantam Doubleday Dell.

Shane, S. (2003). *A General Theory of Entrepreneurship: The Individual-Opportunity Nexus*. Cheltenham, UK: Edward Elgar.

Shane, S. (2004). *Academic Entrepreneurship: University Spinoffs and Wealth Creation*. Cheltenham, UK: Edward Elgar.

Shane, S., S. A. M. Dolmans, J. Jankowski, I. M. M. J. Reymen, and A. G. L. Romme (2015). Academic entrepreneurship: Which inventors do technology licensing officers prefer for spinoffs? *Journal of Technology Transfer* 40: 273–92.

References

Shapira, Z. (2011). "I've got a theory paper—do you?": Conceptual, empirical, and theoretical contributions to knowledge in the organizational sciences. *Organization Science* 22: 1312–21.

Shkliarevsky, G. (2015). Rethinking democracy: A systems perspective on the global unrest. *Systems Research and Behavioral Science*, forthcoming. DOI: 10.1002/sres.2331.

Silverman, D. (2013). *Doing Qualitative Research* (4th edn). Thousand Oaks, CA: Sage.

Simon, H. A. (1955). A behavioral model of rational choice. *Quarterly Journal of Economics* 69: 99–188.

Simon, H. A. (1967). The business school: A problem in organizational design. *Journal of Management Studies* 4: 1–16. Reprinted with "minor revisions" in 1976 in Simon's *Administrative Behavior* (3rd edn).

Simon, H. A. (1969/1996). *The Sciences of the Artificial* (1st edn published in 1969; 3rd edn in 1996). Cambridge, MA: MIT Press.

Simon, H. A. (1973). The organization of complex systems. In: H. H. Pattee (ed.), *Hierarchy Theory: The Challenge of Complex Systems*, pp. 1–27. New York: George Braziller.

Simon, H. A. (1976). *Administrative Behavior* (3rd edn). New York: Macmillan.

Simon, H. A. (1991a). *Models of My Life*. Cambridge, MA: MIT Press.

Simon, H. A. (1991b). Bounded rationality and organizational learning. *Organization Science* 2: 125–34.

Simon, H. A. (2002). Near decomposability and the speed of evolution. *Industrial and Corporate Change* 11: 587–99.

Smith, P. (1990). *Killing the Spirit: Higher Education in America*. New York: Viking.

Sobel, R. S., and R. G. Holcombe (2001). The unanimous voting rule is not the political equivalent to market exchange. *Public Choice* 106: 233–42.

Somers, M., K. Passerini, A. Parhankangas, and J. Casal (2014). Management education and the professions. *Organization Management Journal* 11: 47–56.

Spee, A. P., and P. Jarzabkowski (2011). Strategic planning as communicative process. *Organization Studies* 32: 1217–45.

Spender, J. C. (2007). Management as a regulated profession: An essay. *Journal of Management Inquiry* 16: 32–42.

Spender, J. C. (2015). *An Essay on Method; with Attention to the Rigor-Relevance "Debate" and Its History*, unpublished working paper. Warsaw, Poland: Kozminski University.

Srivastava, R. K., T. A. Shervani, and L. Fahey (1998). Market-based assets and shareholder value: A framework for analysis. *Journal of Marketing* 62: 2–18.

Stablein, R. E., and P. J. Frost (2004). The community of scholars. In: R. E. Stablein and P. J. Frost (eds.), *Renewing Research Practice*, pp. 25–8. Stanford, CA: Stanford University Press.

Stacey, R. D. (1995). The science of complexity: An alternative perspective for strategic change processes. *Strategic Management Journal* 16: 477–95.

Starbuck, W. H. (2006). *The Production of Knowledge: The Challenge of Social Science Research*. Oxford: Oxford University Press.

Starkey, K., and P. Madan (2001). Bridging the relevance gap: Aligning stakeholders in the future of management research. *British Journal of Management* 12 (special issue): S3–S26.

Starkey, K., A. Hatchuel, and S. Tempest (2009). Management research and the new logics of discovery and engagement. *Journal of Management Studies* 46: 547–58.

Sterman, J. D. (2000). *Business Dynamics: Systems Thinking and Modeling for a Complex World*. New York: McGraw-Hill.

Stewart, G. L., and C. C. Manz (1995). Leadership for self-managing work teams: A typology and integrative model. *Human Relations* 48: 747–70.

Stinchcombe, A. L. (1965). Social structure and organizations. In: J. G. March (ed.), *Handbook of Organizations*, pp. 142–93. Chicago: Rand McNally & Company.

Strichow, H.-J. (2013). *Our Ultimate Purpose in Life: The Grand Order of Design and the Human Condition*. Bloomington, IN: Balboa Press.

Strikwerda, J. (2013). Setting the context: Reflections on management consultancy in the 21st century. In: A. F. Buono, L. de Caluwé, and A. Stoppelenburg (eds.), *Exploring the Professional Identity of Management Consultants*, pp. xxi–lv. Charlotte, NC: Information Age.

Stuart, T. E., and J. M. Podolny (1996). Local search and the evolution of technological capabilities. *Strategic Management Journal* 17: 21–38.

Suddaby, R. (2014). Editor's comments: Why theory? *Academy of Management Review* 39: 407–11.

Suddaby, R., Y. Gendron, and H. Lam (2009). The organizational context of professionalism in accounting. *Accounting, Organizations and Society* 34: 409–27.

Sullivan, W. M. (2000). Medicine under threat: Professionalism and professional identity. *Canadian Medical Association Journal* 162: 673–5.

Szopa, A., W. Karwowski, and P. Ordonez de Pablos (eds.) (2013). *Academic Entrepreneurship and Technological Innovation: A Business Management Perspective*. Hershey, PA: IGI Global.

Tadajewski, M. (2009). The debate that won't die? Values incommensurability, antagonism and theory choice. *Organization* 16: 467–85.

Tannenbaum, A. (1967). *Control in Organizations*. New York: McGraw-Hill.

Taylor, F. W. (1911). *Scientific Management*. New York: Harper Brothers.

Teece, D. J. (2007). Explicating dynamic capabilities: The nature and microfoundations of (sustainable) enterprise performance. *Strategic Management Journal* 28: 1319–50.

Tennant, G. (2001). *Six Sigma: SPC and TQM in Manufacturing and Services*. Hampshire: Gower Publishing.

Tetlock, P. C., M. Saar-Tsechansky, and S. Macskassy (2008). More than words: Quantifying language to measure firms' fundamentals. *Journal of Finance* 63: 1437–67.

Thomke, S. H. (2003). *Experimentation Matters: Unlocking the Potential of New Technologies for Innovation*. Cambridge, MA: Harvard Business School Press.

Thomke, S., and J. Manzi (2014). The discipline of business experimentation. *Harvard Business Review* 92(12): 70–9.

Thorpe, R., J. Gold, and J. Lawler (2011). Locating distributed leadership. *International Journal of Management Reviews* 13: 239–50.

Tichy, N. M., and W. G. Bennis (2009). *Judgment: How Winning Leaders Make Great Calls*. New York: Penguin.

Tihanyi, L., S. Graffin, and G. George (2014). Rethinking governance in management research. *Academy of Management Journal* 57: 1535–43.

Timmons, S. (2011). Professionalization and its discontents. *Health* 15: 337–52.

Tisdell, C. (1996). *Bounded Rationality and Economic Evolution: A Contribution to Decision Making, Economics, and Management*. Cheltenham, UK: Brookfield.

Tranfield, D., and K. Starkey (1998). The nature, social organization and promotion of management research: Towards policy. *British Journal of Management* 9: 341–53.

Tranfield, D., D. Denyer, and P. Smart (2003). Towards a methodology for developing evidence-informed management knowledge by means of systematic review. *British Journal of Management* 14: 207–22.

Trice, H., and J. Beyer (1984). Studying organizational cultures through rites and ceremonials. *Academy of Management Review* 9: 653–69.

Tricker, B. (2012). *Corporate Governance: Principles, Policies and Practices* (2nd edn). Oxford: Oxford University Press.

Tripsas, M., and Gavetti, G. (2000). Capabilities, cognition, and inertia: Evidence from digital imaging. *Strategic Management Journal* 21: 1147–61.

TSG—The Sociocracy Group (2012). *The Sociocratic Method: Qualification of Sociocracy Experts* (version October 2012). Rotterdam: Stichting Sociocratisch Centrum.

Tsoukas, H. (1996). The firm as a distributed knowledge system. *Strategic Management Journal* 17 (Winter special issue): 11–25.

Turnbull James, K., and D. Denyer (2009). Historical roots and future directions: New challenges for Management Learning. *Management Learning* 40: 363–70.

Tversky, A., and Kahneman, D. (1981). The framing of decisions and the psychology of choice. *Science* 211: 453–8.

Ulieru, M. (2014). Organic governance through the logic of holonic systems. In: J. H. Clippinger and D. Bollier (eds.), *From Bitcoin to Burning Man and Beyond: The Quest for Identity and Autonomy in a Digital Society*, pp. 113–29. Boston, MA: ID3.

Uy, M. A., M. D. Foo, and H. Aguinis (2010). Using event sampling methodology to advance entrepreneurship theory and research. *Organizational Research Methods* 13: 31–54.

Välikangas, L. (2010). *The Resilient Organization: How Adaptive Cultures Thrive Even When Strategy Fails*. New York: McGraw-Hill.

Van Aken, J. E. (2004). Management research based on the paradigm of the design sciences: The quest for field-tested and grounded technological rules. *Journal of Management Studies* 41: 219–46.

Van Aken, J. E., H. Berends, and H. Van der Bij (2007). *Problem Solving in Organizations*. Cambridge: Cambridge University Press.

Van Burg, E., and A. G. L. Romme (2014). Creating the future together: Toward a framework for research synthesis in entrepreneurship. *Entrepreneurship Theory and Practice* 38: 369–97.

Van Burg, E., and K. E. van Oorschot (2013). Cooperating to commercialize technology: A dynamic model of fairness perceptions, experience, and cooperation. *Production and Operations Management* 22: 1336–55.

Van Burg, E., A. G. L. Romme, V. A. Gilsing, and I. M. M. J. Reymen (2008). Creating university spin-offs: A science-based design perspective. *Journal of Product Innovation Management* 25: 114–28.

Van Burg, E., V. A. Gilsing, I. M. M. J. Reymen, and A. G. L. Romme (2013). The formation of fairness perceptions in the cooperation between entrepreneurs and universities. *Journal of Product Innovation Management* 30: 677–94.

Van der Arend, S., B. Broekhans, and S. Meijer (2013). Professionalizing practices in advisory work: Presenting a conceptual approach to study the relations among institutionalization, reflective learning, and quality in consultancy. In: A. F. Buono, L. de Caluwé, and A. Stoppelenburg (eds.), *Exploring the Professional Identity of Management Consultants*, pp. 141–62. Charlotte, NC: Information Age.

Van der Eyden, R. A. I., A. G. L. Romme, J. Broekgaarden, and A. Reijmer (2015). A circular perspective on public governance and civil participation. Paper presented at Citizenship 3.0 seminar (October 3, 2014), KNAW, Amsterdam. Available at: www.researchgate.net/publication/268489044

Van der Meché, P. (1999). Ontbrekende schakel bij Shell. *Argumenten* 1999(2): 7–8.

Van de Ven, A. H. (2007). *Engaged Scholarship*. Oxford: Oxford University Press.

Van de Ven, A. H., and S. Zahra (2015). Knowledge complexity, boundary objects, and innovation. In: F. Tell, C. Berggren, S. Brusoni, and A. Van de Ven (eds.), *Managing Knowledge Integration Across Boundaries*, forthcoming. Oxford: Oxford University Press.

Van de Ven, A. H., and P. E. Johnson (2006). Knowledge for theory and practice. *Academy of Management Review* 31: 902–21.

Van Fleet, E. W., and D. D. Van Fleet (2014). *Violence At Work: What Everyone Should Know*. Charlotte, NC: Information Age.

Van Maanen, J., and S. R. Barley (1984). Occupational communities: Culture and control in organizations. *Research in Organizational Behavior* 6: 287–365.

Van Olffen, W. (2014). Verandering op heterdaad. Inaugural address at Tilburg University (TIAS). Retrieved via www.tias.edu February 26, 2015.

Van Olffen, W., and A. G. L. Romme (1995). The role of hierarchy in self-organizing systems. *Human Systems Management* 14: 199–206.

Van Seggelen-Damen, I. C. M., and A. G. L. Romme (2014). Reflective questioning in management education: Lessons from supervising thesis projects. *SAGE Open* 4(2): 1–13.

Van Vlissingen, R. F. (1991). A management system based on consent. *Human Systems Management* 10: 149–54.

Vartia, M. (1996). The sources of bullying—psychological work environment and organizational climate. *European Journal of Work and Organizational Psychology* 5: 203–14.

Vaughan, D. (1983). *Controlling Unlawful Behavior: Social Structure and Corporate Misconduct*. Chicago: University of Chicago Press.

Venkataraman, S., S. D. Sarasvathy, N. Dew, and W. R. Forster (2012). Reflections on the 2010 AMR decade award: Whither the promise? Moving forward with entrepreneurship as a science of the artificial. *Academy of Management Review* 37: 21–33.

Vermeulen, F. (2007). I shall not remain insignificant: Adding a second loop to matter more. *Academy of Management Journal* 50: 754–61.

Visscher, K., and J. I. A. Visscher-Voerman (2010). Organizational design approaches in management consulting. *Management Decision* 48: 713–31.

Vohora, A., M. Wright, and A. Lockett (2004). Critical junctures in the development of university high-tech spinout companies. *Research Policy* 33: 147–75.

Von Hippel, E. (2005). *Democratizing Innovation*. Cambridge, MA: MIT Press.

Vroom, V. H., and A. G. Jago (1988). *The New Leadership: Managing Participation in Organizations*. Englewood Cliffs, NJ: Prentice-Hall.

Walrave, B., K. E. van Oorschot, and A. G. L. Romme (2011). Getting trapped in the suppression of exploration: A simulation model. *Journal of Management Studies* 48: 1727–51.

Walsh, J. P., A. D. Meyer, and C. B. Schoonhoven (2006). A future for organization theory: Living in and living with changing organizations. *Organization Science* 17: 657–71.

Ward, L. F. (1892). *The Psychic Factors of Civilization*. Boston: Ginn & Co.

Wareham, J., P. B. Fox, and J. L. Cano Giner (2014). Technology ecosystem governance. *Organization Science* 25: 1195–215.

Warfield, J. N. (1986). Micromathematics and macromathematics. Proceedings of *1986 International Conference on Systems, Man and Cybernetics*, pp. 1127–31. New York: IEEE.

Warfield, J. N. (1994). *A Science of Generic Design* (2nd edn). Ames, IA: Iowa State University Press.

Weggeman, M. (2007). *Leidinggeven aan Professionals? Niet Doen!* Schiedam, Netherlands: Scriptum.

Weick, K. E. (1989). Theory construction as disciplined imagination. *Academy of Management Review* 14: 516–31.

Weick, K. E. (1998). Introductory essay—Improvisation as a mindset for organizational analysis. *Organization Science* 9: 543–55.

Weick, K., Sutcliffe, K. M., and D. Obstfeld (1999). Organizing for reliability: Processes of collective mindfulness. *Research in Organizational Behavior* 21: 81–123.

Wheatley, M. (2005). *Finding Our Way: Leadership for an Uncertain Time*. San Francisco, CA: Berrett-Koehler.

Wheatley, M. (2014). *The True Professional* (poem). Retrieved November 15, 2014 from: http://margaretwheatley.com/wp-content/uploads/2014/12/TheTrueProfessional.pdf

Whetten, D. A. (1989). What constitutes a theoretical contribution? *Academy of Management Review* 14: 490–5.

Whitley, R. (1984). The fragmented state of management studies: Reasons and consequences. *Journal of Management Studies* 21: 331–48.

Wicks, A. C., and R. E. Freeman (1998). Organization studies and the new pragmatism: Positivism, anti-positivism, and the search for ethics. *Organization Science* 9: 123–40.

Wieringa, R. J. (2014). *Design Science Methodology for Information Systems and Software Engineering*. Berlin/Heidelberg: Springer.

Wikipedia (2014). Knowledge. http://en.wikipedia.org/wiki/Knowledge retrieved at December 3, 2014.

Wilensky, H. L. (1964). The professionalization of everyone? *American Journal of Sociology* 70: 137–58.

Wilhite, A., and E. Fong (2012). Coercive citation in academic publishing. *Science* 335 (6068): 542–3.

Williams, M. T. (2010). *Uncontrolled Risk: The Lessons of Lehman Brothers and How Systemic Risk Can Bring Down the World Financial System*. New York: McGraw-Hill.

Williamson, J., C. Driver, and P. Kenway (2014). Introduction. In: J. Williamson, C. Driver, and P. Kenway (eds.), *Beyond Shareholder Value: The Reasons and Choices for Corporate Governance Reform*, pp. 6–15. London: TUC.

Willis, W. (2013). Jack Ma's last speech as Alibaba CEO. *Tech in Asia*, May 13, 2013. Retrieved May 1, 2015 from: https://www.techinasia.com/alibaba-jack-ma-last-ceo-speech/

Worren, N. (2012). *Organisation Design: Re-Defining Complex Systems*. Harlow, UK: Pearson.

Worren, N., K. Moore, and R. Elliot (2002). When theories become tools: Toward a framework for pragmatic validity. *Human Relations* 55: 1227–50.

Wren, D. A., and A. G. Bedeian (2008). *The Evolution of Management Thought* (6th edn). Hoboken, NJ: Wiley.

Wright, M., B. Clarysse, P. Mustar, and A. Lockett (2007). *Academic Entrepreneurship in Europe*. Cheltenham, UK: Edward Elgar.

WRR—Wetenschappelijke Raad voor Regeringsbeleid (2012). *Vertrouwen in Burgers* (Trust in Citizens). Den Haag/Amsterdam: Amsterdam University Press.

Yermack, D. (1995). Do corporations award CEO stock options effectively? *Journal of Financial Economics* 39: 237–69.

Yin, R. K. (2014). *Case Study Research: Design and Methods* (5th edn). Newbury Park, CA: Sage.

Zahra, S. A., H. J. Sapienza, and P. Davidsson (2006). Entrepreneurship and dynamic capabilities: A review, model and research agenda. *Journal of Management Studies* 43: 917–55.

Zbaracki, M. J. (2006). Success, failure, and the race of truth. *Journal of Management Inquiry* 15: 336–9.

Zepeda, S. J. (2012). *Professional Development: What Works*. Larchmont, NY: Eye On Education.

Zundel, M., and P. Kokkalis (2010). Theorizing as engaged practice. *Organization Studies* 31: 1209–27.

General Index

Tables, figures, and boxes are indicated by an italic *t*, *f*, and *b* following the page number, and 'n' referring to a note.

Name Index